TEAM LOTUS

MY VIEW FROM THE PIT WALL

TEAM LOTUS

MY VIEW FROM THE PIT WALL

PETER WARR
With commentary by Simon Taylor

Haynes Publishing

For my wife, children and grandchildren
Yvonne
Susie, Andy
Lucy, Emily, Stephanie, Sebastian

First published in January 2012
Reprinted July 2012

A catalogue record for this book is available from the British Library

ISBN 978 0 85733 123 6

Library of Congress catalog card no 2011935259

Published by Haynes Publishing,
Sparkford, Yeovil, Somerset BA22 7JJ, UK
Tel: 01963 442030 Fax: 01963 440001
Int.tel: +44 1963 442030 Int.fax: +44 1963 440001
E-mail: sales@haynes.co.uk
Website: www.haynes.co.uk

Haynes North America Inc.,
861 Lawrence Drive, Newbury Park, California 91320, USA

Printed and bound in the USA by Odcombe Press LP,
1299 Bridgestone Parkway, La Vergne, TN 37086

Cover photograph credits: LAT (front), sutton-images.com (rear)

CONTENTS

INTRODUCTION   7

PREFACE   9

PROLOGUE   Early Days at Hornsey and Cheshunt   13

CHAPTER 1   Colin Chapman   25
*"The path of a pioneer is strewn with
bloody great boulders"*

CHAPTER 2   Racing Mechanics   47
"You've got to remember it's only a sport"

CHAPTER 3   Drivers   61
*"Love them or hate them, some
are very special"*

CHAPTER 4   Engineers   176
*"Don't confuse me with the facts, my
mind is made up"*

CHAPTER 5   Bernie   204
"If you're absent you get screwed"

EPILOGUE   Leaving Lotus   230

INDEX   236

INTRODUCTION

Such is the extent of the worldwide media coverage of Formula 1 today that another book about Grand Prix racing will always risk being superfluous. Indeed, if you were not satisfied with having seen it on television, read about it in the daily papers, followed that up with a subscription to a specialist magazine and had access in the right places, you could get a print-out of every lap, every gearchange, every subtle change in handling, temperatures, pressures, steering and suspension inputs and who knows what else of your favourite car or driver. You would even be able to spot on the graphics where he went over a kerb or, though he might not admit it, the point at which he made a small mistake.

In this environment another book about Grand Prix racing would definitely be surplus to requirement. So, when I was asked to consider going into print, I had to think carefully whether there was anything I had to say or wanted to say about the activity that has taken up the majority of my life.

And then it occurred to me that there is so much more to Grand Prix racing than just the simple chronological record of races and the spin-off stories that arise from a particular event, which the narrow and time-constrained interface between the sport and its public can never cover. Here, surely, lie the areas which, on the one hand, have occupied so much of my time and which, on the other, might conceivably be of interest.

This then is one person's attempt to fill out some of the background, with the absolute proviso that this view from the pit wall is a purely personal one, probably lacking in impartiality, but an attempt to give the reader a taste of the complex, stimulating, trying, sometimes heartbreaking but always exciting world that is Grand Prix Racing.

It is over 20 years since I last ran the Team and, apart from a brief comeback to Formula 1 as the FISA Permanent Steward for the 1992 World Championship season, I feel that sufficient time has now passed. So if any of the opinions expressed give rise to indignation or offence, they might be excused as those of someone who is not up to speed with the current situation.

But it is certainly not too late to express my thanks to all those colleagues, competitors, business associates and friends who together made it possible for my wife and me, and to a lesser extent our children, to go to places, meet people, see and do things and experience emotions that otherwise we would never have had the chance to do.

Peter Warr
Sainte-Foy-la-Grande
2010

PREFACE

By Simon Taylor

For more than 20 years Peter Warr's tall, restless figure was an essential ingredient at the centre of Formula 1. For most of that time Team Lotus was vying for the very top rung of the ladder, winning Grands Prix, taking World titles, and constantly at the cutting edge of racing car design. While the mercurial genius of Colin Chapman was the Team's fulcrum point, everyone in the paddock knew that it was Peter Warr's energy, commitment, drive and organisation that made it all work. Then, when Lotus was pole-axed by Chapman's premature death, all of Peter's strength of character came to the fore as he ensured that the Team carried on without its founder.

As a working journalist in the world's Formula 1 paddocks throughout Peter's Team Lotus career, I had to pursue, question and interview him on countless occasions. There was always something dramatic or newsworthy going on at Lotus. I knew him to be straightforward and direct, a man to call a spade a spade, and not one to suffer fools. You had to choose your moment, and if there was a crisis unfolding in the Lotus pit you knew to keep out of his way. Yet, provided the approach was right he would be courteous, and as patient with my nosing for fact and comment as his frightening workload and time pressures allowed him to be. And those pressures, however burdensome, rarely seemed to dampen his sense of humour. Unusually within Formula 1 circles, he always told the truth – unless doing so would yield an advantage to another team, for he was above all a totally competitive human being.

In April 2008, nearly 20 years after Peter walked away from Formula

1, I flew to the little airport of Bergerac, in south-western France, to interview him about his career for my monthly 'Lunch With...' series in *Motor Sport* magazine. He and his wife Yvonne had retired some years earlier to a charmingly eaved and turreted house just outside Sainte-Foy-la-Grande, close to the rolling vineyards of Bordeaux. I found Peter fit and well, energetic as ever, very happy to be living in rural France, and full of good humour. His sharp intelligence, excellent memory and relaxed willingness to talk frankly about himself and others in Formula 1 meant that, over a long lunch, we barely scratched the surface. We talked on all afternoon, and throughout an excellent dinner in a Michelin-starred restaurant in St Emilion. Peter and Yvonne gave me a hospitable bed for the night, and the stories kept on coming over breakfast next morning, and were still doing so as he drove me to the airport. "There's plenty more," said Peter, "but for those you'll have to wait for my book."

His book. I knew he'd been working on it for some time. With typical lack of ego, he did not want it to be a conventional autobiography. He felt that a detailed account of his own life and doings would be much less interesting than his unique perspective, from the very heart of the Formula 1 pits and paddock, on the people he had known, worked alongside and competed against. Haynes had already agreed to publish it, unseen. An awful lot of books are written about motor racing these days, but this was going to be one worth waiting for.

Then, in October 2010, came the shocking news of Peter's sudden death from a heart attack. The unfinished manuscript of his book was on his desk. Already completed were his unique and frank assessments of the drivers he worked with, as well as the mechanics – in his view the real heroes of the piece – plus the designers and engineers, and Colin Chapman himself. There was also a very personal view of Bernie Ecclestone, whom Peter knew even before his purchase of the Brabham team set him on the road to becoming a Formula 1 mogul. It was all much too good to lose, and Haynes remained very keen to publish it.

So when Yvonne Warr and Haynes editorial director Mark Hughes jointly suggested I should look over what Peter had left behind, and shade in some of the detail of Peter's own life in an introductory chapter, I felt honoured. Although he didn't himself include much actual autobiography in his book, my recorded conversations with him contained some fascinating personal detail that I knew needed to be added to complete the picture. The combined result is what you are about to read.

PROLOGUE

EARLY DAYS AT HORNSEY AND CHESHUNT
By Simon Taylor

Peter Eric Warr was born in Kermanshah, in the west of what was then Persia, on 18 June 1938. His father had moved to the Middle East six years earlier to work as a banker. When he was eight years old Peter and his older sister Ilma were sent to boarding schools in England, spending the holidays with guardians apart from the occasional trip back to Tehran. Thus, from an early age, he had to learn to be independent and fend for himself. At 13 he was sent on to public school at Malvern College.

"But in 1952, when I was 14, the British got thrown out of Iran, and my father returned to work in the City. As it happened, he bought a house a mile from the gates of Brands Hatch. I was already fascinated by motor racing, but the only book I could find in the Malvern school library was George Monkhouse's *Motor Racing with Mercedes-Benz*. That told me about the pre-war Grand Prix cars, the most powerful racing cars the world had ever known. Later I was to live and work through the period in Grand Prix racing that blew all that away, the turbo era, when we had 1300 horsepower and more." In the school holidays he would bicycle over to Brands Hatch. "I liked the small sports car races. The new thing on the block was the first streamlined Lotus, the Mk VIII. Then the IX and the Eleven came after it. I watched fantastic races between the Lotuses – Colin Chapman, Alan Stacey, Keith Hall – and the bob-tail centre-seat Coopers driven by the likes of Ivor Bueb, Ian Raby and Jim Russell."

When it was time for Peter to leave school, his father pulled some strings to find him a job in a bank. But that seemed to him the world's most boring occupation, and it was the last thing he intended to do. He escaped into his compulsory National Service, which he served in the Royal Horse Artillery: but a freak accident on a firing range in the Brecon Beacons put him in hospital for eight months. Invalided out, he wrote to every motor manufacturer he could think of asking for a job, and while waiting and hoping for his pleading letters to generate some replies he spent five guineas on a one-day course at Brands Hatch with the Cooper Racing Drivers' School. His school report said he was "neat and tidy, lacking only in pace." It was signed by the secretary of the Cooper Car Co Training Division, Andrew Ferguson. Their paths would cross again later...

That June Peter bought a cheap package tour to the 1958 Le Mans 24 Hours. "We flew in an old DC3. In those days people working in motor racing took package trips too, because it was cheap and convenient. Sitting in the next seat to me was Colin Chapman, whom I knew to be the creator of the small sports cars I admired so much. So I took the opportunity to tell him I was a terrific admirer of all things Lotus. A few weeks later I decided to go up to North London and see the place where they were made."

When he got to the tiny, cramped Lotus works behind Chapman's father's pub, the Railway Hotel in Tottenham Lane, Hornsey N8, everything was a hive of chaotic activity. "Somebody asked me what I wanted, and I said I'd just come to have a look around. I was told there was nobody to show me anything, they were too busy, but I if I didn't get in anybody's way I could have a look. After about 40 minutes the foreman, Roy Badcock, said to me, 'Don't just stand there doing nothing, give us a hand.' So I did. Before the end of the day he took me to Colin Bennett, who was the Sales Manager, and Colin offered me a job as his assistant. I started the next morning. How lucky was I! My hobby became my job, and I ended up doing it almost my entire life."

Peter was hired at £9 12s 4d a week, or £500 a year. He was just 20 years old. Early every morning he would leave his parents' house in Kent in his old Hillman Minx and drive through South London, straight over Tower Bridge – "there was so little traffic in those days" – and up the Seven Sisters Road to Hornsey. "There was a little showroom at the front, and behind it what used to be Stan Chapman's beer store, which was now the development shop. Soon sheets of brown paper were glued over the showroom window and it was taken over for more important work. The mezzanine was the drawing office, where Len Terry and Ian Jones were, and a lean-to jutting out into the courtyard was the engine and gearbox shop. Graham Hill worked in there. Beyond the yard was the workshop where the cars were built. Somehow 33 employees were crammed into every nook and cranny, four of them girls.

"There was a complete lunacy about working for Colin Chapman in the early days. One of his philosophies was that there was no reason on God's earth why something he wanted could not be on his cars for the coming weekend, and his ability to motivate people was such that they would start to believe, yes, it can be done for the weekend. Then they would perform way beyond their own self-perceived abilities."

Eventually Lotus Engineering Ltd was split into several companies – Lotus Components, Lotus Cars, Racing Engines Ltd – because to avoid purchase tax on a car at that time it not only had to be nominally assembled by the purchaser, but also the components had to come from several different sources. "In the early days we'd sell a body/chassis unit to a customer and give them a list of parts they had to go and buy. Then we refined it more and more, and eventually a Lotus Seven was a complete kit. But some bits were invoiced from Components, some bits from Cars, some bits from Racing Engines, even though they were all under the same roof, so purchase tax didn't become payable."

Part of Peter's job was to demonstrate the Lotus Seven, the nearest Lotus had so far got to a series production car, to prospective customers. "Every day was an adventure, every day a new experience. We decided to give the Lotus Seven a bit of a zap, so we built up chassis number 436 – the 36th Seven, because they started at 400 –

with single-cam Climax engine, ZF limited-slip diff, disc brakes on the front and wire wheels. Because the standard A35 gearbox might not be strong enough for the power of the Climax, we put the chassis out in the yard – there was no room in the fabricating shop – and drew some chalk lines on the concrete so the lads could fabricate new tubes to accommodate a bigger MG gearbox. But it rained overnight and washed the chalk marks away."

The new car, painted red, was registered 7 TMT, and Graham Hill drove it at the Boxing Day Brands Hatch meeting in December 1958 and won, beating all the streamlined Lotuses and Lolas and Elvas. Then, after it had been road-tested in glowing terms by journalists John Bolster and David Phipps, Peter was able to buy it for £750. He kept it for 18 months, did two seasons' club racing in it, and 30,000 road miles. These included a 1,600-mile European motoring holiday with his sister as passenger, taking in laps of Spa-Francorchamps, Reims, Solitude and the Nürburgring. "I did the Six-Hour Relay Race at Silverstone and the engine stripped the fibre timing gear. I was pretty inexperienced then, didn't declutch in time, and it bent all eight valves."

Mike Costin, the ex-de Havilland Aircraft man who was working in the former beer store as Chapman's Head of Development, somehow also found time to be involved with Keith Duckworth in a little engine business. As an amalgam of their surnames, they called it Cosworth Engineering. On Mike's advice, Peter took his broken engine to Cosworth's tiny premises in Southgate. "Ursula, Keith's first wife, sat at a table downstairs and he worked in the loft. To deliver your engine you needed a block and tackle to haul it up through the window. Keith rebuilt the entire engine, with steel timing gears, for £115." In due course Mike left Lotus to work full-time with Keith, and between them they made Cosworth one of the most famous, and one of the most successful, racing car names of all time.

It seems unbelievable now that a Formula 1 team, a Le Mans sports car team and a racing car production business could all emanate from a little yard behind a North London pub. But inevitably more space had to be found, and in 1959 came the move to much larger premises in Delamare Road, Cheshunt. "It was just a super exciting time. In 1960 the first rear-engined Lotus, the 18, was all-conquering, and we couldn't sell them fast enough. I was badgering Colin to sell me one, but he kept saying 'no' until the new Type 20 was coming out, and then he sold me the last 18. At the 1960 Boxing Day Brands there were so many Formula Juniors they split them into an A race and a B race. Jim Clark won the A race in the works Lotus, and I won the B race in the car I'd bought. So I can say I won a race on the same day and in the same formula as Jim Clark."

One part of the effort towards an increasingly professional image was a stand at the 1959 Motor Show at Earls Court, and Peter was told to design and have printed a series of glossy leaflets for each model. "Colin asked what they were costing, and when I told him he said, 'We're not going to give those away. Run off some roneo'd specification sheets for the plebs.' So I stayed up all night producing those, just single typed sheets, and we kept the brochures for people who looked as though they really might buy a car. On a memorabilia dealer's stand at a recent classic car show I saw one of the rare leaflets for the Lotus 15. The price tag was £115!"

Once the Formula Junior 20 had been succeeded by the 22, Peter got a 20 and somehow found time to race it around Europe. "I was now living at Brookmans Park in Hertfordshire. I'd drive to work on Friday morning towing the 20 on its trailer, leave work on Friday evening, drive to Dover, catch the midnight boat to Dunkirk, then go hell for leather to whichever circuit I was racing at – Rouen, Reims, Chimay, the Nürburgring. It'd be drive all night to get there, practice on Saturday, race on Sunday, rush back to Dunkirk for the midnight boat on Sunday night, drive from Dover straight to work Monday morning. I'd prepare the car during the week after work, and do the whole thing again the next weekend.

"Buying the car, petrol, tyres, getting a bit of start and prize money, and selling the car at the end of the year, I could almost break even.

But people started to complain that, as I worked for Lotus, I must have the best car and the best engine – which I didn't, of course – and it wasn't fair. So we came up with the idea that I'd tow the racer behind a van that could carry a stock of spares, and that way I could provide a sort of Lotus customer service. That's why Colin didn't mind my racing.

"I had a few un-nerving experiences. A Swiss guy living in England called Rudi di Waldkirch was a good friend of mine, with a Lotus 18 that I'd sold him. He went off into the trees at Oulton Park just in front of me, and was decapitated. At Goodwood I remember rushing into Madgwick Corner after the start in the middle of a big group and there was a very serious *carambolage* [one of Peter's favourite words]. I remember Chris Andrews' Cooper going over the top of me upside-down, and being able to look up into his cockpit.

"Some of the European road circuits were unbelievable. Mettet in Belgium was a sort of figure-of-eight of public roads, with a great long honking straight. On the inside of a fast uphill curve there was a row of posts, and stretched between the posts was a single strand of wire to keep the spectators off the track. After practice some of us went to the organisers and pointed out that the wire was precisely at neck level for somebody sitting in a single-seater racing car, but nothing was done. We started the race, and as I led the field down the hill through the village, outside the second cottage on the right a woman was scrubbing her front step, with her backside in the air over the track. A bit further on as I approached the dreaded wire there was an ice-cream vendor standing actually on the track, selling his wares to people over the wire. One of the drivers was killed that day, too."

Some of these sorties were very successful: the morning after the Formula 3 Grand Prix des Frontières at Chimay the headline *Warr is fourth in Belgium* appeared in *The Times*, and two weeks later he was third at Rouen behind the works Coopers of Tony Maggs and John Love. One of his best wins was in the 1962 Eifelrennen on the Nürburgring Sudschleife. Two weeks after that he was back in

Germany, going all the way through the Eastern Sector to Berlin for the Grosser Preis der Nationen on the Avus track. This consisted of two flat-out sections of autobahn, connected at one end by an almost vertical banking surfaced with bricks, and at the other end by a hairpin. "I was battling for the lead with Jo Siffert's Lotus 22, and at 120mph I managed to hit the concrete wall at the end of the straight – fortunately the non-banking end. But some of my wreckage ended up in the Russian zone, and we had to get a special permit to retrieve it."

In 1963 Jabby Crombac, the Swiss-born French enthusiast and journalist who was always a great supporter of all things Lotus, was asked to put together a field of European entrants for the first-ever Japanese Grand Prix. This was to be run for sports cars on the recently completed and superbly elaborate Suzuka circuit. Peter bought himself a second-hand Lotus 23 sports racer from an Irish customer, Mike Costin found him a torquey pushrod 1,650cc Ford engine, the car was shipped east, and on 5 May 1963 he made history by winning the race. "For a short time this British racing driver 'Peter Wall' – because the Japanese had trouble with their Ls and Rs – became quite famous. Most people out there reckon that day represents the birth of Japanese motor sport. It also marked the first appearance of Honda in four-wheel motor racing, because Ronnie Bucknum ran a little S800 in a supporting race. I brought the 23 back home and did a few European events with it, and then I sold it to a museum in Japan. It's still there, on display as the winner of the first Japanese Grand Prix."

A sponsor of the race was the local Coca-Cola importer, and Peter was photographed downing a bottle on the winner's rostrum to echo the famous Indianapolis 500 victor's glass of milk. In fact Peter hated Coca-Cola, and was dismayed when he discovered that part of his prize was a year's supply of the stuff, delivered in monthly batches to his home. Having given away as much as he could, he eventually wrote politely to Coca-Cola and asked them to stop the deliveries.

A year later 'Peter Wall' was invited back to the second Japanese Grand Prix. The frantic pressures of working at Lotus had forced him to bow to the inevitable and call a halt to his own racing, but he arranged to borrow a Formula Junior Lotus 27 from the Ron Harris team, and finished second to Mike Knight's Brabham. It was the last time – apart from a light-hearted Drivers v. Team Managers celebrity Ford Escort race at Brands Hatch in 1978 – that he raced a car.

By now Peter had risen to be manager of Lotus Components, the company that produced racing cars for sale, and effectively the profitable arm of the organisation that had to support the works racing effort, Team Lotus. "I had to make it profitable, because the whole of Lotus was held up by Components. It was a big responsibility, and I reported direct to Colin. They were unbelievably buccaneering days. Roy Badcock was in charge of producing the bloody things, and I looked after the administration, company finances, stock levels, and employing the people. In 1960 we produced 125 Lotus 18s, then the next year 100 of its successor, the 20. There were fewer 22s, but the 23 sports racer was in production at the same time, and the Lotus Seven of course. The Elites were made in the second building at Cheshunt, with the office block in front, and the extension was for the Lotus-Cortina. At the back was the drawing office, and then the Team Lotus race shop."

Lotus Components now needed an accountant to work on the company books, so Peter ran a situations vacant advertisement in the local papers. A girl from nearby Broxbourne, Yvonne Bell, answered the ad, and started work straight away. But before long she decided it would be better if she left, because she and Peter had started to go out together. They were married in 1965.

Although Peter's working life was now taken up with Components, in the tight, hard-pressed little organisation he remained close to what was going on at Team. In the chapters of this book he examines in detail the drivers he worked with during his 20 years at Team Lotus, but within the still extremely compact set-up at Cheshunt he got to know the drivers of that earlier era extremely well. Graham Hill, of course, had first been on the staff at Hornsey as a humble mechanic before he went off to run the Speedwell tuning firm.

"Our image of Graham is compounded of two characters: the Sports Personality of the Year on TV, a wonderful public figure; and a very difficult racing driver, niggly about every detail. You couldn't change ratios on ZF gearboxes, you could only change the crown wheel and pinion to alter the final drive. So we used to take a string of gearboxes to races to give us flexibility. Jimmy [Clark] was always perfectly happy with the ZFs, but Graham would come in and say, 'What I need is a longer fourth gear for that corner'. So he made us switch to Hewlands. And he was forever asking for another quarter-inch on the roll-bar, or the ride height up a bit, or down a bit. He got the job done because he worked extremely hard at it, but he was difficult to work with because he imposed a high workload. Of course after Jimmy's death he was the man, and was so valuable to Team Lotus that he got what he wanted.

"The other side of him was the way he could get the public to love him. He was a wonderful after-dinner speaker. I remember him at a South African Grand Prix prize-giving dinner in a very grand building, very stuffy and colonial with everybody in black tie. He gets up to speak, looks around the room, and says, 'I knew a bloke once who thought F*** All was a stately 'ome.' There was a shocked silence for about 10 seconds, and then the whole room erupted into laughter, and after that they were in the palm of his hand. One of his favourite openers when he stood up to make a speech was to say, 'This is the second time today I've got up from a warm seat with a piece of paper in my hand.'

"Jim Clark was just an ordinary guy, shy, a bit timid really. I remember him sticking his head round the door of the Components office apologetically asking the girl who looked after the petty cash if he could borrow a fiver – 'I've just got to drive back to Scotland' – and signing an IOU. But he had in spades the key characteristic of all the great drivers I worked with: an unbelievable competitive spirit. At any sniff of competition, in a car or out of it, he became somebody different. I remember a party at Colin and Hazel Chapman's house. Somebody found a pogo stick in the garage and started laying £5 bets on who could go upstairs to the landing on it. It all got a bit rowdy, Hazel's wall lights got knocked down and there was a lot of mess, and then Jimmy rather spoiled the game by going boing, boing straight up to the landing without touching anything. Then they found another of the kids' toys, a woggle board, a plank across a log, and the wagers became who could stay balanced on it for one minute. Everybody had had a few drinks and they were all crashing to the carpet and making more mess, with Hazel crying out, 'Mind my furniture.' Then Jimmy got on, and after he'd been on it perfectly steady for two minutes he said, 'Can somebody pass me my drink, please.' So he rather spoiled that one, too.

"Jimmy was just nice to everybody, although by the end he'd changed a bit. He'd seen the world, he'd been living in Paris with Jabby, and maybe he'd decided that Colin had been taking advantage of him in some things. By then he was prepared to stand up to him over money and things like that. I wasn't at Lotus when Jimmy was killed, thank God, but it affected everybody in motor sport in different ways. I can't remember anything happening to any sportsman that had quite that terrible impact. Drivers did get killed in those days, it happened a lot, but what made his death harder to bear was there was always this unspoken feeling in the back of your mind: it'll never happen to Jimmy.

"The tragedy was that during that spring and summer of 1968 we managed to kill a racing driver a month, with depressing regularity: Jimmy on April 7th, Mike Spence on May 8th [in a Lotus 56 turbine at Indianapolis], Lodovico Scarfiotti on June 8th, Jo Schlesser on July 7th. It was a wonderful time for racing, but it was a dreadful time in terms of survival rates. You just had to think that it was something they wanted to do, otherwise it got very hard to accept.

"Alan Stacey was already a Team Lotus driver when I joined in 1958, and I got to know him very well. A lovely man, and a very, very good racing driver. In the great mid-50s days of small sports car racing he was unbeatable, and I think he had the makings of getting to the very top. He had a false lower right leg because of a motorcycle accident when he was younger, but that never slowed him down in any way. We fitted a twist-grip accelerator onto his gearlever so he could blip the throttle on down-changes. At Spa in June 1960 he was hit in the face by a bird, it smashed the visor on his Herbert Johnson helmet, and it must at least have knocked him out. The car plunged over a steep drop and caught fire. The 'queerbox' used a special oil, and when it burned it had a vile odour. The wreckage of his car sat in the Team Lotus shop for a week with this terrible smell.

"Innes Ireland's contract was famously terminated by Team Lotus straight after he had won the United States Grand Prix in October 1961. For the rest of Innes' life, all the time he was around Formula 1 as the Sports Editor of *Autocar*, he loathed me because he thought I had something to do with him being sacked. Of course I had nothing to do with it at all. It was entirely Colin's decision, and it was because Jimmy was inevitably going to be his number one. Trevor Taylor, who became Jimmy's number two, had the right attitude, always professional, and got on very well with Jimmy and everybody else. He was a fine driver: I suppose it was his misfortune to end up in the same team as Jimmy, because Jimmy would always outshine anybody."

Almost as soon as Lotus got to Cheshunt it began to outgrow its new premises, and by 1965 a disused airfield at Hethel, near Norwich, had been bought as the site of a new, purpose-built factory. "I was involved in some of the planning of this and went up there several times. The more I did so, the more I felt I didn't fancy it. When the move to Hethel came in 1966 about 150 Lotus employees went with it, and I was one of the ones that didn't. Yvonne and I were married by now, and we wanted to stay closer to London. But the real ulterior motive in my going was that the one job I really wanted, which was to run Team Lotus, I wasn't going to get. As long as I was doing a good job at Lotus Components, and I suppose I'd made myself pretty indispensable there, it wasn't in Colin's interests to move me. I needed to break the chain."

So, with mixed feelings, Peter left Lotus, where he had spent the first eight years of his working life, to set up a new enterprise of his own. Slot car racing had become fashionable and lucrative in America, with big public layouts drawing enthusiasts who paid per session to race the model cars against their friends. Peter believed it could have a big future in Britain. Commodious premises were found in the old Harold Radford coachbuilders' premises in Hammersmith, West London, but despite strenuous efforts the business did not prosper. When the already steep rents came under review, Peter decided to call it a day. But he wasn't out of work for long.

Since 1961 Colin Chapman's right-hand man at Team Lotus, looking after the organisation and logistics of the racing programme, had been Andrew Ferguson – the same man who had signed Peter's Brands Hatch school report back in 1958. Andrew did the job extremely well, but after eight years he had started to find working for the mercurial Chapman unbearably stressful. During the summer of 1969 Peter had written to him asking for advice on where there might be vacancies in the motor-racing world. "Next thing was, Andrew phoned me and said, 'I've had enough. I'm off.' So I phoned Colin, he offered me the job, and we moved to Norfolk. On Monday October 6th 1969 – the day after Jochen Rindt's Lotus 49B won the US Grand Prix at Watkins Glen, and Graham Hill crashed his 49B and smashed his legs – I started with Team Lotus."

Peter was to be the Team's manager, first time round, for seven remarkable seasons, during which time Team Lotus won 22 Grand Prix victories, two Drivers' World Championships and three Constructors' World Championships. There was glory, but there was tragedy too; there were battles on the track, and inevitably battles off it. Which is a good moment to hand the baton to Peter, who unsurprisingly and quite correctly starts *My View from the Pit Wall* with his appreciation of the relentlessly brilliant and frequently difficult man he knew better than most: Anthony Colin Bruce Chapman.

CHAPTER 1

COLIN CHAPMAN

"The path of a pioneer is strewn with bloody great boulders"

The night before he died, Colin Chapman and his wife Hazel kindly invited my wife and me to join them at the Wroxham Hotel where an old friend, racer and keen Lotus enthusiast, Chris Barber, was performing with his famous and long-lived jazz band. After a pleasant meal, Chris joined us for a couple of beers and we sat talking and reminiscing until after midnight.

Very early the next morning Colin left with Fred Bushell, Group Lotus Financial Director and his right-hand man for many years, for Paris where they were required for meetings at the FIA headquarters in the Place de la Concorde. They flew direct out of Hethel in the company aircraft flown by the company pilot. As Fred was on duty first, Colin took a room at the Hôtel de Crillon and spent much of the morning resting before taking up the cudgels in the afternoon session.

As soon as the meeting was over, late in the evening they hurried back to Le Bourget and took off for Hethel. Tired and exasperated, as was often the case when confronted with lengthy meetings and intransigent people who he felt were impeding progress, Colin impulsively reacted when the pilot, nominally in charge of the aircraft, told him that the crosswind at Hethel was over the aircraft's limits and that they would have to divert. It was his company, his aircraft and his airfield, so he assumed command of the aircraft and made a competent if slightly hairy landing. Returning home a mile down the road, he made himself some soup before retiring to bed where a couple of hours later he suffered a massive heart attack.

So ended the life of one of the most charismatic, influential and successful engineers, entrepreneurs and competitors this country has ever seen, and certainly the most dominant British force in post-war motor racing.

It fell to me, after an early morning call, to rush to Snetterton where the race crew were testing to tell them of the night's events. I then hurried back to Ketteringham Hall, where by then the staff had arrived for work, to make sure that Colin's very own Team Lotus people did not hear through the rumour mill.

The devastated look on the face of each and every person bore witness to the fact that this was in every case a very personal loss, not just of 'the Guv'nor' but of someone who was held in the highest esteem and whose enthusiasm, drive and sheer brilliance affected every facet of their lives. An eerie shell-shocked silence pervaded the workshops and offices throughout the remainder of the day. The next day, as was the practice at the Team, all the talk was of how we were to go forward from this low point and how we could possibly live up to the standards and ideals set by the man who was no longer there in person.

What was it about the man that evoked these feelings in all the people with whom he came into contact? By the time of his death he had a standing and presence, not to mention a track record, that commanded respect. But this was 1982, and he had been active in one primary field, motor racing, since 1948.

I first met Colin on a charter flight to the Le Mans 24-hour race in June 1958, and by August I was working for him at the then Lotus works in Hornsey. It was immediately apparent to an inexperienced youngster that he was the driving force of every aspect of the business. There was absolutely nothing going on in the place, or down the road at the Team Lotus workshop in Edmonton, in which he did not wish to be involved or indeed in which he was not involved. This was also the time when the company, in addition to the base business of building racing cars for sale to the public, was racing its own works cars in many international categories. The three works Lotus Elevens had just returned from the Sebring 12-hour race and were parked forlornly and almost discarded in the yard on the day I started work, as there was no room anywhere to get them indoors – and Colin was immersed in the birth pangs of his revolutionary first real road car, the stunningly beautiful Lotus Elite.

There were 33 of us working at Hornsey, and about another eight at the Team workshop in Edmonton. The production of about 100 race cars a year, a full racing programme and a research and development programme on an entirely novel type of car construction was considered par for the course by a man who could in any 24-hour period get through more work than one could possibly imagine.

Perhaps his greatest attribute was his ability to motivate people to achieve more than they would for themselves think possible, and that is often overlooked when reviewing his engineering and design achievements. But the fact is that both of these were the result of a mind that was fertile, hyperactive, intensely competitive, retentive and above all boundless in its limits. He would never accept 'no' for an answer, would always ask 'why?' when told that something was impossible, and if you really wanted to see him explode you had only to tell him that something was 'good enough'. 'Good enough' was certainly not 'good enough' as far as he was concerned, and if you did not wish to be shown the door in short order you had to learn in quick time that 'getting it right' was all-important. This learning process set standards for everyone in the organisation, and in turn the maintaining of these standards built a loyalty to the man and a team spirit unequalled in my experience.

If the above in any way suggests that his style was re-active to problems put to him, then a totally wrong impression has been given. He was the powerhouse from whom a constant stream of new and very often seemingly unattainable ideas would pour forth – with the added proviso that he usually wished to see the results by tomorrow!

In conversation Peter enlarged thus on Colin Chapman's management technique:

"He had this aura of, I'm a bit busy, but I could do that if I had the time, so why can't you do it? I did my best to be a buffer between him and the workforce, because they had to take so much workload, so many changes of direction, so many last-minute ideas needed by this afternoon. I was the shock absorber. His temper was fairly violent, he had a very short fuse, but he'd recover very quickly. His rages were a momentary thing.

"His most annoying characteristic was that he'd come up with some suggestion that was complete madness, and you'd say, 'He's really gone off his rocker this time, I'm going to go and have it out with him.' He did drop some big ones occasionally, but nine times out of ten you'd find he was right. If you survived working for him long enough to understand him, you realised what an incredible mind the man had, and it all started to make sense.

"He'd come into the drawing office, stand over the draughtsman and say, 'What I'm after here, the overall concept, is this,' and then he might come back and say, 'No, no, that's not what I want,' and grab a pencil and sketch something on the edge of the draughtsman's board. If the draughtsman didn't produce exactly what he had in mind he'd keep on and keep on until he got it.

"If somebody else had an idea he'd listen. Then he'd go away, and come back after a while and say, 'Why don't we take it a step further, why don't we do it like this?' And suddenly you'd realise, he'd done it again."

Colin had a clarity of mind that brought with it an amazing ability – even when faced with seemingly very complex problems, either engineering or administrative – to cut through all the irrelevancies and go straight to the core of the problem. And yet he was not too arrogant when confronted with something new and outside his field of expertise to take himself off to a library or a research establishment, study all the available material and come back with an answer. The phenomenon that usually followed, however, was that something he had read or seen started his own mind working, and the chances were that his solution took the new process, material or technology to an even more advanced level.

To top it all, he had a photographic memory and, years after his initial study, he could quote verbatim whole paragraphs or even pages of a piece of work that he had read. He really was the prototype of what is known today as a lateral thinker.

And as one worked for him over a longer period of time, in spite of the many occasions when any member of the Team was utterly and completely convinced that this time they were right and he was wrong in his judgement or solution, the really annoying thing about him was that nine times out of ten he *was* right. It only served to increase the respect in which he was held. This became a kind of reverence, not fear, and resulted in the sort of loyalty and effort to achieve that meant that if he came into the workshop or office and said, "Right, lads, now today I want you to follow me and jump off this cliff", most of them would have done it. Not because they were stupid and following blindly, but because they believed that yet again he knew something they did not, and so they trusted his solution.

In all humans the mind is the person, and it is housed variously in bodies of different shapes and sizes. Colin's mind was housed in a body of fine proportions, of medium height and raffish good looks very much in the mould of the film star David Niven, and which at various times was slim, fit and lean but could easily get overweight, usually as a result of eating binges which very often accompanied times of great stress or worry. Nonetheless the pace at which he lived his life kept him very fit, and in his youth the outward sign of this was his outstanding ability as a racing driver. Many will remember his sports car drives and victories in the early series of small-capacity Lotus sports-racing cars when the Six, Eight, Nine, Eleven and Fifteen models were a force to be reckoned with, and even more so if they were driven by A.C.B. Chapman. Fewer might remember that he was offered a Grand Prix drive in the Vanwall team. Unfortunately his drive in the third car at Reims ended in brake problems in practice and a coming-together with a rather ugly piece of French architecture down the escape road. Pictures of the shunt (the car could not be repaired for the race and, as the new boy, he had to sit it out on the pit counter) reached the insurance company carrying the life risk of the head of this burgeoning new car company, and they unsurprisingly took a dim view. Nonetheless there were many who thought that Chapman was as good as Hawthorn, and perhaps even Moss. This is yet another clue to his future understanding of race cars and empathy with their drivers.

Nevertheless he continued all his life to subject the body to the profuse and high speed output of the mind – indeed when his hair turned first grey and then almost white he was known as 'The White Tornado' after a detergent advertisement of the era, which accurately depicted the manner in which he would rush through the office or the workshop. If you did not look up quickly enough all you got was a sense of swirling mist, air movement and a swinging door. Presumably it was the stresses to which he subjected himself continuously, coupled with business affairs that tended to swing wildly from great success to impending disaster, that eventually caused the body to let down the mind on that December night in 1982.

This brief sketch of the life and style of one of the titans of his era does not, of course, tell the whole story. As an employer he was incredibly demanding, unwilling to accept that anyone else was not capable of working at the same pace or output as himself, and as a result he could be short-fused, intolerant and given to extreme outbursts of temper. This made for a very lively atmosphere in the workplace, and everyone had perforce to be on their toes at all times. At Hornsey, where his office was on the left at the top of the stairs in the then new 'showroom' building that fronted onto Tottenham Lane, he was protected by his secretary in an outer office. On the same floor in Fred Bushell's Accounts Department and elsewhere in the building were housed the two or three other female staff, and many was the time that they would all gather in the yard or seek a cup of tea in one of the other buildings while the language emanating from 'The Guvnor's' office would turn the air blue at a very considerable number of decibels.

On the other hand, if one attempted to get behind the sometimes outrageous and seemingly impulsive decisions which could affect every aspect of the business, changes in design after sign-off, setback of R&D schedules, loss of production, hours and hours of overtime for all involved and usually some fairly serious knock-on effect on the company's finances, it was usually possible to arrive at the conclusion that he was right to have made the decision at the moment he did, as hindsight would show that the earlier path would have led to a less elegant engineering solution or a less competitive position.

Indeed elegance was at the forefront of Colin Chapman's engineering philosophy, and he would spend hours and hours searching with his designers and draughtsmen for the solution that was pleasing as well as efficient. Thus rarely did a Lotus use a bracket that did not serve three functions instead of one, or a structural member that did not serve more than its own single purpose. This fluidity gave his cars a style which incorporated simplicity with elegance and which bore his unmistakable signature. It was also this philosophy, which was borne out of his obsession with light weight, that gave rise to the very often unwarranted reputation for fragility that early Lotus cars earned in the reports of the day. What was so often overlooked was that it was not in him to build a 'conventional' or 'conservative' car. Most of his designs were at the cutting edge of technology and the knowledge of the day, incorporating the latest materials as well his thoughts on how to get the best out of the then current rule book. Once built, they were competing at the highest level in their class, driven by the best drivers who were constantly at or beyond the then current standards of speed, cornering force and indeed stress. No wonder then that at times when exploring these limits, like so many pioneers in other fields, he had to suffer the indignity and hurt of something going wrong with his cars.

Chapman's early cars were all of necessity small-engined: there were no large-capacity engines available. Their lack of power made the other three parameters of racing car design – grip, drag and weight – of the utmost importance in his work. Later in Formula 1 as the regulations became more and more restrictive, very often as a result of some innovation of his which was deemed to be an unfair advantage, his views crystallised even more on the parameter of weight, as this was the only thing that one could get, as it were, for free. Most of the field were using the same engine for power, the same tyres for grip, and the aerodynamic package was so closely regulated that most of our competitors' solutions were of the same size if not efficiency.

Through the late 1970s he would fret continually at the restrictions being imposed on the freedom of design of race cars, and the freedom of their engineers to come up with ground-breaking new ideas. Chapman's ideal formula for the Grand Prix car was one with but three performance-related rules. He would say, "Pick the maximum capacity of the engine, choose the type of fuel and specify that the resulting car has to fit in a box so long, so wide and so high. Then we can really get down to making a car." All other rules were to be safety-related. Perhaps he would not admit to himself that in many cases it was his own design solutions that had brought about the newly imposed restrictions!

But, analysing the multiplicity of Chapman innovations, quite soon one comes to the conclusion that he was not so much an inventor, that is to say the creator of completely new and original inventions, but more a developer of things someone else had thought of previously. His genius was in the way his mind could find a better application for an already extant idea and fine-tune it, or incorporate it to provide an exciting new solution.

The early sports-racing cars – the Eight, Nine, Ten, Eleven and Fifteen – were examples of stiff, lightweight structures using the space frame (which was not new) in extremely aerodynamic bodywork (which also was not new) with suspension systems (which were not new) designed into one cohesive whole that was at the same time of extremely efficient high performance and beautiful to look at.

The Twelve, the first single-seater, used the Chapman strut rear suspension. This incorporated a MacPherson strut (which was not new) but this time in the rear suspension and thus reduced the suspension to just three links. It was later used in production on the original Elite.

The Lotus 25, one of his most stunning creations, was provoked by the need to dispense with the simply awful and difficult-to-manufacture aluminium fuel tanks that wove their way in and out of the chassis tubes on the 24 and were always leaking and never interchangeable from one car to another. Chapman's solution, the monocoque (also not new) utilised this type of construction in an entirely new application and allowed the introduction of rubber fuel cells (not new, but used for the first time in a racing car).

The backbone chassis of the 26, the original Lotus Elan, was also not new but allowed a departure from the complex monocoque hull of the original Elite and was something that could be relatively easily productionised while allowing a bolt-on glassfibre body to be kept, for the cost of tooling for a metal body was too high for the company to contemplate.

The 29 and 38 Indy cars resulted from his realisation, after a test with the 25 at the famous oval, that the following year would be the first after the original brick surface was repaved. This fact alone would permit cars with European-type road racing suspension to survive 500 miles and corner at speeds the front-engined dinosaurs could not achieve.

The Lotus 49 was a package that was possible because of his success not only in persuading Walter Hayes of Ford to fund a Formula 1 engine but also in negotiating a position where his input into the final layout of the engine permitted it to be used as a structural part of the chassis, and from which to hang the rear suspension. And what a package it was! But Chapman was not the first to use the engine as a stressed part of a vehicle.

The 72 was the first all-new design of a Formula 1 car to attempt to maximise the performance of the recently introduced wings in Grand Prix racing by incorporating aerodynamics into the fundamental design rather than treat them as bolt-on afterthoughts. But the various features that made it different, the torsion bar rising-rate suspension, the inboard front brakes, the side radiators and indeed the overall wedge shape, had all been seen before. And while the 78 and 79 ground-effect cars used for the first time in Formula 1 the motion of the car to suck it to the ground, the theory had been used before, but not with quite the same incredible effect, giving Colin his last World Championship.

Indeed over his career he took out remarkably few patents and the ones he did were mainly to do with processes rather than particular parts or products. But the measure of his impact can best be judged from the fact that there is hardly an idea of his on a car that has not been extensively copied or utilised by other designers. Enzo Ferrari preferred to be addressed as 'Ingegnere' rather than the title 'Commendatore' bestowed on him later, and I think that Colin would prefer to be remembered by his engineering achievements: taking what was often a remote and unlikely idea and engineering it into something which would work, and more importantly work better than those of his competitors.

In completing this analysis of some of his innovations – and there were many, many more – it is somewhat sad to reflect that because he was ahead of his time and the rest of the field so often, and his mind worked at such an incredible pace, frequently he did not stick with the development of ground-breaking design but preferred to go on to the next thoughts in his mind. As a result, very often the copies of his cars turned out to be more successful than his own. There is no doubt, for example, that the Patrick Head-designed Williams ground-effect cars were far better race cars than the

Lotuses of the same period, yet they were simply beautifully engineered copies of Chapman's concept.

Grand Prix racing can be divided into four sequential periods from the end of the 2½-litre formula in 1960 to Colin's death in 1982. There was the 1½-litre formula from 1961 to 1965; the 3-litre formula in its pre-aerodynamic phase from 1966 to 1969; the surface aerodynamics phase from 1970 to 1976; and the ground-effects period from 1977. All were profoundly influenced by Colin Chapman's cars and, even though there were odd variations on the theme, every car on the grid owed something to the ingenuity and design concepts of this one man. In fact there were those in the late 1970s who went further and said that there was not a car on English roads that did not owe something to his original thinking in the design, structure, layout, handling or performance of his own cars, whether road or racing. That by anyone's standards is a very considerable legacy.

As a businessman Colin had something of the 'second-hand car dealer' about him and, while later in his life he was perfectly at ease in the offices of the Chairmen of very large corporations, he could not resist a 'deal' – mainly, one felt, because his confidence in his own quick-thinking mind made him feel he could always get one over on the other party. This somewhat cavalier attitude led to some fairly major disasters that usually resulted in the summoning of the faithful right-hand man, Fred Bushell, to sort out the ensuing mess while, as with the racing cars, Colin was off and on his way to the next deal. It has to be said that he came from a fairly hard school of knocks. While building the business he was dealing with a clientele of budding and established racing drivers who would go to extreme lengths to get themselves into a Lotus at the least possible expense, and who thought as little of cutting the odd corner in business dealings as they did on the track.

It was a characteristic of his business ethic that, for all the years that I had occasion to be summoned to his office at Hornsey, Cheshunt, Hethel and finally at Ketteringham Hall, there was a framed sign facing you on his desk that said: "I know you believe that what you think I said is what I want, but are you sure that what you heard is really what I meant?".

This was made clear in the early 1960s when, with the Elan coming into being, there remained just over 100 of the original Elites unsold, many finished ones standing deteriorating in the field next to the factory. Colin summoned the then Lotus Car Company Sales Executive, Ron Richardson, and me to his office where with his usual charm onslaught he persuaded us to add to our existing responsibilities and get on and sell these remaining cars. The carrot was a commission scheme that appeared on the face of it to be generous and potentially rewarding. We worked long and hard, wheeled and dealed, cajoled the dealers, advertised and dealt with the retail customers and pressured the production department to get the cars out in the right but frequently changing colour and specification order, making ourselves extremely unpopular around the factory in the process. Came the day when the last one was gone and Ron and I presented ourselves in Colin's office for what we hoped was a fairly substantial pat on the back and, who knows, perhaps even a drink out of the drinks cabinet. All was going well until we presented our claim for commission. Colin point-blank refused to pay out that much money to any employee, and the realisation dawned on us that "what we had heard was not really what he meant".

On another occasion, this time in 1970 at Hethel and while Team Lotus was still housed in the main factory building, Colin was leaving on a trip to the USA when he noticed in the yard the crates containing the returned four-wheel-drive Lotus 64s that had gone to Indianapolis in 1969, but were not raced because of Mario Andretti's practice accident. This triggered his mind to conjure up a list of all the old and obsolete cars on the balance sheet at that moment; they offended his sense of tidiness not to mention the cash he could see tied up. "I'm off to the States for a bit," he said. "When I get back I don't want to see any of these – I don't care what you do with them, sell them, give them away, do anything you like, but if they are here when I get back I am going to cut them up and throw them in the bin. And that goes for those others over the road as well." So saying he dashed off to the airport. When he returned I was quite chuffed to be able to tell him that the bandsaw would not be necessary as I had managed to sell the job lot to one customer, Robs Lamplough, for a not inconsiderable sum of money, given their alternative destination. "You've done what?" he exploded. "Well, get on the 'phone and tell him it was all a big mistake and get the cars back." Dumbfounded and entirely at a loss to grasp what had changed his mind, I telephoned a distinctly unimpressed Robs. The ensuing lawsuit went on for years and was eventually settled mostly in Robs' favour, but included among other things getting a Lotus 49 back from the National Motor Museum at Beaulieu, where it was on indefinite loan on a covenant. These complex negotiations, the administration involved, coupled with the legal fees paid to the ever-eager lawyers who could see another golden goose coming their way, must have more than eroded all the money from the sale. After a great deal of soul-searching I came to the conclusion that his remarks prior to his departure to America were no more than a cunning plan to ascertain whether there was indeed any residual value in the cars. He certainly succeeded in winding me up to get the answer in the short time he was away, and as a priority over the other perhaps more interesting work on my job list.

As with any fast-growing company, and particularly one involved in technology, the pressure to expand was relentless and the demands for fresh money continuous, either for new plant and machinery or greatly increased space and premises. In the early days of road car production Colin's view, when presented with another criticism of the build quality or cost-cutting component-purchasing policy, was that we were selling to a very specialist market – 'the lunatic fringe' he used to call it – where in return for the blistering performance, fantastic handling and graceful good looks the customer was quite prepared to put up with some inconvenience, even if this did entail getting out and getting under from time to time.

If asked what we would do when we had exhausted the 'lunatic fringe' he would reply that we were not to worry. In his estimation the client pool was capable of absorbing about 4,000 cars a year, and as some grew out of their youthful, enthusiastic, sports car-owning period they would be replaced by a fresh intake at the bottom end of the age bracket. In retrospect there was not a lot wrong with this philosophy. Had it not been for his ambition to become the size of Porsche, who were at the time producing in the region of 14,000 cars a year, one could have seen a continuation of a steady and profitable run of exciting and affordable sports and GT cars. Unfortunately, as Colin's family grew up he seemed to drift off into the need for 2+2s and ever more sophisticated cars with leather upholstery, air conditioning and, heaven forbid, automatic gearboxes. What he seemed to have missed was the fact that the customers for these cars were by nature professional people, rather than enthusiasts, who did not take kindly to spending a sizeable portion of their large salaries only to find that reliability was not the car's strong point and that their nearest dealer was not necessarily just down the road. So after the heyday of the original Elite, the Elan and the Europa, how refreshing it was to see the beautiful Lotus Elise once more capturing the true Lotus market. Colin would surely have been immensely proud of such an outstanding little car created in the true spirit of his early concepts and bearing the ACBC badge.

Needless to say it was his foray into the whole range of second-series Elites, Eclats and Esprits that forced him to seek funding from outside sources, first with David Wickins of British Car Auctions – who had as a background partner Michael Ashcroft of ADT security systems fame – and then Toyota. When Colin died the control of the company was finally lost with the sale of Group Lotus to General Motors. Happily at the Stock Exchange flotation in the late 1960s the city in its infinite wisdom decided that shareholders, and particularly institutional shareholders, would not want to be involved in the risk of owning a racing car company, and so Team Lotus was kept as a wholly and privately owned separate entity.

Little did they know that they had backed the wrong horse, for not only was Team Lotus healthily profitable in all the years in which I was involved except one (1987, when we promised Ayrton Senna an unlimited development budget), but for year after year Fred Bushell, who wore Team Lotus and Group Lotus hats, also passed over some of our hard-earned money to keep the car company from yet another crisis.

There was another side of Colin Chapman that a few of us were privileged to see: a man intensely occupied with his family, and of quite unbelievable generosity. It is said that behind every great man there is an even greater woman and Colin's wife Hazel certainly fulfilled this role. Hazel provided the solid base and the calm, measured advice that on many occasions prevented some of Colin's more headstrong and impetuous schemes, but between them they succeeded in putting together a home and a family environment that would be the envy of us all. To visit Colin and Hazel at their house was to pass into an oasis of calm, comfort, warm hospitality, exquisite taste and enjoyment of life that was as refreshing as it was a complete contrast with the madhouse that was the office. Now it would be easy to say that an achievement of that sort is not so difficult if you have money. But I believe that at home lay the entire object of Colin's ambitions in business, and that his continual and manic drive for success was primarily to benefit his family. Undoubtedly he could be as difficult to live with as he was to work with in the business, and it is certain that there were from time to time some pretty tempestuous moments. But in spite of his burning wish for his children to be as successful as he was, which resulted in their all being driven quite hard, he built this oasis to which he could return from the rigours of another day, week or month of high tension and usually drama.

Of his generosity there are too many examples to list, but one or two stories might put things into some sort of perspective. In 1974, well into my period of managing Team Lotus, he and I were flying into London Heathrow in the company's single-engine Piper

Cherokee to get to a meeting in London. I was wearing, as I always did, the traditional watch that was given to employees after so many years of service and that had been on my wrist for some years already, as I had started in 1958. As we let down on finals on runway One-Zero Right the controller in the tower was screaming at Colin to keep his speed up to 140 knots as there was a 747 behind us and please would we try and take the very first off-ramp to the right to clear the runway for the following 'heavy'.

Colin was not flustered at all and popped the Cherokee down on the first 50 yards of the tarmac, applied the brakes hard and promptly burst a tyre. The aircraft was now stranded on the right half of the main Heathrow incoming runway with a stack of jetliners behind, getting closer, and the first was a big Jumbo. Colin shouted to me that he had to stay on the radio and that I should get out and push. As will have been understood from remarks earlier in this chapter, he was not one with whom to argue. So I unfastened the door, leapt out and pushed like hell. Reaching the first off-ramp totally finished, I jumped back in the right-hand seat, naïvely thinking that this would offer some degree of protection from the incoming 320 tons of Boeing. After the noise of its reverse thrust had died away Colin turned to me and spoke.

"Are you all right?"

"No, I am not," I replied. "Actually I am really pissed off."

"Oh, why is that?" he said. "Well, somewhere in that kerfuffle I've gone and lost my watch and it was the one you gave me."

"Well, you're not going back to look for it – I've got the breakdown wagon on its way to tow us in."

The next day, late in the afternoon, he popped his head round the door of my office and told me he had something for me. The package contained a solid gold Rolex Oyster Perpetual Day-Date Chronometer wristwatch which had already been inscribed 'From the Guv'nor' and which, needless to say, I wear until this day.

One day in April 1975 I left the factory at Hethel at 6am in my company Elan Plus 2, picked up our designer Ralph Bellamy, and set off for a Silverstone test. We were still in Norfolk, travelling down the A11, when the lead vehicle in an army convoy decided that at that time in the morning there was unlikely to be any traffic about, and drove straight out of a side turning into the path of the Lotus. Ralph was perfectly all right but I was less fortunate, being trapped in the right-hand side of the car with both legs broken in several places and a nasty head wound. The ambulance took me to Bury St Edmunds hospital where they operated on my legs, and when I came round there was Colin standing beside my bed with an enormous box that hardly fitted between the next bed and mine.

"You'll be needing something to pass the time," he said. "Now where are we going to put it?" He promptly started reorganising the furniture in the ward so he could position the portable colour television he'd bought me (remember that colour was still fairly new, and a portable would have been hugely expensive). Having shifted everything around to put it where I could see it, he then tested to see if the reception was of decent quality. This was a man of decent quality.

On another occasion in November 1973 he asked if my wife and I would like to take his place at the FIA prizegiving in Paris to receive the World Championship Trophy for Constructors. Just before we left in the company aircraft he caught up with Yvonne and slipped her an envelope saying, "That's for you to blow on something really nice for yourself." In the envelope was a not inconsiderable sum of cash in French francs. And when we got home he insisted that I keep the original World Championship trophy and have a replica made for him.

But these examples are only a very few of the many, many cases of his generosity and consideration towards me and my family. Following the championship season he flew everyone who worked for Team Lotus, and their wives, to Majorca for a week's holiday. At the conclusion of an earlier championship year he gave everyone on the crew a Ford Cortina! There are many others who worked for him who were on the receiving end of this typical generosity of mind.

On the other hand he could at times be the most difficult, intransigent, uncompromising and downright rude b*****d it was possible to imagine. In 1976 we had started the year badly with the Lotus 77, which was his then current idea of a car for all seasons and circuits. Although the master design was followed as faithfully as possible by the designers of the time, Martin Ogilvie, Geoff Aldridge and Mike Cooke, the constraints of the multiple variability of wheelbase, track, weight distribution and aerodynamic configuration, not to mention the ever-present "must be 50lb under the weight limit" laid down by Colin for his infinitely adjustable race car, left us with something that was fragile and complex; it had 108 different settings for the rear wing alone. Furthermore, due to the sub-frames carrying the inboard brakes as well as the suspension links being well out in the airstream, it unfortunately had the aerodynamic efficiency of a Norfolk barn.

After losing Ronnie Peterson to March after the Brazilian Grand Prix, the Team arrived at Long Beach for the USA West Grand Prix with Gunnar Nilsson and rookie Bob Evans, whose only previous outings had been South Africa and the Race of Champions at Brands Hatch. No wonder, then, that the Team did as badly as it ever had with Bob Evans failing to qualify (only 20 starters were allowed) and Gunnar languishing on the back row of the grid. What was already a débâcle promptly turned into a disaster when Gunnar crashed into the unforgiving concrete wall, the car turning sharply and without notice when a rear radius rod mounting failed on the first lap. There followed the most unholy row with Colin, who was dejected beyond belief, completely losing control and shouting and screaming and basically blaming me for every ill that had befallen the Team and many that had not. What finally caused me to lose my cool was that he was blaming me as well for the design deficiencies of the car. Only the intervention of the cool-headed Swedish submariner, Gunnar Nilsson, prevented blows actually being exchanged. I resolved there and then to jack it in. Colin must have got the vibes being given off by my quivering disbelief at the perceived injustice of it all, for when we got back to base there was a long hand-written letter of apology, followed soon thereafter by a gift of an immaculately tooled leather briefcase inside which was a card with a further personal note. So the b*****d had changed back into a nice guy just as quickly as he had gone the other way.

Nonetheless it was after the Long Beach episode that I came increasingly to consider whether I was suffering from what had become known as 'Cosworth syndrome': when the engine won it was a Ford and when it blew up it was a Cosworth. In this case, if we did well it was Chapman, and if we did badly it was Warr. Also, after so many years under the Chapman umbrella I did not really know if I could get things done for myself. When at the British Grand Prix that year I was approached in broad daylight behind our mobile home by a loud and larger-than-life guy who said he was going to start his own racing team, asked me if I would come and run it for him, and would not take 'no' for an answer, I decided that the time was right to see if I could do it without the all-pervading influence of Colin Chapman. The guy's name, by the way, was Walter Wolf, and his team included the late Dr Harvey Postlethwaite as his chief engineer, and Jody Scheckter was to be the driver. But that is another story.

When Colin came back from his holiday at his villa in Ibiza that summer, Hazel was complaining that as usual he quickly became bored with relaxing and lying in the sun. What he had done was to spend the time insulated from the pressures and mundane irritants of the office to produce in 30 handwritten sheets of his standard 'Oxford' feint-ruled and margined note pads (on which his job lists were always kept) the thesis and design philosophy that was the basis for the Lotus 78 'ground-effect' car. This was to set the standard for the next complete generation of Grand Prix cars of every manufacturer. I call it a thesis because the first considerable part of it was concerned purely with the theory of obtaining downforce from below the car with less drag than had been possible hitherto with surface aerodynamic devices.

With Colin's typical verve and enthusiasm a new division was set up at Ketteringham Hall, previously used as a staff training area by the car company and where the original model of the Esprit was made. There throughout the summer, while still developing and racing ever more successfully the 77, the basic configuration of the new 78 car was honed. In September at Monza I thought it only fair to tell Colin, with three months to run to the end of my contract, that I would be joining Walter Wolf in 1977, leaving him sufficient time to organise a replacement. With typical generosity of spirit, when he realised that he was not going to be able to change my mind he said, "Well, off you go then. Good luck and let's not treat it as farewell, just a leave of absence." I was not to know at the time how fortunate I was to have an employer and friend like him.

When I returned to Team Lotus in late 1981 there had been a radical change in the man I had known in 1976. In the interim there had been the glory days of Andretti's World Championship, but also a less attractive period of intense commercialism, untold pressures in the car company business, and a succession of other distractions that come from running a growing and diversifying group of companies.

Colin had had a brush with an outrageous character called David Thieme, whose company, Essex Petroleum, had sponsored the Team for a couple of seasons. Gone were the days when it was important to stay in the same family-owned hotels as the drivers and team, in order to dine with them and extend the discussion time with them. Gone were the days when he was still in the garage at 9pm working out yet another ingenious solution to the problem of the day, or writing a personal job list of sometimes more than 90 items to be finished by the next morning. And certainly gone were the days when his energy and drive were directed so exclusively towards his racing team because of growing complaints from other areas of the businesses about getting access to his time.

It was also during the period from 1977 to 1981 that he came into contact with John DeLorean. The aftermath and consequences of that adventure were just starting to spill over when I came back to the Team for the 1982 season. However, it looked like things were looking up and in much the same way that fortuitously our previous association had ended with Mario Andretti's glorious victory in the Japanese Grand Prix of 1976, 1982 rolled towards its close with Elio de Angelis scraping that narrowest of wins over Keke Rosberg in the Austrian Grand Prix at Zeltweg by five hundreths of a second.

Although that was to be the last time that Colin saw a Lotus take a Grand Prix win, the last time he was in the pits with his cars he saw one of them crash. By special arrangement we laid on a Lotus 92, in fact Elio's race winner from Austria, at Donington in early December for Prince Michael of Kent to try. The day was cold and the circuit just damp with dew. In spite of repeated reminders that the tyres would be very difficult to warm up, if indeed they could be at all at the speeds at which the car was likely to be driven, His Royal Highness let it get away from him and bumped the earth bank backwards. We had lunch in the Redgate Lodge with Prince Michael and then Colin dashed off back to the factory leaving me to sort out the mess, as we had another commitment for the afternoon. A young Japanese driver had won a test drive in a JPS Formula 1 car as his prize for winning his series in Japan. His name was Satoru Nakajima. But Colin did not meet this young man who was to play an important part in his race team in the 1980s, because a few days later he was dead.

Thus ended an era in motor racing dominated by the personality and genius of one man, the possessor of an outstanding mind, someone who lived life to the full and who achieved in 53 short years far more than many to whom a full lifespan is granted. What we all missed is just what he would have made of the eras that followed him: the turbos, the flat bottoms, the second coming of active suspension, the electronic aids, the clutchless paddle-operated gearboxes and the politics. We can be sure that he would have revelled in the technology explosion, would have found his own, probably astonishing, way of extracting the maximum from the regulations, and through his ingenuity would probably have caused yet a few more rules to be written to stop him doing what he had just done and no-one else had thought possible.

CHAPTER 2

Racing Mechanics

"You've got to remember it's only a sport"

It is ten o'clock on Saturday evening in the pit garages at a Grand Prix circuit. It could be any circuit. Some eight hours have passed since the end of qualifying. The mechanics have been working to a set pre-race preparation schedule that will include changing the engine and fitting the race rear end (gearbox and rear suspension). They will also change any 'lifed' components and complete a checklist that might have upward of a hundred specific tasks. In addition they will be keeping an eye on the idiosyncrasies of 'their' chassis. Then they must tackle any other jobs written out on a job list by the race engineers. These could include anything from settings changes to improve further the performance of the car, via modifications to a component that has given trouble during practice, to repairs to mend any parts which have been given a beating by the driver, the kerbs or even the Armco barrier. The extra items have to be woven into the work programme in a cohesive and time-efficient way.

There are two things the mechanics hate above all else. The first is being kept waiting by the manager, engineers and drivers in one of their interminable debriefs for the list of work to be done. The second is to be given the work list in a way that means they have to strip and rebuild something twice.

But that friction-filled time has long since passed and the car is now sitting on the trestles. It is finished bar the bodywork and wheels. The suspension geometry and aerodynamic settings can only be done when the car is on the floor. The mechanics stand back waiting for the electronics man to finish peering into his laptop, the engine men to finish their installation checks, the race engineers to fuss over the interpretation of their settings sheets and be given the word to fire up the new engine.

It is now a quarter to eleven and, far from being filled with exhaust fumes, the garage is filled with grim-faced technicians indulging in a great deal of head-scratching. The computer guys are busy connecting their umbilical cords to the black boxes on the chassis. The engine men are taking out spark plugs and peering down borescopes. Someone is trying to reach the engine shop on the telephone and the mechanics, sure that they have done their bit right, are rapidly losing patience. If the bloody thing is not going to start they want to get on and do something about it so they can get off to their hotel, which may be 30 miles away, have a beer, shower and get their heads down, for they know that race day is a 6am start.

Finally the chief mechanic intervenes. He sends the crew from the spare car, the other race car, and the tyre men off in the second minibus. He tells the engineers in no uncertain terms that the time for research and fault-tracing is over and that they had better make a decision. Perhaps relieved that someone has taken the lead and that some gremlin will be discovered back at the ranch that will not have been down to him, the race engineer confirms that a second engine change is needed. The truckie and the spares man, both old hands at viewing the decision-making process, have anticipated what was inevitable in their eyes. They have already unloaded the next engine, stripped it out of its travelling frame and popped it on a wheeled engine stand. They now deliver it instantaneously to the scene but not without bumping, accidentally of course, into the engineer in question. This is a gesture of support for their mates, the race mechanics. Then the two of them head off to the mobile home to drum up another tray of teas and coffees, getting a perverse enjoyment from the fact that this means the mobile homers will be up late as well.

Among the mechanics, some subdued muttering and some not so

subdued about the ancestry of all engineers, electricians, engine builders, suppliers and anyone else involved in the chain of supply is to be heard. From outside comes the sound of roller shutters going down on yet another team that has finished for the night. This is followed by a quick head or two round the door of the garage from the friends from other teams who are unable to resist a quick "Goodnight" wind-up.

The muttering from the mechanics, however, is not bitchiness or overt criticism but an inbuilt way of gearing themselves up for a quick and efficient engine change. There is no way that any of them would accept sending a car to the grid the next day in anything but the best condition that they are able to achieve. And what makes it tolerable is that, sarcastic "Goodnights" or not from their competitors, their car is on the pole.

At this moment, to settle things down and recover concentration on the task in hand, chief mechanic Bob Dance is heard to say, "You've got to remember, it's only a sport."

The tension is relieved and the task begins. The crew gets to bed just after 3am, any thoughts of a beer long since banished. It would be great to finish the story by saying that the race was won but of course this does not always happen.

So who are these heroes who make up the engine room of Grand Prix racing? Of the several hundred who passed through Team Lotus during my time there, it is amazing to observe the variety of backgrounds from which they came. There was one who had been a milkman. One was the son of an Oscar-winning film director. One was an American Airlines cabin attendant. Many were frustrated racing drivers. Quite a few were Antipodeans looking for a fix of something they could not get at home. Many were apprenticed garage mechanics in search of a more colourful and glamorous existence than the local car dealer could offer. And many were ex-servicemen, particularly from the Royal Air Force, who at the end of their spell of service were not convinced by what the careers office put before them. Then there were the nationalities. Australians,

Kiwis, Swedes, South Africans, North Americans, South Americans, French and Japanese in addition to the home-grown Brits who were, not unnaturally, the vast majority.

Disparate characters from disparate homes and backgrounds, by and large they all had one common interest – motor racing and an enthusiasm for things mechanical, preferably high-speed things. Not for them the mundane routine of a clock-on, clock-off job with set hours, set location, set mealtimes and a set home to which to return at the end of the day. They looked for something extra, the adrenalin buzz of an instant result to their week's effort, the highs of success and the lows of failure, something to talk about with their wives or girlfriends or simply something to mull over with their mates over a pint in the team's favourite hostelry. Or at least, if they had taken the job with any other preconceptions or expectations, that was what they soon learned it was all about.

Mostly young men, they tended to burn out in three to five seasons of the Grand Prix treadmill or their priorities changed with the advent of families – they say that the second thing a Team Lotus mechanic did when he got home was put down his suitcase. Others felt that they had got the experience they needed to go off and start something on their own. Many used the Team Lotus experience, which proudly stood out on their CV, to gain advancement in other fields.

Others, though, stuck at it with simply amazing endurance, resilience and grit, and spent their working lives racing, season after season. Then they would build next year's cars during the winter off-season. Many of these have a quite staggering list of achievements to their name. These include World Championships, impressive numbers of individual Grand Prix wins, pole positions, deep and lasting relationships with the most famous drivers. But, most remarkably, they had a way of dealing with everything that was thrown at them with intelligence, intuition, versatility, experience, application and never failing good humour. And yet none has a cabinet of medals recording their successes. They should have.

Of course their other really outstanding deeds rarely even got a mention, even in the weekly race reports. They built complete race cars from scratch between the end of practice on Friday and first practice on Saturday morning. They changed engines in minutes when needs must. They replaced components buried deep in the engine bay with minutes to go to the end of practice, all the while smelling their own flesh scorching. They found ways to repair parts in the field with none of the equipment available at the factory. They could turn their hands to skills in which they were not specifically trained: panel-beating, composite lay-ups, electronics, machining, in fact anything that needed to be done on a race car. They achieved *Guinness Book of Records* times from circuits all over Europe to the channel ports in huge trucks. They left the English sub-zero temperatures in January and started work in the 37 degrees C – blood heat – paddock of Rio de Janeiro an hour after stepping off the aeroplane. And then they continued with five consecutive 18-hour working days in those oppressive conditions. Many times from a total of, say, 120 hours spent in such a country, they could count on the fingers of one hand the number of hours spent in bed at their hotel. This was particularly true of the early-season races.

During the second week of October 1969, Team Lotus was much pre-occupied on the one hand with a drama of considerable magnitude and on the other with a crisis that could have far-reaching effects. The previous weekend the Team's lead driver Graham Hill had had an enormous accident at Watkins Glen. After spinning off on oil he undid his seat belts to get out and push his Lotus 49 back on to the circuit. Positioning it on a downwards slope, he jumped back into the car, bump-started it and set off back into the race. Noticing some chunking in a rear tyre, probably due to a slow puncture picked up during his off-road excursion, he signalled the pit that he was coming in for tyres. He never made it, for that lap a sudden and complete deflation of the rear tyre caused him to go off the road again this time with disastrous results. The car dug in, rolled over and half-threw Graham out of the car. It landed with his legs half in and half out of the cockpit, causing him injuries of such severity that his career to all intents and purposes was ended. It was little consolation that Jochen Rindt won the race, the richest on the calendar, in the other works car. So that week everyone was concerned that Graham would recover and with the enormous help of Walter Hayes of Ford arrangements were being made to get him home to England as soon as he could travel.

The crisis developing at the same time was an undercurrent of grumbling among the race mechanics about their wages. It came to a head when Mike 'Herbie' Blash, then a number two mechanic on one of the race cars, asked for a rise in his wages from £29.10 to £29.50 per week. In our second full season with the sport's first commercial sponsorship from John Player & Son, there was a feeling abroad that the Team could afford better pay and conditions. Whether Herbie was pushed forward as the junior fall guy to jump in and test the water will never be known but the ramifications could have a serious effect on the 1970 budget. At that time Team Lotus was involved in running no fewer than five race programmes with five different race crews. The year started with the Tasman series in Australia and New Zealand with 2½-litre Lotus 49s; there was a team doing Indianapolis with the four-wheel-drive Lotus 64 cars; the Formula 1 Team was committed to the full World Championship season; while in England we were running a Gold Leaf team of two cars in both GT and Formula 3. So any wage review did not just affect one or two people.

By 2000 a number two mechanic with one of the leading teams was earning a salary of £32,000, while his number one would be getting over £34,000. The 1969 mechanics received a share of 10 per cent of the prize money earned by their car that might amount to a £2.50 to £5 bonus for a Grand Prix win. In 2000 each of the crew got a bonus of some hundreds of pounds per World Championship point.

So it is refreshing and pleasing to see that, hard school though it was – many think that Team Lotus was the toughest training ground of all – so many of the class of 1969 went on to make such successes of their careers. The 1969 Racing Manager, Dick Scammell, previously mechanic and then chief mechanic, became the Managing Director of Cosworth Racing. Herbie Blash went on to be Team Manager of Brabham, then Managing Director of Yamaha F1, and is now Bernie Ecclestone's right-hand man. Eddie Dennis, then Herbie's number one, ran his own successful business for many years before returning to Classic Team Lotus and working again with the cars from that era. Derek 'Joe 90' Mower created his own team, Nordic Racing, as did Dave 'Beaky' Sims and Hywel 'Hughie' Absalom, though for many years Hughie designed and built his own successful race cars. Jim Pickles built up an excellent gun restoration and repair business. His erstwhile partner on the Formula 3 team, Ian Campbell, has run a successful and expanding engineering business for many years.

Bob Dance is still motor racing. After 40 years in the sport, most of which he spent with Lotus, March, Brabham and then again Lotus, this doyen of chief mechanics joined the Audi Le Mans effort. From the very early days Bob would keep a diary of the hours he worked, not from a unionist point of view but purely for his own interest.

When he was with March in the early 1970s, soon after that team was formed, he averaged 53 hours per week. By the late 1980s that figure had risen to over 70 hours per week, in spite of greatly increased crew numbers. A 1969 long-distance overseas Grand Prix saw Team Lotus taking a total of nine people. The numbers were made up of Colin Chapman, the Team Manager, the two drivers, two mechanics on each race car and one mechanic on the spare car. By 1979, the heyday of the ground-effect era, the number of personnel travelling to long-distance races had risen to 15. The extra people now included a race engineer, bodywork and sliding skirt specialists, two dedicated tyre men and a spares man. The latter task had previously been undertaken by the chief mechanic. For European races the number went up still further with the inclusion of an extra mechanic, a truckie to drive the second truck and the couple to run the catering in the mobile home. By 1979 the paddock had also seen the first of the species known as the PR man or Commercial Manager. In 1989 Team Lotus took an average of 32 people to Grand Prix events. Ten years later, for the first race of the season in Melbourne, Australia, both McLaren and British American Racing took 80 people. That was almost exactly twice the *total* number of people employed, both at the factory and as race crew and in the offices, by Team Lotus in 1969 when the Team undertook five separate race programmes.

In the 1970s the travel arrangements and cargo aircraft capacities limited teams to 1,000kg of spares for intercontinental races. In the 21st century the main players take some 20 tons of spares.

But the cars are infinitely more complex today. Specialists have to be in place for most aspects of a car's engineering. Specialists need their own equipment to collect, download, analyse and illustrate their data, whether it be sent by telemetry or gathered by on-board black boxes. The World Championship series is now up to 20 races instead of the 11 of 1969, quite apart from testing. So it is not surprising that the heroes, the race mechanics, are working still longer hours.

Studies have shown that above 55 hours per week at work, people start to become less efficient. Quite how this relates to the race mechanic is incomprehensible. For a European Grand Prix the transporters would leave usually on a Tuesday. So having done a day's work on Monday and perhaps an even later one on Tuesday finishing with the actual loading of the truck, the mechanics might have worked as many as 28 hours before their day off on Wednesday. This free day did not apply to the truckies, two in each truck. Then on Thursday morning the crew would set off very early to the airport, catch a flight, drive to the circuit and finish the immediate pre-race preparation and setting up of the garages and pits. That would add up to another 14-hour day if there was no drama, such as an unfinished car having left the factory due to late arrival of parts. So before the race meeting proper started on Friday morning the mechanics had already worked 42 hours. If it was a completely straightforward meeting with no further dramas they could expect to put in two 16-hour days on Friday and Saturday, the days of official practice. This would be followed by at least an 11-hour day on race day to the point at which the truck was once again loaded. Race day became another 16- to 18-hour day if one included getting back to the airport, the flight home and the drive back to the factory. So depending on whether travel time is included in the working day, the best case was a 75-hour week, the worst case substantially longer.

Even in these most testing of circumstances it was impossible to detect any loss of efficiency from the crew. Their physical tiredness could easily be masked by the exhilaration of their car doing well, though on some occasions the cameras did catch the odd one catnapping in the pits during a race.

Furthermore, if the race had been at one of the nearer circuits, the truck would be back at the ranch on Monday. The race crew would be back into work straight away to get engines out and returned for rebuild. This process had the feel of yet another out-and-out race because the system, for example at Cosworth, worked strictly on a first-come, first-served basis. The long haul of stripping, modifications, repairs and preparation would start all over again for the next departure six or seven days later. The intervening weekend was treated quite simply as normal working days.

From time immemorial it was the practice to pay the race crew a flat rate per week as it was impractical to calculate the hours actually worked. Their overtime was supposedly compensated by their share of prize money. The factory-based personnel who were 'on the clock' received overtime rates for their hours over and above the standard working week of the factory.

So it is fair to say that the Team got exceptional value from the £29.10 a week paid to Herbie Blash.

Before Bernie Ecclestone and Bob Dance introduced the first articulated transporter to the Formula 1 paddock in the early 1970s a different system applied. The cab of the articulated lorry held only two people, thereby prompting the system of flying the rest of the crew to meetings. Prior to that the custom-built team transporters incorporated crew cabs with seven or eight seats and the race crew travelled to and from meetings in the transporter, further lengthening their working hours. The range of commercial chassis available meant that the basis for most transporters was a coach chassis.

In 1970 the Team Lotus transporter was a Leyland Leopard chassis fitted with a purpose-built crew cab and bodywork fitted with ramps that could carry three race cars. Lockers accessed from inside and out carried the spare engines, gearboxes, suspension and chassis parts as well as an ever-increasing number of wheels. The introduction of the slick tyre necessitated extra sets of wheels for wet-weather tyres. The transporter also carried equipment such as a lathe and a welding set and there was also a large-capacity concealed tank. This was separate to the truck diesel tank and was used for transporting high-octane racing fuel, the local supplies being distinctly dodgy in some parts of Europe. During its service this transporter also saw the introduction of new-fangled wings and other aerodynamic parts that added to the pressure on space and gross weight.

I remember hitching a lift once with the crew back from a non-championship race at Oulton Park. The whole plot, valuable personnel and virtually all of the Team's assets represented by the race cars and spares was proceeding down the M1 at a speed somewhat in excess of the limit. Dozing like the rest of the crew, I heard a clearly stated "Ready?" from Eddie Dennis, who was driving at the time. An equally clear "Ready" came the response from the guy sitting to the left of the driver's seat. Whereupon to my complete astonishment Eddie stood up, vacated the driver's seat to his right and was immediately replaced by the new driver. With very little time with no foot on the throttle, the truck lost hardly any momentum.

Seriously concerned by this cavalier attitude to the safety of the crew and the valuable cargo, I remonstrated with Eddie. As usual the explanation was succinct, logical and irrefutable. It seemed that the truck was so overweight that if one stopped with the tyres very hot the weight caused 'flats' to form on the contact patches with the asphalt. It then took four to five miles to run them out round again. In the meantime the vibration was such that the load could be loosened, the race cars could shuffle about and the transporter itself could suffer. With race mechanics I quickly learnt to dispute something in their area of expertise at my peril.

It will be obvious by now that my admiration and respect for the men who plied their trade as race crew have no limits. Indeed, I consider it the greatest privilege of my working life to have had them as colleagues and friends.

Few football managers, when interviewed after a big game, like to single out individuals for particular mention, the sport being a team game. Formula 1 is the same and every person on the team makes their own individual contribution, and their input is as valuable as the next person's. This is true whether their responsibility is highly academic and technical, administrative, or physical as in working with their hands.

So who is to say that the contribution of a star designer or engineer, while being more visible, is greater than that of the Lotus inspector who once tried to get to work in a snowstorm. He found all the roads were blocked and walked four miles across snow-covered fields and Norfolk lanes full of drifts to be sure that the parts needed urgently that morning were passed through his department on time.

The story of Team Lotus's famous factory cleaner also illustrates the point. Brian Leighton, or 'Brian the Broom' as he was universally known, kept the whole factory area clean and ready for work for nearly 30 years.

An almost total absence of schooling left Brian unable to read or write. But he was as strong as an ox, had an unfailingly cheerful disposition, worked very hard and long, and took great pride in his work. He took the practical jokes played upon him in good spirit. He

was once persuaded that if he stood in a dustbin he was strong
enough to lift his own weight off the floor. He had the last laugh,
however, for he tore the handles off the bin. We took him to Brands
Hatch in the 1980s as a treat, and it was the first time he had been
out of Norfolk in his life. He was over 50 at the time.

And yet he could be reduced to tears by some of the sadnesses
that go with motorsport. While his financial rewards seemed to
place a different value on him to that of, say, an engineer, his
contribution to team spirit and morale was equally important.

So the preceding paragraphs have been used as a justification to
single out a few of the stalwarts in this chapter on racing heroes.
But where does one start, and how does one choose? The list of
Team Lotus chief mechanics reads like a programme for a Hall of
Fame. There was Willy Griffiths, who suffered the most dire sequence
of seasons when the Team first started in Grands Prix. He was
followed by Stan Elsworth, who came to us from BRM. There was
Jim Endruweit of white socks fame, who aged from a fresh-faced
youngster to a hardened campaigner in just a few short years, and
who after he retired was still willing to make a comeback when he
was needed. Jim was followed by Dick Scammell, whose innate
understanding of engineering took him on to greater things. Gordon
Huckle had the job the year we lost Jochen Rindt, and was never the
same again. Eddie Dennis followed Gordon, having been the
number one on Jochen's car, and held the job with great equanimity
through the difficult times that followed to go on to achieve two
World Championships.

Keith Leighton, previously of March, whose close relationship
with Ronnie Peterson from those days more than qualified him to
take on the role, was next. But it was his intelligence and ability to
read any given situation that actually got him the job. Keith's volatile
nature and on-the-edge lifestyle took its toll, and he has the
distinction of being the only chief mechanic to have been fired. He
failed to turn up for work at Monaco one morning having overdone
things a bit in the Tiptop Bar the night before.

But his understanding of racing and his devil-may-care attitude also had its plus side. At a Formula 2 race at Interlagos in front of a huge and partisan crowd, while looking after Emerson Fittipaldi in the works car, he spotted that Emerson's brother Wilson had had a push start on the grid, something that the rules did not allow. So he walked over from one side of the front row to the other and, in full view of the Brazilian nation, leaned into Wilson's cockpit and flicked the ignition switch off. Wilson, with a similarly fiery temperament, tried to get out of the car to do serious injury to Keith even though his seatbelts were still fastened.

Keith's place was taken by Rex Hart in doubly difficult circumstances, mid-season and at a time when the Team was struggling to find some form. Then, just prior to my leave of absence to run the Walter Wolf Racing team at the end of 1976, it became possible to secure the services of Bob Dance as chief mechanic. Bob finished his stint with the Team as racing manager in the early 1990s. His was easily the longest continuous occupation of one of the most stressful jobs to be found anywhere in motor racing.

His successor as chief mechanic was Nigel Stepney, who went on to be chief mechanic at Benetton and then Ferrari. Then it was the turn of Paul Diggins, an ex-RAF airframe technician who started with the Team in the 1980s. Such was the quality of the forces training that Paul personified one of those mechanics who knew there was only one way to do things: the right way. His greatest attribute was that he continued to do things right even when under the greatest pressure, and when a short cut might have been the easier solution. Finally Richard Taylor took over, a quiet and extremely intelligent young man whose apprenticeship had taken place in the new very high-tech era. He was therefore used to having to share his domain with the computer whizz-kids, engine specialists and other boffins who doubled the number of people in his garage.

It's quite a list, and together they formed the basis for a record of 79 Grand Prix victories, over 100 pole positions, six World Drivers' Championships and seven World Constructors' Championships.

CHAPTER 3

D~RIVERS~

"Love them or hate them, some are *very* special"

There is little to be gained from adding to the debate. Everyone has their own very personal opinion. But it is nonetheless a debate of interest. It is a debate of emotion. And one of passion, bias and bigotry. In most disputes that go further than discussion, it is usually the lawyers who add to their wealth. In this case the publicans simply sell more rounds of drinks in the pubs where the heated conversations take place. So at least the activity is harmless. There is never a victor, never a loser. No-one is able to say categorically, "He was the best of all time."

Thus any set of personal observations may at best add a little to a legend or by contrast nibble away at the fabric of the pedestal on which another stands.

Many a pundit has, in order to make his own view more emphatic, worked out a formula – a formula that, however it is based or however complex its workings, somehow contrives to place that pundit's favourite in first place. That senior statesman of the profession of motor racing journalism, Denis Jenkinson, had a formula. His was a serious attempt to resolve the debate. It needed to be, for nowhere does the argument rage more fiercely than in the ranks of the motoring journalists.

Jenks's formula was simple: take the number of Grands Prix in which a driver participates, and divide it by the number of wins. The resulting ratio, or strike rate, may be used as a rule-of-thumb. If nothing else, he would say, it would always start a jolly good argument. So using the Jenks formula Juan Manuel Fangio comfortably tops the list of drivers who have completed their careers with 47 per cent (24 wins out of 51 races). He is followed by Jim Clark with 34 per cent and Jackie Stewart with 27 per cent. Alain Prost is fourth with 25.62 per cent and Ayrton Senna fifth with 25.46 per cent.

"But there were only 10 Grands Prix a year in Clark's era whereas Prost and Senna took part in 16 each season!"

"Fangio always had the best car!"

"The formula does not work with an unfinished career such as that of Michael Schumacher. He might still go four seasons without a win!"

"Are we looking for the best racing driver or the fastest racing driver?"

"What if Ayrton had not had the accident?"

"Why is the number of pole positions not taken into account?"

"What about Nuvolari?"

"Fangio and Clark won in many categories, the others were single-seater specialists!"

"If you think any list is complete without Stirling Moss, you must be joking!"

By now the flames of yet another long and invigorating session are well and truly alight. Non-footballers may readily accept that a fair comparison between Sir Stanley Matthews, Pelé and George Best is not possible. They came from different eras, used different equipment and played at different stages in the development of the game. But try and tell a motor racing enthusiast that comparisons of drivers from different eras are invidious and they will immediately launch into the reasons why such comparisons are possible, reasonable and valid. Football fans are probably the same.

During a career in which I was fortunate enough to work with 12 drivers who were, had been or were to become World Champions, it was easy to understand the compelling appeal of all great drivers to their most steadfast supporters. However, they fell into two distinct categories. There were those who were either loved or hated in almost equal measure. These included Stewart, Hunt, Prost and

Mansell. And there were those who were universally loved and admired. On this plateau we find Fangio, Moss, Clark, Rindt, Andretti, Peterson, Lauda and Senna.

The love-them-or-loathe-them brigade as exemplified by Stewart and Prost were almost too clinical in their approach to be judged by the public as having any real warmth of personality. There were too few outrageous overtaking manoeuvres, breathtaking pole position laps or sensational last-gasp victories – simply routine and often predictable wins. Hunt enjoyed an abrasive and non-conformist lifestyle too strong for some tastes and Mansell suffered from personality flaws too blatant to fool a far-seeing public. All of them often had too much to say for themselves outside their field of competence, and it showed.

The brilliance of their performances on the track was the foundation of the reputations of Fangio, Moss, Clark, Rindt, Andretti, Peterson, Lauda and Senna. Their driving did their talking, and the public responded wholeheartedly and without reservation. The natural modesty of the Argentinian and the Scot endeared them to a far wider audience than merely those who followed motor sport. Stirling's spirited and dogged pursuit of success was done with flair and energy very often against odds that would have daunted lesser mortals. And the lesser mortals warmed to him and his attitude. Andretti's versatility, the span of his career and his success in almost every category of the sport sets him aside as one of the all-time greats. Anyone who had the privilege to see Rindt or Peterson behind the wheel of a race car at one of the world's classic circuits immediately knew they were seeing something very special. The great Austrian World Champion, Lauda, won the hearts of whole nations with his bravery and skill. His uncompromising commitment to straight talking also won him respect and innumerable friends because what he said made sense. And the public eventually realised that what they had mistaken for arrogance in Senna was nothing more than the supreme confidence in his own ability that is a trait of true champions. Their presence, style, comportment and humility backed up by their incomparable actions behind the wheel allowed them to cross the boundary from national to truly international superstars, from heroes for motor racing fans to heroes that inspired the common man.

Not all Team Lotus Formula 1 drivers fell into either of these categories. Some were chosen because of a promise for the future that they did not fulfil. Some got the drive as a reward for services in a lesser formula. Some were picked specifically as the supporting act to a 'great' in the number one seat. Others were picked to give the guy in the number one seat a continuing reminder that his was not necessarily a long-term tenancy. The sponsors influenced some choices, the budget others. It is gratifying nonetheless that, when the argument does start and formulae like that of the late Denis Jenkinson are used, there are usually several Team Lotus drivers included in the list under discussion.

Picking from among them is more testing than singling out mechanics and it would be a failing of human nature if the list was impartial. Too much of one's life and emotions are wrapped up in the relationship that a team has with its drivers for any commentary to be truly objective.

JOCHEN

In the late spring of 1962 an unhappy Jo Siffert called at the Lotus factory in Cheshunt, north of London, for some parts. As usual he was driving 'the paddock hotel', a very large American estate car towing a trailer on which sat his Formula Junior car and spares. Instead of rear seats the estate car had a 300-litre fuel tank in the rear footwells, the price of petrol in Switzerland being half that of the rest of Europe. To conceal the tank a large double mattress covered the whole of the rear compartment, and Jo and his mechanics, Jean-Pierre Oberon and Michel Piller, would take it in turns to drive, navigate or sleep. The ensemble could go from Switzerland to Sicily and back without refuelling. 'Seppi' was now getting ready to go to the Grand Prix de Bruxelles for his first race

Peter Warr, aged 17, in his study at Malvern College in 1955 – within only three years he would be working for Lotus. Courtesy of Ilma Moss

National Service in the Royal Horse Artillery – Peter is third from left, back row. After this photo of the cadet school was taken, in December 1957, a freak accident on a firing range put him in hospital for eight months. Warr family collection

Soon after starting work at Lotus during 1958, Peter was able to buy this ex-works Seven with Climax 1,100cc engine for £750; he raced it for two seasons and also did 30,000 road miles in it. Warr family collection

Peter's Ford Anglia van and trailer carrying his Lotus 18, outside the Cheshunt factory in 1961; the van wears the 7 TMT cherished registration from the Lotus Seven. Warr family collection

In the Formula Junior Lotus 20 during 1962; Peter was too tall for this car and the top of his head is rather higher than the roll-over bar. Warr family collection

The Lotus 20 on its side for inspection, with the Lotus Developments van – used to carry spare parts for Lotus customers as well as to tow Peter's race car – in the background. Warr family collection

In 1963 Peter took part in the first-ever Japanese Grand Prix, for sports cars – and won it driving his Lotus 23. Warr family collection

In deference to a local sponsor, Peter forced down a Coca-Cola – which he hated – after winning the Japanese Grand Prix, and was later dismayed to learn that one of his prizes was a year's supply of the stuff. Warr family collection

When Fangio visited Cheshunt, probably in 1963, Peter showed him round: here the five-times World Champion examines a new Lotus-Cortina. Atricia Industrial Pictures

Mike Costin, Chapman's number two in the early days of Lotus, was a good friend to Peter. Having moved to Cosworth, he built Peter's Japanese GP-winning pushrod engine. LAT

Jochen Rindt talks to Colin Chapman from the Lotus 49 cockpit at the 1970 Brands Race of Champions. LAT

Opposite: Rindt and Chapman discuss the 72's practice form at Zandvoort in 1970. Maurice Phillippe, responsible for the car's execution, is in the background. LAT

At Zandvoort that weekend Rindt took the 72 to its maiden victory. sutton-images.com

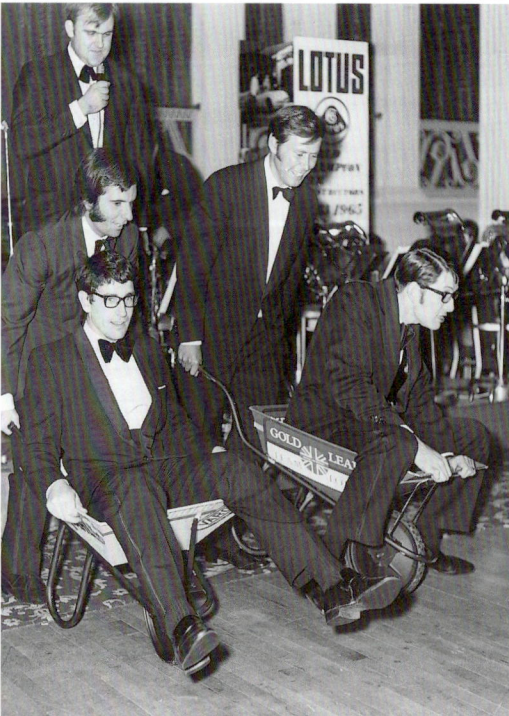

Four weeks after the shocking tragedy of Rindt's death at Monza, Emerson Fittipaldi's fine win at Watkins Glen in the US GP helped restore Team Lotus morale. LAT

High jinks at a black-tie dinner in London at the end of the 1970 season: Dick Scammell pushes Peter in one wheelbarrow, Emerson Fittipaldi and journalist Mike Doodson crew the other. Warr family collection

in the company of the big boys in Formula 1, but he would drive a Lotus 22 Formula Junior car fitted with a 1,500cc engine arranged with the help of the factory. He was upset because he had just returned from a couple of Formula Junior races in Italy at Cesenatico and Lake Garda where he was defending his victories in the same events the previous year. Having won at Cesenatico he retired at Lake Garda with no water left in the radiator. Inspection after the race revealed a water hose had been sabotaged with a knife cut. "Well," he said, "I will just have to go back next year and get the job done – we cannot let them get away with that." He was too naïve to know then that the following year his Formula 1 schedule competing in the World Championship would not permit such distractions.

His top place on the podium at Cesenatico in 1963 would be taken by a crazy young Austrian driver called Jochen Rindt. Reports from other drivers in the race suggested that Rindt straightened the car up after corners by bouncing it off the straw bales. They also reported that he was amazingly quick and this in a Cooper that was not thought to be the fastest of the Formula Junior cars then available. He had beaten established drivers on a circuit new to him in his first season in single-seaters. "If he doesn't kill himself by the end of the year I think he'll be World Champion," opined one seasoned and respected journalist who witnessed these events. That reporter, not unnaturally, became reluctant to use his prophetic quote when Jochen did become World Champion, for by then he was dead, killed in an accident at Monza during his championship year.

A Formula Junior race is one thing, but taking on the cream of the then Formula 1 establishment in Formula 2 and beating them is something altogether different. This is precisely what Jochen did in 1964, racing against opponents like Clark and Hill, who between them were to share three of the four World Championships between 1962 and 1965. Small wonder that the team owners and team managers sat up and took notice. What they saw out of the car was a tousled-haired, fresh-faced youngster. His gangly gait almost gave the impression that he was not that well co-ordinated, and then there were those stories about his wild youth and bad driving habits. What they saw in the race car was an out-and-out racer, smooth, very fast and daring his car to do something he could not control. Decisive overtaking passes were executed in a flash of intuition and with complete commitment. The driver seemed to make the car dance to his tune. The book about respecting those whose reputations were greater than your own had obviously not been on the required reading list in the Rindt household. Could anyone this inexperienced be this good? Jochen came to believe so in 1964 and felt that he had made the grade, proved the point. That year he also resolved to become World Champion. He had discovered that race driving suited him better than anything else he could do.

The attitude of most Austrians is a carefree one, and life is there to be enjoyed to the full. They have disciplined family lives, live in beautiful countryside, breathe fresh air and indulge in pastimes such as strapping two long, flat boards to their feet and launching themselves the shortest and fastest way down a snow-covered mountain. When this gets too tame they try other things. Jochen's gang of school friends tried tobogganing towed behind cars and then skiing in the same fashion. Gerhard Berger used to get a friend to lie down on the icy, snowy road from school to his home to get a passing car to stop. Gerhard would slip over the snowbank at the side of the road and crouching down, knees bent, hold the rear bumper. This way and on the soles of his school shoes he would get a tow the two kilometres to his home village. The only tricky bit, he would tell you, was where the road bridged a stream. The air circulation under the bridge would thaw the road and he would have to try to anticipate the 10 to 12 metres of tarmac across which the car would drag him at whatever speed the driver of that particular car chose to do on that particular trip. It is through tales like these that the 'crazy Austrians' stories take root. By and large they may like to perpetuate the myth but, like the other Austrian legends of Formula 1, Lauda and Berger, Jochen had in good measure the attributes of intelligence, a highly competitive nature, a very well developed business sense and a great awareness of the risks of his profession.

By the time he reached Formula 1 the rebellious nature that had caused him to leave more than one school ahead of schedule was evident only in an attitude of single-mindedness to achieve the target he had set himself. He was insistent in contract negotiations to get the conditions that gave him the best situation. He placed a reasonable value on his services, arguing that ultimately the championship was worth more to him than financial reward. He monitored his situation within a team closely and was never reluctant to intervene either verbally or in writing if he believed there was some area to which attention should be paid. The fact that he'd had Bernie Ecclestone looking after his interests since his Formula 2 days may have had something to do with this very business-like approach.

His Formula 1 apprenticeship was served in the somewhat abrasive atmosphere of the Cooper-Maserati team as run by Roy Salvadori. In a controllable and sturdy chassis propelled by a heavy, out-of-date and unreliable engine, Jochen could drive adventurously but without any serious winning prospects. Progressing to Jack Brabham's team he found himself in a very happy environment. He was supervised and fussed over by 'Black Jack' himself, the father figure of Formula 1, and drove a nimble, modern and well-engineered car that Jack himself also drove. There could be no better guarantee of assiduous attention to safety matters. And in that terrible year of 1968 when the world seemed to be losing a driver a month, safety was starting to play an ever more important role in Jochen's mind. His mechanic, who went on to make quite a name for himself, was Ron Dennis, and there was a happy-family feel to the team that suited their star driver. But here too the Repco engine had outlived the simplicity and underpowered reliability that had seen it win the 1966 and 1967 championships for Jack Brabham and Denny Hulme. Overstressed, it let Jochen down in race after race in 1968.

So, in spite of having never won a Grand Prix, the name at the top of most teams' 'wants' list for 1969 was Rindt. Few doubted that he was the fastest driver of his time. He signed for Team Lotus having had approaches from nearly every other team, and also having given serious consideration to starting his own. At the time he signed he had no reason to disbelieve what he thought he was going to get: equal number one status with Graham Hill, a Lotus 49 with a race-winning pedigree and factory-supported Ford-Cosworth engines, fully contracted and sponsored works deals with tyre, fuel and a host of accessory makers, and a budget reinforced by the sport's first alliance with a commercial sponsor.

What he got was a team owner in turmoil. Colin Chapman would never fully get over the loss of Jim Clark and now, just months later, he had to build a new kind of relationship with the first non-British driver Team Lotus had ever contracted. He had resolved never to get too close to a driver again, and at the same time he had to cope with Jochen's distinctly European and therefore, to him, un-British behaviour. On the other hand he had signed Jochen to put himself back in a championship-winning position, something he felt Graham Hill was unlikely to be able to deliver again. How was Colin to get him on board as a team player, and at the same time maintain the distance he now wished to keep between himself and his drivers? It did not help that Jochen had been a particularly close friend of Jimmy.

Simultaneously Grand Prix racing was going through a sea change of a magnitude similar to the switch from front to rear engines of a few years earlier. As the 3-litre formula settled down, the sudden surplus of power over grip was exercising the minds of designers, and none more so than Colin. The first taste of how this might be overcome, not counting the attempt to 'be-wing' Jimmy Clark's Tasman Lotus at the start of the year, emerged out of the back of the Ferrari and Brabham trucks at Spa in 1968 when embryonic wing structures appeared, mounted on the engines and forward of the rear axle. These were apologetic enough in scale to not worry the rule makers, but once thought through by Colin were considered pathetic in not tackling a man-sized problem with a man-sized solution. His solution, as often in his career, was to lead to a ban. But not until the wings were bigger, higher and wider, and mounted front and rear on the unsprung part of the suspension. They led directly to the two enormous accidents that Graham and Jochen were lucky to survive in Barcelona during the Spanish Grand Prix. The ensuing ban, actively promoted by Jochen in his safety mode, caused the designers to consider other solutions to gain more grip. One of these was four-wheel drive.

Colin, always in the vanguard and desperate not to lose the technological initiative, launched the Team into a four-wheel-drive programme. To concentrate minds fully on the new car, the Lotus 63, he not only threatened but actually did start to sell off the 49s. The nadir of this approach was reached at Silverstone for the British Grand Prix, at home and in front of the sponsors, when the Team entered four cars, two 49s and two four-wheel-drive 63s, the latter to be driven by Joachim Bonnier and John Miles. Bonnier was given the drive in return for 'lending' his 49 to Graham Hill for the race! Colin, who had already categorised Jochen as "impossibly demanding", something he had not previously encountered with a driver, had earlier experienced the self-same driver "refusing" to drive the Lotus 63. Now he watched the unedifying sight of Jochen, yes Jochen, and any other able-bodied person close by, wheeling tyres and other bits around the paddock in an effort to get the completely overstretched Team to the start.

Jochen drove a brilliant, bullish but smooth and very fast race, battling with Stewart until the rear wing endplate broke. The pit stop took a long time but he was still second. And then he ran out of fuel shortly before the end, eventually finishing fourth. Meanwhile Hill and Siffert in the other two Lotus 49s also ran out of fuel, but their plight was due to insufficient fuel tank capacity rather than a fuel measurement error as was the case with Jochen. So a season that had started in Levin in New Zealand with an overturned and brake fluidless Tasman car and continued with formation flying in

Barcelona hit rock bottom at Silverstone in a race Jochen should and must have won.

That 1969 British Grand Prix was neither the first nor the last time Team Lotus cars ran out of fuel near the end of a race. Peter's further comment was this:

"Weight, of course, was always a preoccupation with Colin. He used to throw the most enormous wobbly at the famous Team Lotus 'mechanic's gallon'. Colin would never do a Ken Tyrrell and run loads of laps in practice to get the race set-up. It was always: get the car as fast as possible to put it on pole, and we'll sort out the rest later. Some decent full-tank running was needed to calculate fuel consumption on a given circuit, and six laps plus one out and one in certainly wasn't enough to estimate it accurately. So we'd do our best to work it out with a slide rule – Colin gave me one, which I still have – and then we'd say, 'Right, it looks as though we'll need 34.5 gallons for this race, and we'll put in 10 per cent safety margin, so that's 38 gallons.' But then the mechanics would put in 39 gallons – adding the 'mechanic's gallon' to be on the safe side.

"If he found out, Colin would go raving mad. 'A gallon weighs 0.75kg. We spend thousands trying to save three-quarters of a kilo, and now the mechanics are adding it back on.' If you've spent a lot of time and money making your engine mountings out of 20-gauge steel, then 18-gauge, then 16-gauge to get the one that's just strong enough to do the job, the last thing you want is a mechanic throwing another bloody three-quarters of a kilo into the car.

"Even so, we still had cars running out of petrol before the end of a race, and it was not unusual for a driver to have to weave on the last lap to get the last bits in the tank up to the fuel feed. Nowadays, of course, they've got electronics to tell them how much they're using – just another challenge that's gone out of Grand Prix racing."

After Silverstone Jochen's relationship with Colin, which had never been brilliant, now degenerated to a point where a conversation between the two was virtually impossible. Perhaps this was the reason that, unlike any other Team Lotus driver before or since, rather than use the telephone Jochen would communicate by letter. Jochen knew he had what it took to be champion, but felt blighted by bad luck and bad decisions. Colin continued to wrestle with his inner demons and throw himself at the technical challenges with an energy level set to keep other matters out of his mind. But Colin was now to start on a concentrated campaign to keep Jochen for 1970. He admitted the errors of the frenetic 1969 season and promised a complete re-jig for 1970. Jochen was to be undisputed number one with a genuine number two in John Miles. A dream of a new car was the only priority, and gone would be the distractions of other racing categories. And Colin acknowledged that, while the relationship was troubled, he was sure that it would mature and build into something special.

What Colin did not know was that, even as he wooed Jochen, his driver was making plans to be involved with his 'own' team in 1970 that would include Robin Herd and his friend Alan Rees, erstwhile team manager and driving rival from his Roy Winklemann Formula 2 days.

Then three things happened to change his destiny. The first was when Jochen discovered that the new March team, as it was to become, was a vastly bigger and more commercial set-up than the small, intimate and personal team centred around himself that he had been led to believe.

The second was that, with the intuition that saved the day on so many occasions, Colin offered Jochen the possibility to have and run his own Formula 2 team. Jochen immediately envisaged his mentor, Bernie Ecclestone, running this with him. His opinionated view, showing that at heart he was still an out-and-out racer, was that only a few of the top drivers still competed in this exciting division of single-seater racing because the others were frightened of getting beaten by the newcomers.

The third thing was his win in Watkins Glen in the US Grand

Prix, the race in which his team-mate Graham Hill had been badly injured. Although he had already signed for the 1970 season, something had happened to ensure that all the shenanigans of the previous season would not be repeated. Firestone had come up with a new super-wide and only marginally treaded rear tyre – the forerunner of the slick. Jochen said it had so much grip that it was extremely hard to get the car away from a standstill, even on the downhill start at Watkins Glen. This was music to Colin's ears: he immediately saw the chance for a really radical weight distribution on the new car for 1970 to complement the integrated, as opposed to bolt-on, aerodynamic package he had in mind.

With his first victory after five and half seasons in Formula 1, Jochen seemed to undergo a personality change. The burden of being so often the 'nearly man' vanished. He was relaxed, less contentious and more philosophical. Though he was still on 'top dollar' for a leading team, he wanted the income only to secure his future after he stopped driving. He still loved to race, but was devoting more time to his life after racing. The Jochen Rindt Show, his Austrian racing car exhibition, was getting bigger by the year and its success was a huge source of pride. His unbelievably beautiful wife, Nina, had given him a daughter, Natascha; the family was finally settled in Switzerland, and a home of their own was soon to be finished. No less demanding, he had developed a way of communicating that contained a little more lubricant and a little less emery paper, particularly where Colin was concerned.

This 'new' Jochen was therefore better able to handle the trials and tribulations of the birth of the Lotus 72. These started the day of the launch to a large group of journalists and sponsors on the airfield at the Hethel factory. After it had been shaken down for a few miles the day before, essential assemblies were stripped and checked prior to Jochen demonstrating the car to the guests. Unfortunately the torsion bar suspension was so novel that the 'set' taken by the springs when first loaded up was overlooked and the bars re-installed on opposite sides of the car from where they had been originally fitted. Jochen duly set off to do some laps around the test track for the benefit of photographers but stopped after just three. The earlier Rindt would have stopped in the middle of the crowd and sounded off, but the latest mature version pulled the car up away from the biggest concentration of people, jumped out, quietly explained to the crew that the car had settled with its belly on the ground, and hoped aloud to the press now gathering round the car that they had got their pictures as it was far too cold to drive again.

In Spain the first signs emerged that all was not well with the handling. The radical anti-dive front and anti-squat rear suspension, designed to keep the chassis from pitching under braking and accelerating, was in fact rather good at picking up the inside front wheel turning into a corner, and picking up the inside rear wheel when accelerating out of it. And there was trouble too with the Teflon-type material used as insulation to stop the front brake heat soaking into the constant-velocity joints of the front drive shafts.

Jochen handled with equanimity the decision not to run the car again until the suspension was modified. He was less impressed when he found out that, due to the immensely complicated construction, particularly of the front end, the delay would run into weeks. But the forced reacquaintance with the 49 at Monte Carlo gave him the chance once more to show that he was the best racer in the field. Sure that he was on a hiding to nothing he started from the fourth row, and in his own words "drove like a chauffeur". Never interested in driving races he considered lost, he only needed a sniff of victory for something inside him to be unleashed. And a sniff he got at half distance. In the greatest race of his career, and one of the races that form the foundation of legend, Jochen attacked. He attacked like crazy and, with Jack Brabham in his sights, drove an unbelievable series of laps to win, having forced Jack into a mistake on the last corner of the last lap. On that final lap he broke the 1969 lap record by 2.3sec and bettered Stewart's pole time of the day before by 0.8sec.

The heavily revised 72 was ready for Zandvoort and the Dutch Grand Prix. But Jochen's joy at having a car that improved his own pole position of the year before by 2.5sec and led the race for all but the first two laps was completely overshadowed by the fatal accident of his closest pal, Piers Courage. He considered retiring mid-season, but inside he now knew that this could be his year. He had two victories in the bag and a car that had the beating of all the others out there. And winning the championship and getting it out of his system would allow him to go on and do all the other things he wanted to do.

Wins followed at Clermont-Ferrand, where after Ickx and Beltoise dropped out he only had to demoralise Amon with a couple of quick laps to win comfortably, and then Brands Hatch. The British Grand Prix was quite the reverse of Monaco. This time Jochen dominated and Jack hung on. As his Goodyears coped with the changing track conditions better than Jochen's Firestones, Jack got past with 12 laps to go, only to slow two laps from the end and gift the race to the championship leader. But this time the win was nearly gifted back to Jack, who had coasted over the line in second place.

After the race the scrutineers checked the winning car in the pits area and found the rear wing too high. As a delaying tactic we insisted that the car be checked in the scrutineering bay in the old paddock, which is where it had been checked prior to practice and where the nearest thing to a flat surface could be found at Brands Hatch. The scrutineers agreed. Suddenly several mechanics were needed to push the 500kg car through the tunnel to the paddock. All of them were pushing on the rear wing, as they had been instructed to do, and noted that the two tubular stays supporting the trailing edge of the rear wing had been bent. It took two hours to convince the scrutineers (who were now getting very different readings to those obtained in the pits) that this was how the car had started the race, and finally the win was confirmed.

At Hockenheim Jochen won again, this time in a classic slipstreaming battle with Ickx's Ferrari, but his innate racecraft and ability to think things out while driving on the limit allowed him to work out how to out-fumble the Belgian. The crowd thought it was another devil-may-care, all-out attack from the Austrian, who still held a special place in their hearts from his Formula 2 races there, but in reality it was a calm, professional and measured approach that won him the race. Afterwards Ickx, always the gentleman and a true sportsman, told Jochen how much he enjoyed racing against him and how the greatest reward a competitor could have was to earn the respect of his opponent. Jochen told Colin: "Today a monkey could have won in your car."

For someone who could now see the championship beckoning, Jochen was not looking forward to his home race at Zeltweg. He was sure it was going to turn into a circus of media attention, and he positively disliked being bothered by the press and the intrusive attentions of the public during a race weekend. And yet in what was the final chapter of his transformation he was at ease with himself, outwardly happy and relaxed, and made real efforts to be friendly to everyone at an event at which the huge weight of public expectation was on him to win. He had reached a plateau of calmness akin to one of those yellow-robed Middle Eastern holy men. When he dropped out of the race early, he did not even seem to be disappointed.

At Monza Jochen's mathematical situation was straightforward. If he won and Jack Brabham finished lower than fifth, the championship would be settled there and then. The Team Lotus game plan, as usual, was less straightforward. The mechanics, worn out again by building a third 72 in record time, arrived just before practice. Jochen's car had a well-used engine in it but there was a 'special' in the truck. Emerson Fittipaldi, signed before the Brands Hatch race as a prospect for the future and a 'banker' should Jochen retire, would have one of his outings, starting in the new car. Once this was shaken down, Jochen would try it and choose which chassis he preferred. This would then get the 'special' engine for final practice.

But Plan A did not work out as planned. When Emerson did finally get out in the new car in the second session he shunted it beyond immediate repair, while Jochen had had some engine misfire problems in the first session that left him a lowly 22nd. The three-tier wing of the 72 was a high drag, high-downforce affair that worked in perfect conjunction with the car's 70 per cent rear weight distribution and massive rear tyres. It was also becoming responsible on the higher-speed circuits for a lower top speed than that of its competitors, particularly the Ferraris. In the second practice period on Friday Jochen, in common with some other drivers, tried removing the rear wing altogether. John Miles came in after two laps in the same configuration and said the car was altogether too "squirly" and tried the wing with the middle tier removed. Jochen on the other hand, could not believe the extra speed the stripped-down aerodynamics gave him, some 800rpm before the engine limiter cut in. After practice he was buoyant beyond belief, saying that with the new 'special' engine and the right gear ratios he would not only be on the pole, but a whole 1sec faster than the Ferraris.

At dinner in the Hôtel de la Ville he arrived elegantly wearing a prototype of the new range of suits he was about to add to his Jochen Rindt clothing range. It was maroon and white, with a sort of paisley pattern to the weave, and it was hard to believe that he was not a model but the world's leading race driver – until he regaled the table with the story of the tallest top gear ever fitted in a Lotus Formula 1 car (204mph), and the 1min 23sec lap he thought was easily possible the next day. Much of the rest of his conversation that evening was bubbly and full of excitement for the future of his commercial activities, particularly his Racing Car Show, and he even confided that his mind was now firmly made up – he would retire at the end of the season and would announce it as soon as the championship was won. And this was the night that initial discussions about next year's contract were supposed to have started!

Italian law is based on Roman law, and says that the blame for any happening must be laid at someone's door. They tried to lay the blame for Jochen's death on Colin. The charge of culpable homicide that they used in the Senna case in 1994 was the same one they used in 1970. With Ayrton they said that the steering column failed; with Jochen they said it was a drive shaft. Does it really matter? Will it bring them back? Does anyone in their right mind believe that anyone made a conscious decision to send a driver out in an unsafe car?

What were the facts and what were the factors that influenced these facts? First let us look at the car:

- The Lotus 72 was the first of a new type of race car designed to incorporate within the overall concept the new aerodynamics that were revolutionising race car performance, and not utilise bolt-on appendages.
- It had a very different and exaggerated weight distribution – 70 per cent on the rear and 30 per cent on the front.
- The wings were designed to apply downforce front and rear in these same proportions.
- The braking balance was distributed in these same proportions.
- The car took advantage of the new range of taller, wider rear tyres to apportion grip front to rear in these same proportions.
- It had rising-rate suspension to give it a soft and supple ride at low speeds and a soft and supple ride at high speeds, even though the aerodynamic forces greatly increased the effective chassis weight from one condition to the other.
- The anti-dive front suspension and anti-squat rear suspension, designed to prevent the car pitching under braking and squatting under acceleration, had been abandoned earlier in the year. The advantage of lack of pitch sensitivity had been outweighed by the disadvantage of poor handling, though the rising-rate springs still gave a reasonably stable platform for the aerodynamics.

Second, let us look at the circuit:

- Pre-chicanes, Monza was almost entirely right-handed. Only the

Ascari curve was a left-hander. The tyre mix chosen as the best
compromise in 1970 with no wear worries was a durable hard-
compound tyre on the left and a soft-compound tyre on the right.

- The hard-compound tyre took seven or eight laps to get properly
  bedded in and up to the best operating temperature.
- The compromise between handling in the corners and top speed
  for overtaking and slipstreaming was crucial.

And finally the driver:

- A veteran of epic slipstreamers, Jochen knew exactly what was
  needed to win a race like Monza.
- Crucially, he always refused to wear the crutch straps of the
  mandatory six-point safety harness, and these were tucked under
  the leading edge of the seat squab.

So now most of the relevant parameters for that last practice session
are in place:

- The latest development and more powerful Cosworth engine
  is fitted.
- The longest top gear ever used is installed.
- The wings are removed, changing significantly the dynamic weight
  distribution of the car and the effective spring rates at
  high speed.
- New hard tyres are fitted to the left side and new soft ones to
  the right.
- The ride height is not altered for the lesser dynamic weight of the
  car, nor is the rising rate of the springs altered.
- The brake balance is left unchanged.

It would be hard to imagine a less stable package, yet Jochen
was confident of being able to master it. And what happened?
Already down to a lap time of 1min 26sec by his fourth lap, but
still with fewer miles than it was accepted were needed to bed in
the hard tyres, Jochen passed Denny Hulme and headed towards
the braking point for the Parabolica corner on his fifth lap. As he
hit the brakes to slow for the corner, the rear of the car started to
swing out of line (consistent with having too much braking effort

on the rear, uneven grip right to left, and very little downforce). The car gripped on the soft right side tyres and speared into the Armco barrier on the left.

So what killed him? The environment in which he found himself at that moment was his downfall. The Armco barrier was poorly installed in soft sandy soil with no firm anchorage. The wedge nose of the 72 slipped under it and raised it out of the ground. The car whipped to its right and, now facing backwards, careered down the barrier, raising successive posts as it went, all the while with the right front suspension trapped on the spectator side of the barrier. Then it came to the 10ft upright in the barrier. The circuit operators had chosen to extend every tenth or so upright to carry the loudspeaker system. The trapped suspension got snagged on this heavier upright and the enormous force tore the entire front suspension subframe with brake, drive shaft and steering assemblies off the front of the car. Unfortunately the driver's feet were trapped in the foot box within this frame and, in addition to amputating a foot, the absence of the crutch straps meant that his entire body was dragged down the cockpit well by the separating subframe. As a result there were terrible neck injuries inflicted by the inside edge of the shoulder straps of the seat belts. Jochen was dead within 15 to 30 seconds of the impact.

Now the farce started. Italian law requires that in the event of such an accident an inquest must take place on the spot. This would have caused the organisers to cancel the race. So they went through the motions of bringing Jochen to the medical hut at the circuit. After some staged attempts at 'resuscitation' he was transferred to an ambulance to be taken to hospital. Conveniently he 'died' on the way so the inquest could be held away from the circuit.

It is a sound belief that accidents are rarely the result of one event, but rather that an accident happens when two or even three things conspire simultaneously. Here we had an unstable platform in the car, a less than satisfactory installation of the safety barrier, and a driver who from personal choice elected not to use all six straps of the seat belts.

After Rindt's death there was much paddock gossip about the significance of the failure of one of the hollow tubular shafts connecting the front wheels to the inboard front brakes. Three weeks earlier in the Austrian GP, Rindt's team-mate John Miles had retired when one of these shafts failed. When pressed about this, Peter said:

"That brake shaft failure in Austria came back to haunt us. But I am convinced it was a manufacturing fault. After Jochen's Monza accident the wreck was impounded by the Italians but we needed to get that Cosworth experimental engine back, so I persuaded the authorities that the engine wasn't involved, and I flew Maurice Phillippe down and we took the engine out. While Maurice was there he had a good look at the remains to try to assess just what had happened. I can guarantee that Jochen's accident was not caused by brake shaft failure. The right-hand shaft was broken by the impact with the big post, which tore off the front of the car and did all the damage.

"But, as a knee-jerk reaction, we had solid brake shafts made up for the next race at Watkins Glen. It was a wrong engineering decision because they had no torsion in them, they put too much stress on the rest of the drive line and started breaking the constant-velocity joints. So by the time we got to Mexico in late October we were back with the original brake shafts, which had a certain amount of twist. And we continued to use the same shafts on the 72s for five seasons, without problems."

As recounted later in this chapter, Emerson Fittipaldi saved Jochen's posthumous championship for him by winning the US Grand Prix at Watkins Glen, thus preventing the possibility of Jacky Ickx overtaking his points total.

And the final word on the 1970 World Champion? There will never be a final word, for no-one will ever solve the enigma that was Jochen Rindt. How could someone so committed and outspoken about safety and the hazards of his profession drive so sublimely fast, and engage in some of the most torrid battles ever seen on a race track? How could someone with such a devil-may-care image hide the intelligence that taught him that at nine-tenths he was faster than his contemporaries at ten tenths, and to manage the risk this way? How could someone be so much fun and yet so serious? How could someone who vacillated so wildly and frequently between jacking it all in and driving because he loved it have not allowed his inner fears and worries to dim the brilliance of his track craft?

We shall never know, for this is the stuff that gives us our heroes.

EMERSON

Exactly a year after Jochen's death, once again at Monza, three things of significance took place. With the charges against Colin still hanging in the air he had to stay away. A single car was entered for the Italian Grand Prix for the driver who had taken over from Jochen as team leader, Emerson Fittipaldi. But it was a Lotus 56B turbine car and not a 72. Furthermore it was painted gold and black and entered by Worldwide Racing and not Gold Leaf Team Lotus. The entry was a ploy to leave the Team without risk of impoundment. The turbine, it was felt, would have a better chance at Monza than any other circuit. And the gold and black colour scheme was a trial run to gauge reaction to a major change in image for the 1972 season. The third and most significant thing, however, took place in that same Hôtel de la Ville where I persuaded Emerson in one of the upstairs rooms to sign for the 1972 season. The initial contract was barely enough to cover two sides of a piece of headed Team Lotus notepaper, and the basic driving fee was £30,000 plus success bonuses. Thus the 1972 World Championship was in part secured.

Emerson had come to England to pursue his career. He was the first of the modern Brazilian drivers and all those who came after followed his route. By mid-1970 he had a formidable reputation from Formula 3 and was doing well in Formula 2. With teams not constrained as they are today over the number of entries they make, it was easy to put a marker down for the future by offering him a third car, a Lotus 49, for the British Grand Prix and a few other races. He did not disappoint, and finished eighth in his first Grand Prix with a steady drive in a not quite competitive car. By Watkins Glen he was perforce team leader in a 72.

Still reeling from the impact of Rindt's death, and with two 72s destroyed, Team Lotus missed the next round after Monza, the Canadian Grand Prix. But Fittipaldi's victory at Watkins Glen, still only four weeks after the tragedy, was crucial in rebuilding the morale of the Team. It was a bit like Graham winning the 1968 World Championship after Jimmy's death. Something happens to people in the aftermath of a shattering event like that, something makes you get your head down, shut out the rest of the world, not talk to anybody, just get on with the job.

Poor John Miles had not only been overlooked but actually replaced. Though he dines out to this day on his 'sacking', the decision to replace him was not for lack of any quality as a race driver. It was simply that in the heavily charged atmosphere following Monza we decided that the only way forward for the Team with any chance of putting recent events out of our minds was to start with a clean sheet of paper. The last two races gave us a chance to see if the new set-up would gel.

Thus Reine Wisell came in to be Emerson's team-mate for Watkins Glen and Mexico as well as for the 1971 season. Reine's third place at the Glen, when added to Emerson's victory, which secured Jochen's championship, also secured the Constructors' Championship for the Team. So, in spite of the most ghastly of years just ended, the 1971 season held much promise – a well developed car, the youngest-ever Grand Prix winner backed up by another young man of promise.

It was the first all-foreign driving line-up in the history of the Team. Emerson, who was living with his wife Maria-Helena in a miserably cold bungalow in Bunwell, Norfolk, seemed to have little more success in learning English than he did in keeping warm. He struggled particularly with technical English, the construction of whose words was more remote from his native tongue than conversational Portuguese was from conversational English. In fact he had been driving for the Team for nearly six months before we asked him to point on the car to the things he called 'chuckers-overs' and discovered that he meant the 'shock absorbers'. To this day he calls ride height 'high ride'.

With these communication problems and a steep learning curve in front of both drivers, the Team embarked on the 1971 season. Neither had driven all the circuits and both had little experience in the testing and adjustment of a Grand Prix car. An unspectacular start to the season, with retirements in South Africa and Spain, had just begun to turn around for Emerson with his first points-scoring finish in Monaco when he had a very nasty road accident in France. He suffered a very painful broken sternum and Maria-Helena, who was with him in the car, was also injured. Luckily we were able to get that staunchest of friends and founder member of the Lotus fan club, Jabby Crombac, to attend and it was just as well he did. In the front passenger footwell he found two of Maria-Helena's teeth still attached to a piece of her jawbone. Rushing to the hospital with them wrapped in tissue he was able to get them to the surgeon in time for them to be replaced.

Although Emerson only missed one race he was not fully fit for some weeks, and he was showing signs of being back to full speed only by the British Grand Prix in July. But he had finished third in France, did so again at Silverstone, and when he was second in Austria he had stepped onto the podium three times in four races. He was at last starting to put a season together.

Monza saw the diversion with the turbine car where, without Colin or 'Flame-out Fred' (Fred Cowley of Pratt & Whitney), none of the few of us who were there could find a way of disconnecting both the electrical and mechanical governors on the engine to get it to run at a higher output than 98 per cent. Emerson was eighth, a lap down. Retirements rounded out a not entirely satisfactory but nonetheless not wasted year for the young man from Sao Paulo, who returned home for a holiday during the winter with the prospect of better things to come in 1972. He had incidentally also won three Formula 2 races.

It was hard for the Team to assess his true ability as his team-mate, Reine Wisell, turned out to be one of those drivers who blew hot and cold. He could be very impressive one day and give the appearance of really struggling the next. This made it difficult to make comparisons or have a benchmark by which to judge Emerson. And it was only at the end of the season that we came to realise, from information received from an outside source, that Emerson's injuries had in fact been more serious than we thought. Indeed the crafty political nature of the guy was just beginning to reveal itself, for so keen was he to hold onto his seat that he let us think he was less injured than he was.

That season had been the first one for Team Lotus without a Grand Prix win since 1960. But for 1972 everything was different, and not just in the change from red, white and gold to black and gold colours. New Firestone tyres that were in effect designed specifically for the still radical car allowed an even higher performance aerodynamic package to be used, together with winter developments on the rear suspension.

> Peter explained those suspension changes thus: "During the first part of the season we made a big breakthrough with the 72. At the back the front leg of the wishbone was attached to the bellhousing, and the rear leg was attached to the gearbox. When they got hot the bellhousing and the gearbox expanded at different rates, and the wishbone was bending. We switched to double-link rear suspension, and at the same time we threw away the Armstrong 'chuckers-overs' and changed to Konis, and it transformed the car."

It was soon clear that it would be difficult, given reasonable reliability, for anyone but Stewart to give Emerson a run for the championship. As it turned out, Emerson won five Grands Prix, finished second twice and third once to top the points table with 61 points to Stewart's 45. He was fit, enthusiastic, fast (with three poles and a total of six front-row starts) and fully committed to his racing.

Emerson's 1972 team-mate, the Australian Dave Walker, never scored a championship point. Peter remembered: "He had done a brilliant job for us in Formula 3, winning a string of victories and championships. He was fit, he was aggressive, he was an excellent racing driver – although maybe he hadn't developed good throttle control, because in Formula 3 you treated the right-hand pedal like an on-off switch. The Cosworth DFV engine was still quite peaky in those days, and he never quite got to grips with that. But there was nothing else wrong with him.

"The year before, for the Dutch Grand Prix at Zandvoort, we put him in the 56B turbine car. It was pouring with rain, he had four-wheel-drive, and with 75 gallons of fuel on board it was so heavy you couldn't have spun it if you tried. He was 22nd on the 24-car grid, and I said to him: 'Dave, take it easy for the first 20 laps, let the race come to you." But it was his first Grand Prix, he got excited, he went from 22nd to 10th in the first five laps, and then went straight off the road at the Tarzan Hairpin, filled the turbine with sand and it had to go back to Pratt & Whitney for a rebuild. If he'd stayed on the island he could have finished way up at the front."

In 1972 the Team also took part in six non-championship races and Emerson won three of those, was second in another and set fastest lap in four. He won the Rothmans 50,000, strictly a *Formule Libre* race, driving a Formula 1 Lotus 72 with extra fuel tankage non-stop for nearly 120 laps of Brands Hatch, and was victorious in four Formula 2 races. As he headed home to Brazil and a ticker-tape welcome in his home city after securing the title at Monza as the youngest ever World Champion, he could reflect on a superb job, supremely well done.

But his reflections no doubt included thoughts about his situation for 1973. After its low point in 1971, Team Lotus had bounced back in no uncertain terms. The car was still the class of the field, and

Colin's thoughts turned to dominating the opposition in 1973 with two top drivers, ideas that had been floated with Emerson. His favourite driver after Jimmy Clark, Mario Andretti, was not available. Ever since Ronnie Peterson had taken over the mantle of Jochen Rindt in Formula 2, he'd had the eyes of the leading teams on him. They did not know just how poor his English was, and when Alan Rees of the fledgling March team had mentioned the words "Formula 1" Ronnie's eyes lit up and he said "Yes", even though there is some question as to whether he had understood what he'd heard. His brilliant second place in the 1971 championship had further reinforced his reputation and, when the signs were that he could be prised away for 1973, we pounced.

But Emerson had a selfish streak, a not unnatural characteristic of many great sportsmen, and his competitive instincts were more than usually well developed. He was not particularly impressed, therefore, by the arrival in the Team of someone who he knew, before he had even sat in the car, would be a threat to his situation. Having no background as a team player, he immediately set about trying to ensure his position remained pre-eminent within the Team. The early tests confirmed his worst fears, for Ronnie was formidably quick. These tests also showed that despite having to change from the 'customised' Firestones of 1972 to Goodyears that had been by and large developed for cars like the Tyrrell, which had far more weight on the front wheels, the Lotus 72 was still going to be the class of the field.

This was never more evident than in the first two races of the year in South America. Emerson won in Argentina, but when Ronnie put in one of his rear-tyre-smoking pole laps in Emerson's back yard in Brazil it was obvious that, unless sense prevailed, the two black and gold Lotus front-row sitters would race each other into oblivion. So a complex 'deal' was struck. If Ronnie 'allowed' Emerson to win in Brazil, Emerson would return the favour in Sweden and finish behind Ronnie. The first half of Ronnie's season was bedevilled with an engine seizure, a wheel breakage, gearbox problems and the odd accident, and it was not until June that Ronnie scored his first points at Monaco. Then came Sweden and, true to his word, Emerson ran second to Ronnie until an engine seizure made his 'deal' irrelevant. In all honesty Emerson never looked like threatening Ronnie, and had his work cut out to hold off the Tyrrells of Stewart and Cevert. Ronnie, however, suffered the most cruel blow when, in front of his King and 50,000 of his countrymen, he had a puncture, which lost him his first Grand Prix win just one and a half laps from home in an 80-lap race. By now Emerson had 41 points to the 10 of Ronnie.

But Emerson was already feeling pretty miffed. He worked hard and steadily through practice periods setting up his car while Ronnie, due to his lesser understanding of things in the handling department, would generally head off in an entirely different direction. Then, lost and without a time of which he could be proud, he would stop 15 to 20 minutes before the end of qualifying, ask for Emerson's settings to be put on his car and then go out and beat Emerson's time – and usually pop it on the pole into the bargain. In nine out of the 14 races Ronnie was on pole, and in three of the remaining five he was on the front row. And now Ronnie had learned how to win. In fact it must have been doubly galling for Emerson to know that he had effectively gifted Ronnie his first victory in France when an aggressive dive up the inside of Scheckter resulted in both Emerson and Jody not finishing.

Emerson retired in Britain, and then suffered the setback that probably cost him a second championship when a front wheel failure at Zandvoort in practice on one of the fastest corners left him trapped in a destroyed car. His feet, caught in the footbox amongst the pedals and brake mountings, took the most fearful knocking about and left him unable to drive more than two laps in the race. At the Nürburgring a week later he managed a gritty and courageous sixth place while still very unfit and in pain, knowing that to let Stewart get any further ahead in the points table would ruin his championship chances. Then the circus moved to Austria with Stewart on 60 points and Emerson on 42, and Cevert between them on 45. Ronnie at this moment languished on 25 points, having failed to score in Holland (he led for 64 of the 72 laps) and having succumbed to distributor failure on the first lap in Germany.

So once more Emerson needed the help of the Team, and of Ronnie. The likeable Swede demonstrated, not for the last time in his career, that although he knew he was the fastest he could also be a team player, and he readily agreed to give up the race to Emerson to help his championship bid. This he did, waving Emerson through, only to find himself back in the lead and taking victory when a fuel line failed on Emerson's car.

Now the plot really thickened. Going into the Italian Grand Prix at Monza, Stewart, who had been second in Austria, led Emerson by 24 points with three races to go. With five wins to Emerson's three, Jackie needed three points from Monza to make the championship safe – provided Emerson did not win. For Emerson to become champion, on the other hand, he needed three straight wins and Jackie to score fewer than four points from three races. After considerable discussion with Colin Chapman it was decided that, while it had been reasonable to ask Ronnie to give up Brazil and then Austria, it would be neither reasonable nor fair to ask him to give up Monza, Mosport and Watkins Glen as well. While Ronnie appeared to be the easiest going of personalities it was hard to believe that the relationship with the Team would not suffer if his joint number one status was sacrificed to out-and-out favouritism for his team-mate. Similarly there was a strong feeling that Emerson would not have done the same for Ronnie if their roles had been reversed. It was also known that Emerson had been somewhat scarred by the continuous and relentless extra speed that Ronnie could produce, apparently at will, and had made initial moves to investigate seats in other teams. Team Lotus's future in all probability therefore lay with Ronnie.

We resolved not to close our minds – there was after all still the possibility of a championship – but to play it by ear on the day. When Stewart recovered from 20th place to fourth after a puncture (good enough for three points and the championship if Emerson stayed second) Colin was reminded that, if he did signal Ronnie to let Emerson through, Ronnie would also have to give up the last two races. Colin's assessment came from the other direction: it was inconceivable that Stewart, who had finished in 11 out of the season's 12 races, would fail to score one point in the remaining two, and that the championship was to all intents and purposes lost. So the instruction was *not* to put out the signal.

Ronnie took the victory, an out-and-out race between the two drivers was avoided, and Emerson had an enormous sulk. It never entered his head that a championship in which he had been waved through by his team-mate five times could not really have been called a championship, and he now went further by bad-mouthing the Team to the press. Ronnie, who been very good friends with Emerson throughout the season, started to feel that Emerson was in some way blaming him as well and did not enjoy being caught in the cross-fire.

The Team were not to know that Stewart would announce his retirement early after Cevert's fatal practice accident at Watkins Glen, altering the mathematical possibilities, but the prediction of Stewart getting enough points to win anyway proved right when he finished fifth in Canada. By this time the damage was done and Emerson had not only firmed up on his move to McLaren for 1974 but also further revealed his political nature by scheming with his friend from Team Lotus's fuel sponsor Texaco, John Goossens, and McLaren boss Teddy Mayer to take that sponsorship with him.

In assessing Emerson it is fair to call him a very worthy champion, but not one of the greats. His early blistering speed was put into perspective by Ronnie's performance in the same car, but he was an intelligent, thinking driver in the mould of Stewart and later Prost. Most annoyingly, like Stewart and Prost, and particularly when we were racing against him from 1974 onwards, he was one of those drivers who never set the world on fire but whom one could never discount, whether he was fourth or eighth on the grid. He would, like Stewart and Prost, always be there at the finish, usually in the points and often in the winner's circle. Thus he scored his second championship victory.

By the time he was persuaded to throw in his lot with his brother, Wilson, with the all-Brazilian team building their own Fittipaldi cars, one could be forgiven for thinking that his judgement was being overruled by temptations of serious monetary gain. His low point came in 1981/82 when, instead of leaving the business side to Wilson, who was an astute professional out of the cockpit, Emerson wanted to be all things to all men and drove the race car, attempted to run the business and tried his hand as team manager, all at the same time. Happily the disaster that was inevitable helped turn his mind back to the thing he did best, which was driving, and he forged a new and very successful career in CART/Indycar racing. Perhaps his greatest achievement was to adopt the mantle of the father figure whom subsequent Brazilian race drivers could look up to, respect and try to emulate.

RONNIE

In complete contrast to Emerson, Ronnie Peterson was the most non-political and most uncomplicated of all the great Team Lotus drivers. He lived, breathed, ate, slept and dreamed motor racing. There was nothing else he did better, and nothing else on his priority list. All he wanted was a race car to drive, a full schedule of races in which to take part, and preferably someone else to organise all the nitty-gritty details like travelling, hotels and other essential amenities, so that he just had to think about his racing. He only knew one way to drive, and that was flat out. There was no difference at all between testing and racing – the object was to see how fast he could make it go. And here was a driver whose out-and-out speed was so astonishing that, like Clark and Rindt before him and Senna after him, the Team knew immediately that if he was not on the pole then something was wrong with the car.

This is the most vital and valuable bonus that any team can enjoy.

Never is there the temptation to suggest that perhaps the car is all right and that the driver is having an off day. Never can one be complacent that there is nothing more that can be done to improve. Never do the crew get demotivated, or feel they are doing their work for nothing. Their reward is to know that every time the car is on the track it is going as fast as it is possible for anyone to drive it. If Ronnie was vulnerable as a race driver at all, it was in two areas. The first was that his constant exploring of what happened beyond the limit led inevitably to quite a few 'offs'. Not even his innate skills, incredible reactions and uncanny car control could bring back some lost causes, though he could usually talk you through the accident in great detail. More often than not the eventual cause could be analysed as being an outside agency. Ronnie's somewhat naïve belief, therefore, that it was in order to assume that track conditions would be constant, that the tyres would maintain their grip in spite of the punishment he was giving them and that an unforeseen mechanical glitch would not intervene, put him in some very compromising situations at circuits everywhere.

His second shortcoming was his complete conviction that he was a sound and reliable tester and sorter of cars. In fact his natural skills were so great that, whatever a car's failings, he would subconsciously and almost immediately adjust his driving style to drive around the problem, and he never appreciated this. Nowhere was this better illustrated than during a test at the Circuit Paul Ricard in the south of France, where the kilometre-long straight is followed by the dauntingly fast corner called Courbe de Signes.

Driving the 72, Ronnie returned several times to the pits complaining that the car was understeering badly. The tyre temperatures, with the rears hugely hotter than the fronts, did not bear this out. In an effort to unravel the mystery I paid a visit on foot to the outside of Signes, which was taken at over 160mph. As Ronnie approached at very high speed there would be a momentary feathering of the throttle, after which the car would lurch sideways and exit the corner on some opposite lock with a trace of smoke coming off the inside rear tyre. I hurried back to the pits to explain to Ronnie that this was called 'oversteer'. He countered immediately by saying "No, you are wrong. The car is understeering so much I have to throw it sideways to get it round the corner!" Of course he was right, but on the one hand no other driver would have attempted the same thing at that speed and take that risk lap after lap. On the other hand it did make it pretty hard to understand what he would say about the behaviour of the car and apply the appropriate adjustments. Perhaps he was actually a very good test driver, and we mere mortals could just not get our heads around what he was doing with the car...

We did get to know when the car was well set up for him, though. At the Curva do Sol on the old unmodified track at Interlagos – like Eau Rouge at Spa, Woodcote at pre-chicane Silverstone and Signes at Paul Ricard, among the truly great corners in Formula 1 – Ronnie would have smoke coming off both the rear tyres, a sign that he was happy with the balance. Another sign would be the huge margin by which he achieved some of his most memorable pole positions. In an era when everyone but Ferrari was using the Cosworth DFV engine and times could therefore be expected to be very close, he amazed us by putting large chunks of time between himself and the rest.

In 1973 his pole lap in Brazil, only his second race for the Team, was 0.4sec quicker than Emerson's – and Interlagos was Emerson's home circuit. The next five places on the grid were covered by 0.7sec. In Barcelona at the Montjuich circuit, which, being a street track, was not available for testing, Ronnie's fastest lap in practice was an unbelievable 0.7sec faster than anyone else. At one stage he was 1.75sec better than the next driver during final practice. At Zolder for the Belgian race his margin to Denny Hulme, who was second, was over half a second. The margin covering second to tenth places was less than that. Again in Holland he was half a second clear of the field. It was the same story at Monza and Watkins Glen, but at Mosport for the Canadian race that year he beat Peter Revson in the

McLaren by over a second to take the pole and put his absolute superiority in speed over a single lap beyond any possible doubt.

Add to all of this the fact that Ronnie was the most lovely man, friendly, uncomplicated and completely committed to his work, and it is not hard to understand why the whole team adored him. Always accompanied by Barbrö, who helped him enormously by taking much of the strain of the organisational bits of his life which were not race driving, he projected a laid-back and easygoing approach that put everyone around him at their ease. His personality and behaviour were never tainted by his fame and success. Indeed he seemed to prefer a pretty low-key existence and was happiest among friends over a meal talking about – what else? – motor racing. But his enthusiasm for driving even when his situation in a race was a lost cause engendered fierce and unswerving loyalty from those around him. He did crash a number of times, but the Team did not mind. The extra work was easy to do if the reward was the car being driven to the maximum of its potential.

Only once did the Team start to show signs of despair. The Lotus 72 was a very complex car, and only after a long period of the factory working horrendously long hours to maintain, modify and update the current race cars and try to build up new chassis was the Team able to field four cars at a race. This happened at Zolder in 1973 when, fulfilling the obligation to the drivers for equal number one treatment, four 72s were unloaded from the transporters for the very first time. In fact this was such a notable occasion in the car's fourth season of Grands Prix that the whole lot were lined up in front of the pits and a posed photography session with the Team was held. This took place while delays in the schedule were happening due to the surface of the track breaking up and frantic discussions were going on to see if a race was to be held at all. Once resolved, extra practice was arranged at the drivers' request for Sunday morning. In spite of being on pole and leading the race initially, by that afternoon Ronnie had crashed three of the four 72s! In practice he had put both of 'his' cars on pole but one had suffered a brake hydraulic failure on Sunday morning and he went off the track. Taking the other car, he crashed out at the same place, suffering mild concussion. His eventual race car was built up from half of one of his chassis and half of Emerson's spare car. Thus the ticking off he got was as much for reducing the Team from its first-ever four-car level to a singleton running 72 as it was for his having concealed that he had been suffering from a virus infection all weekend and probably should not have been driving anyway. He was that sort of person.

As for his laid-back approach and the new-found self-confidence that he gained during that year, this was never more clearly illustrated than in Canada. By this time he had learnt to his surprise that, although he had always known he was quick, in fact the quickest, he was actually quicker driving in a relaxed manner than he had been at the start of the year when he had been overdriving the car. Now, with him on the pole by that incredible margin, the weather had turned distinctly dodgy. Goodyear hand-cut some slick tyres to make them intermediates, but time was so short that only one set per team was available. It seemed logical that Ronnie on the pole should have them, but this produced a fairly major sulk from Emerson. Ronnie, sensing that there was a less than harmonious mood in the pits, volunteered without hesitation or being asked: "Give them to Emerson. I will win whatever tyres you give me." (He was chasing Niki Lauda for the lead when a rear tyre punctured, and he crashed.)

Similarly, his reaction to being told that Jacky Ickx had been signed to join him for 1974 was: "Well, I hope he and I get on as well as I have with Emerson. And it's good because he is very quick at the Nürburgring, and he will be able to show me a thing or two." Such natural and unrestrained bonhomie towards his fellow competitors was typical of his attitude to life, and further endeared him to everyone with whom he came into contact. His trusting nature did play against him later in his career, when he found that some people were inclined to take advantage of his easygoing ways, and he always responded with hurt and indignation to some of the stories printed about him, particularly by the Swedish press who were ever eager to emphasise his accidents.

"I always knew I could win races," he would say, "but they did not want to give me the chance." But he was entirely philosophical, too, with no sign of frustration or anger. When reviewing the 1973 season he said, without a trace of emotion, "If the car had not let me down in Barcelona and Zandvoort when I had things completely under control, I would have been World Champion."

For 1974 the Lotus 76, called officially the JPS 9 for sponsorship reasons, was supposed to be the car that gave Ronnie his real chance at the championship.

The 76 had an advanced transmission system, with no clutch pedal. Peter explained how the Team tried to get Ronnie to adapt to it. "There was a button on top of the gear lever to actuate the Automotive Products electric clutch, and a forked brake pedal so you could use either your right foot or your left to brake. Ronnie wasn't getting on with it very well, so we built him an Elan Plus 2 road car with an AP electric clutch and a button on the gear lever so he could get used to it. We were at Silverstone for a test and it was pouring with rain so we'd stopped for a bit. Ronnie said to me, 'My Plus 2 is making a funny noise.' I said, 'Is it engine or transmission? If you put it into neutral and the vibration is still there you know it's in the drive line, the drive shafts or the diff.' So he asked me to come out with him to listen. We were rocketing through the old Woodcote in pouring rain at 125mph, and he put it in neutral, steering with one thumb on the bottom of the steering wheel, and said, "There, can you hear it?' Ronnie was priceless."

By Monaco the 76 had not lived up to its hyped expectations and the 'old nail', the 72, was dragged out of retirement. Unfazed, Ronnie drove it to victory. Although he won again in France and Monza, he could do no better than fifth in the championship. In winning the championship for McLaren, Emerson also won three races, as did

Carlos Reutemann, who finished sixth behind Ronnie. Jody Scheckter and Niki Lauda, who finished ahead of Ronnie, only won two races each. Four retirements and only three further points finishes for Ronnie meant a meagre total of 35 points, all achieved after the 72 was brought out of retirement at Monaco.

And so what was supposed to have been his best championship chance slipped past. Worse was to come, as the team sponsor threatened to end the relationship before the 1975 season started due to pressures it was being put under regarding tobacco advertising. This crisis, scarcely averted prior to the new season, led to another that was to knock the stuffing out of Ronnie and leave him depressed and ill at ease with his team. Drastic economies were necessary, as the sponsor had been persuaded to continue only on the basis that its withdrawal just six weeks before the season would effectively mean the end of the Team. With no time remaining to find a replacement sponsor and insufficient resources of its own to continue by itself, Team Lotus managed to persuade John Player & Son to provide just sufficient funds to let the Team tick over and not go to the wall while re-grouping for the following season. Ronnie and his team-mate Jacky Ickx were asked if they would consider taking a voluntary drop in their contract fees, even as it was pointed out that the new financial regime meant another season with the now heavy and uncompetitive Lotus 72, there being insufficient budget even to consider a new car.

Even if the championship is out of reach for whatever reason, a driver can and will fall back on his 'worth' to establish both in his and the various teams' minds his place in the pecking order. The contract fee, while essentially confidential, is normally known fairly accurately within Formula 1, as the driver has in all probability spoken with other teams before getting his deal. They, particularly if they have been unsuccessful in signing a driver, will make what mileage they can from telling everyone else what his demands were. Thus the retainer is like a badge of rank. Not unnaturally, Ronnie was not so easygoing as to wish to give up his place as the number

The tension of qualifying shows on the faces of Peter and Colin Chapman. This was 1970s F1: breeze-block pits, a picnic chair and a hand-held stopwatch. LAT

In 1972 Fittipaldi won five Grands Prix in the now black-and-gold 72, becoming at 25 the then youngest-ever World Champion. This is at the French round at Clermont, where he was second to Stewart. LAT

With Fittipaldi at Silverstone in 1972 for the non-championship International Trophy, which Emerson won; mechanic Eddie Dennis is on the right. Courtesy of Eddie Dennis

A stern, long-haired group in team garb at Brands Hatch in 1972: with Peter are, from left, mechanics Eddie Dennis, Trevor Seaman, Stevie May and Vic McCarthy. Courtesy of Eddie Dennis

The 72's replacement, the 76, wasn't a success. At an early 1974 Goodwood test Ronnie Peterson talks to Stevie May, designer Ralph Bellamy stands pensively by the rear wheel, Keith Leighton sits against the pits and Peter models some period bell-bottoms. LAT

Paddock pow-wow in 1974 among F1's big men: the tall figures of Peter and Ken Tyrrell flank the compact Bernie Ecclestone while Ferrari's Luca di Montezemolo, right, keeps his own counsel. sutton-images.com

By 1975 the 72 was no longer competitive, but Peterson, here leading team-mate Ickx in front of his home crowd at Anderstorp, still gave his all. LAT

Opposite: Peter, still on crutches after the road accident that broke his legs, at the 1975 British GP at Silverstone with Ronnie – 'an absolute favourite of everyone on the Team'. sutton-images.com

At Kyalami Peterson, Ickx, Warr and Chapman ponder a lean season. During 1975 Ronnie scored just six points, Jacky three. LAT

Through all the highs and lows of Colin Chapman's motor-racing life, no-one worked with him more closely than Peter. sutton-images.com

Solemn faces. At Interlagos in 1976 Mario crashed and took out Ronnie too; they listen as Colin delivers his thoughts to Peter and race engineer Nigel Bennett. LAT

Gunnar Nilsson, left, was Mario's team-mate for two seasons, until illness ended his career. Peter called it 'A tragedy: he would have become very, very good.' sutton-images.com

Peter was very competitive in the team managers' race run at Brands Hatch in 1978 as one of the support races to the British Grand Prix. Gerry Stream

Mario's 77 won the wet Japanese GP at Fuji in 1976, Peter's last race at Lotus before departing for Wolf. Vittorio Brambilla's March follows. sutton-images.com

Tony Southgate with Colin and Mario before Mario's victory at Jarama in 1977. In the 78 that year he won more GPs than anyone else, but his championship title only came the following season. LAT

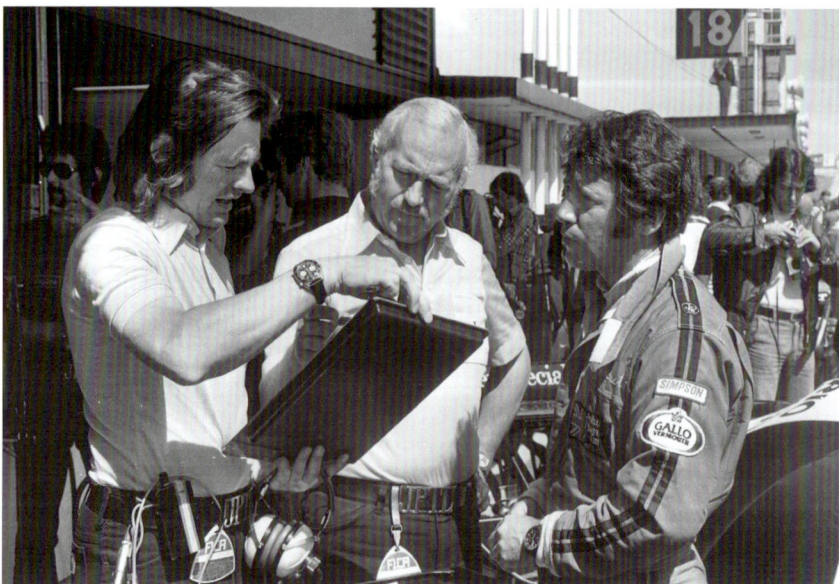

one championship contender as measured on the dollar scale. His business sense was remarkably well developed, and he knew that his future financial wellbeing depended on holding firm. In desperation we had to look at the option of trading our most valuable commodity away to cover the forthcoming budgetary disaster. Weeks of unsatisfactory discussions followed, mainly with Shadow, whose team manager Alan Rees was the original founder member of the Ronnie fan club from his March days. He couldn't wait to get his favourite pilot back. And from Team Lotus's standpoint the new youngster at Shadow, Tom Pryce, looked to be, if not a fair exchange for Ronnie, a much cheaper one with a great deal of promise for the future.

Driver contracts were not then and are still not like footballers' contracts, where a club may buy and sell a player. In the end Shadow and its owner Don Nichols were not prepared to pay a premium to Team Lotus for the release of Ronnie and, in spite of the talks having progressed to the point where Ronnie himself let slip in Brazil that "he was now a Shadow driver", the deal undid itself at the eleventh hour. Ronnie now had to face up to a season of frustration driving a car which in anyone else's hands would have been back-of-the-grid material, but in his hands was midfield but still hopelessly uncompetitive with the newer cars. To add to his downcast demeanour as he saw his career fall apart, his old team-mate from March, Niki Lauda, who had paid for his drive back in 1972 and never been anywhere near Ronnie in the speed stakes, was to win the 1975 World Championship.

While the turn of events had not been the fault of Team Lotus, the relationship with Ronnie was now showing signs of strain. Colin Chapman was inclined to let his frustration at not being a front-runner show by turning on and bawling out the nearest person to hand and some of his remarks in the hearing of Ronnie seemed to imply that he thought his driver could do better. Nothing could have been further from the truth and Colin made the mistake of thinking that all Ronnie's flair and outstanding ability was being compromised by an attitude that was short on work ethic. He did not understand that was the impression Ronnie always gave and that when he was doing well this outwardly relaxed approach merely served to add to the mystique surrounding the man. When things were not going well the same approach could give an impression of indifference. And yet on a couple of occasions during that dreadful season, in Monaco and Austria when it was wet, there were glimpses of the real Ronnie.

The 1976 season started with the promise of a new car at last, but as with his first outing with Jacky Ickx as his team-mate, when the two of them collided, his first outing with Mario Andretti as his team-mate in Brazil ended when the two of them collided in the new Lotus 77. It was with a sense of *déja vu* that negotiations got under way which ended with Ronnie going back to March in time for the next race, and March's young hopeful, Gunnar Nilsson, being released for Team Lotus to sign.

In spite of the troubled nature of the three seasons that Ronnie spent with the Team and the fact that subsequently he was to lose his life during his second stint at Lotus, it is hard to convey the excitement and anticipation he brought with him. He was worshipped by those who worked with him, became a good friend to many of them and had an uncomplicated outlook that everyone found refreshing. Here was the driver who recreated the adrenalin flows brought on by Rindt. His car control was probably better than anyone before him and may well have surpassed those who followed him. He was a man of his word, whose love of motor racing oozed out of every pore in his body. His background of a hard-working family and the struggle to get established was reflected in the way he dealt with people. Never the superstar, he always had time for others whether they were fans, friends, press, colleagues or rivals. His relationship with Barbrö whom, after many years together, he married in 1975, gave him the loving and stable base of a warm and supportive home life that was further reinforced when their daughter, Nina, was born. A racer's racer, he would drive anything and everything that was on offer – single-seaters, sports cars, GTs, saloons and American stock cars – something few of his top-flight contemporaries in Formula 1 did.

So confident had he become in his own ability and so relaxed was he about what he could do that he could make unselfish gestures towards his team-mates without remorse or rancour. In contrast he found it hard to understand why other drivers were not like him and could be so egocentric. No wonder, then, that he was an absolute favourite driver for everyone on the Team when he drove the black and gold cars.

MARIO

There was no-one better than Colin Chapman at spotting true race driving talent, probably because his own outstanding ability in this field made it easy for him to recognise a kindred spirit. In the case of Mario Andretti this was not really necessary, as he was an established and successful professional when Colin started enthusing about him. What was different was that Mario's domain was the USA and that, unlike Phil Hill and Dan Gurney, two Americans whose potential talents had singled them out for trials in Europe and subsequent stardom in the Formula 1 arena, Mario was already a star in his own widespread world of Stateside racing. No more versatile or experienced driver existed, possibly since the days of Fangio and Moss. He was and remains the consummate professional.

Although he stunned the Formula 1 world by putting his Lotus 49 on pole position in his first outing as a guest of the Team at Watkins Glen in 1968, he remained tantalisingly out of reach to his greatest fan, Colin. This was purely because his standing, reputation, personality and success rate had already made him the highest paid driver in the US, and when we discovered the real extent of his earning power over there it seemed inconceivable that such an income could be supported out of a typical Formula 1 budget. Nonetheless, having been first choice to take the place of Jimmy Clark in 1968, and the subject of strenuous efforts to sign him for

1969, he remained in the thoughts for much of the 1970s.

He did come to Formula 1 first with the newly formed March team, but the STP-sponsored car was run somewhat unconventionally by the Granatelli brothers. Then he was lured by the magic of Italy, his country of origin, and even more by the magic of Ferrari. For neither did he race a full season. When Maurice Phillippe, the Team Lotus designer responsible for the Lotus 72, was given the task by his then team owner, Parnelli Jones, to design a Formula 1 contender, he came up with a car that fitted exactly the brief that Colin Chapman had given his designers for 1974. This brief was for "a car with all the good points but none of the bad points of the 72, and 100 pounds lighter". While the Ralph Bellamy-designed Lotus 76 was consigned to the scrap heap and the faithful 72 brought out of retirement, Mario, with his astute approach to everything in his professional life, quickly recognised the Parnelli car as the true successor to the one he had been hard pressed to beat for the previous two seasons. Nonetheless after two North American races in the new Parnelli at the end of the 1974 season, he did not enjoy the results it should have given him.

One can never be certain why an approach at a particular moment in time suddenly has a chance of succeeding where previously it did not. Mario certainly did not need the money, and his success in dirt-track racing, quarter-mile ovals, champ cars on the big ovals, sports cars and stock cars needed no confirmation in another category. Also there was no way that he was prepared to give up his life in his home town of Nazareth, Pennsylvania, in the street that was named in his honour. So the negotiations were tricky and the courtship prolonged.

Indeed, Mario's contract broke new ground in many respects for the Team. Amongst these were the inclusion for the first time in any Team Lotus driver contract of first-class air tickets to each race. As these were nearly always transatlantic, they represented a considerable on-cost. And excluded for the first time was the usual requirement for a driver to be at the circuit the day before practice started. In spite of warnings that the continual transatlantic travel imposed on Jackie Stewart in 1972 by his management team of Mark McCormack may have contributed to the ulcer that laid him low, and so to his failing to win the championship that year, Mario brushed such excuses to one side almost as a sign of weakness. Indeed many was the occasion when he stepped off an overnight transatlantic flight, jumped into his hire car, drove to the circuit and was out to practice at ten o'clock with all the others. And yet we never saw any sign of jet lag or tiredness.

Two things occurred, however, that may have tipped the balance finally in favour of Team Lotus. The first was that, with a natty piece of lateral thinking, we came up with a solution to the continuing problem of parity of pay in Formula 1 compared to the value of his contracts in America. By paying a smaller retainer than he would have expected in the States but adding a bonus of $5,000 per championship point, we were able to promise a scale of pay that, if he were to become World Champion, would reward him with a World Champion's money. This system, which was to become the norm in Formula 1 until the astronomical retainers of the 1990s, resulted in a bonus in respect of the 22 points Mario scored in 1976 and the 47 points for the third place in the championship achieved in 1977. By 1978 the bonus level was even higher and the 64 points that were good enough to win the World Championship gave Mario remuneration on a par with what he might have expected had he stayed in the States.

The second persuader was an overtaking move that was done to Mario rather than by him. This occurred during the *Daily Express* Trophy meeting at Silverstone in the spring. Before this, however, Team Lotus had asked Mario on a one-off basis to start the year for them in the Brazilian Grand Prix. With Ronnie, he was to drive the new 'all-things-to-all-circuits', infinitely adjustable Lotus 77. Ronnie crashed his in practice (not his fault) and Mario failed to get his recalcitrant chassis to respond to his set-up either. What could have been embarrassing reports about the 77's lack of performance quickly turned into sensational stories when Ronnie and Mario managed to take each other off in the race. Emergency eating of humble pie took place when chassis and suspension flexing were found to be a major component of the 'infinitely adjustable' element of the car, and the extreme and hitherto unthinkable step of contracting a quick fix to an outside design house was taken. Like other well-known designers, Len Terry had served his time under Colin Chapman and was running his own successful company, Design Auto, down in Dorset. His fix was to junk the inboard brakes (too powerful, too heavy, too much drag and too cool in the airstream) and put conventional smaller outboard brakes inside the front wheels where they at least helped the front tyre temperature. The wheels were carried on a Ralt front upright, and the whole assembly was supported on a traditional front rocker and lower wishbone. In the non-championship race at Silverstone the 77 was on the way to being sorted, although after some carnage at Long Beach only one car was entered for Gunnar Nilsson. And who should turn up at Silverstone but Mario, now driving one of the ex-Hesketh 308E cars being run by Frank Williams. When Gunnar overtook Mario during the race, having qualified fourth in only his fourth outing in a Formula 1 car, it was in a way and at a rate that impressed Mario sufficiently to re-open talks and sign for us.

Of Gunnar Nilsson, Peter had fond memories. "Once they became team-mates, Gunner adored Mario. The two of them got on extremely well. Having spent time in the Swedish Navy, Gunnar was worldly-wise, he could handle himself, and I think he would have learned a whole new level of things from working with Mario, like François Cevert did by being Jackie Stewart's team-mate. I think he would have become very, very good. He wasn't talented in the way of a Clark or a Senna, but he was professional, he applied himself, he worked very hard. It was a tragedy that he got ill." Gunnar contracted testicular cancer and, having scored his only Grand Prix victory in Belgium in 1977, left the Team at the end of that season. He died in October 1978.

Having signed Mario Andretti at 36 years of age and eight years after our initial interest, what sort of driver had we finally got? We had got the very best: the ultimate professional who never had an 'off' day and whose vast experience meant there was rarely a situation with the car, the tyres, the track or the race that he had not encountered before. Add to this that he was quick, very quick, and surprised us most when we least expected it – for example, in the rain. All in all, none of us could believe how lucky we had been to get him at a point when the Team was not at one of its all-time highs. When his inherent talent, courage and race-driving ability was added to his unfailing charm, politeness and sensational sense of humour, as well as his capacity for hard work, it is easy to see why all who came into contact with this great driver were immediately captivated and became fans for life. Mario added something to every team with which he came into contact, and enriched the lives of all those who were lucky enough to have a spell working with him. This applied in equal measure to all those drivers who drove in the same team as he did. You will not find one who has anything but the highest praise and who does not value greatly his friendship. It was one of the proudest moments for Team Lotus to be able to say that they had contributed in some small way to Mario adding the title of World Champion to all those other championships he so richly deserved.

It would take a very lengthy book to re-tell the many and side-splittingly funny stories that roll so freely from Mario's huge store of personal experiences. Once started he can hold any audience spellbound. When and if one wonders how it could be that they are all so funny, when life has a way of dealing out some bad as well as some good, the realisation comes that he can make even a serious crash – and he has had a few of those – sound amusing. Perhaps this is part of an in-built mechanism that always gives him the outward appearance of someone who lives life to the full and enjoys every minute. One story he told many years ago seems to sum up the man and the standards he has set for so long.

Soon after he started competing at an impossibly young age, he was 'the new kid on the block' in the harsh and hierarchical world of quarter-mile oval racing. The ranking guy, the star, the champ of the time was a driver whose name I forget but whose image was enhanced by running his single-seater entirely in white. Mario, the newcomer, was starting to make his mark and the race programmes involved heats, quarter-finals, semis and the final. A driver might do eight races in a meeting. The champ would keep an eye on his competitors and anyone who was perceived as a threat would find things getting tough. "This guy was so smooth you didn't feel it when he put you in the wall," Mario would say, "but finally, after he had had me off for the umpteenth time, I decided it had to stop." The next time they clashed Mario found that, though in the wall again, his car was still a runner. Timing his run to perfection, he set out across the infield of the oval and T-boned the white roadster right in the side. "And ya know what?" Mario recalled in that lazy but melodious drawl of his. "He never did it again!"

Modern teams' PR output plays down the relationship between the two drivers in a team while journalists, seeking marketable copy, play it up. The quest to be the number one driver is actually simple in the extreme. The one who is fastest earns the spot and the respect of the team, the journalists and the fans. In Mario's apprenticeship and the environment of American short-track racing he found himself, as the rising star, teamed with the biggest name in US racing, A.J. Foyt, in the Holman Moody team. Very closely matched, they had each other off the track so often that Mario realised his career might end prematurely, as the mechanics could hardly keep up with the repair schedule. After yet another 'team' coming-together A.J., who until then did not really speak to the youngster, was surprised to be approached by Mario. "A.J.," said Mario, "You and me had better step outside and settle things." And they did.

Mario remains one of the sport's more modest heroes, a gentleman, one of the great drivers and quite correctly a legend.

JODY AND JAMES

As recounted elsewhere, Peter left Lotus at the end of the 1976 season to be team manager for the new Wolf team. While he was there, his drivers included two strong but very different characters, Jody Scheckter and James Hunt. Talking in 2008, he told me:

"I liked Jody a lot as a driver. He was very brave, and he concentrated on what he was doing, planning all his practice sessions and his races in great detail. He always gave his best in the car, and he was supremely fit. He always looked pretty nonchalant to the outside world, but inside he was a seriously professional race driver, and the boys on the team loved him for it.

"It was always clear to me that when he won the World Drivers' Championship he would stay around for one more year for the money, and then move on to something else. He was a sound businessman, and he did very well."

For 1979 Jody Scheckter went off to Ferrari and duly won his World Championship, and the new Wolf driver was James Hunt. "James stayed on at McLaren after winning the Championship in 1976, but during the summer of 1978 I signed him to come to Wolf for 1979, for a retainer of £150,000. Then we all went to Monza, and Ronnie had his accident.

"James was a pretty brave straight-up sort of guy, and when the accident happened right after the start he jumped out and ran to Ronnie to see if he could help and lift him out. Then there was a long delay while they cleared everything up before they restarted the race, and instead of going back to the McLaren motorhome he came into the Wolf one, and started to plead with me to let him out of his contract for the next year. He'd finally had enough after what had happened. James was too intelligent, he was always thinking, 'There but for the grace of God go I.' He wanted out. I didn't tell him he couldn't, I just said we should wait a week or two for things to settle down and then talk some more. What we didn't know, of course, was that Ronnie would be dead by the next morning.

"Anyway, we did meet and talk some more. James's brother Peter was *there too, because he was always involved in all his contracts and arrangements, and in the end we decided to go ahead. I do remember having the feeling that we were making a mistake, because the stuffing had gone out of James, really, and I was concerned that we weren't going to get value for money from him. At Long Beach the following April he retired on Lap 1 of the race with a broken driveshaft. I found out later he'd said to one of the mechanics, 'I've discovered something: if I run the car along the barrier and give it a squirt in second gear, it breaks a driveshaft.' The following month at Monaco he stopped on Lap 5 – with a broken driveshaft. Then he announced he was retiring from racing."*

ELIO AND NIGEL

Among the 40 or so drivers who have appeared in Formula 1 cars for Team Lotus, neither Elio de Angelis nor Nigel Mansell come near the top of the rankings. Elio won but two Grands Prix in his time with the Team, while Nigel won none. However, they represent most ably the majority of Grand Prix drivers who never achieve true greatness, but make their mark transiently. Stars but not superstars, they are included here because of the almost total contrast of their backgrounds, personalities and approach to their work, and the comparison is all the more stark because they both drove for the Team at the same time.

Elio was the eldest son of a patrician, wealthy and old-established Roman family. He raced because it was something he really liked to do, and was actually rather good at. He gave the impression that he was never hungry enough to devote himself completely to his profession, but that may have been a false impression because of his inherent good manners. One doubted nonetheless whether he would have been prepared to give up the other aspects of his easy and elegant lifestyle and to exclude his other pleasures for the cause of a championship.

Nigel's background was more modest, more Costa Birmingham than Costa Esmeralda, and not much had been handed to him on a plate. In spite of having the in-house backing of Peter Collins, the then Competitions Manager, and that of journalist David Phipps, who was often used by Colin as an out-of-house sounding board, Nigel then and throughout his time with the Team made it clear that he felt the whole world was against him. It did not help his case that in many instances his demeanour and his behaviour did nothing to convince the Team that anything they did would help change his attitude to one where he was not continually suspicious of their real intent.

Elio breezed through life, was open and friendly with everyone he met and was a very social animal. He was equally at home at the keyboard of a concert piano or in a disco. Such was his passion for football and his beloved Roma that he once injured his fist punching the air when they scored in a European Champions Cup match. The ceiling of the bar where he was watching the game on TV was too low to jump and punch at the same time. This was Saturday, the evening before a race, but happily he had remembered to put down his cigarette and the glass of J&B whisky he always had in the evening. He would have been far more concerned about spilling the whisky than the prospect of driving with a painful hand the next day.

He was naturally at ease in the company of royalty, show business personalities, other sports stars, politicians and high-powered executives. As a result he was superb with sponsors and their wives. His laid-back approach meant that often he would turn up for practice having left his helmet behind or having forgotten where he had put his gloves or driving boots, but that did not worry him. He just went off and borrowed what he needed from another of his driver friends in the pits. He had a calm, solid and enduring relationship with Ute, his German girlfriend, who accompanied him to all the races and who helped as far as she could to get him organised.

Nigel enjoyed the solid support of his wife, Roseanne, who had already had to grin and bear it through some very tough times early in her husband's racing. He also had a Mum and a Dad who not unnaturally wished to be in as close proximity to their son's advancing career as possible – never something that is easy to handle for either the son or a team. Nigel also developed a propensity for listening to those people who said things he wanted to hear, and in no time at all he was surrounded by a large group of hangers-on, sycophants, the odd journalist and others. The others included a California policeman who stopped Nigel for speeding when we were at Long Beach for the race there. All of a sudden the policeman was a bosom pal, turning up at all the races, requiring a pass and probably advising Nigel on the set-up of his car, his contract negotiations, his fitness regime and who knows what else.

Strong as a bull and a good athlete, Nigel did not appear to have a fitness regime at that time in the early 1980s, though in common with most drivers this had to follow later. The ground-effect and subsequent high G-force cars put ever greater strains on a body that had been subjected to some brutal shunts earlier in his career: the neck support he always wore bore witness to this.

In contrast to his team-mate, he neither drank nor smoked and rarely, if ever, partied. One often felt that if perhaps he had some relaxations in his life the tension that kept the chip on his shoulder might have melted away and he might have been more at ease with himself and others.

Elio had been signed from Shadow as a real young prospect for the future. At 23 he was the youngest driver in the Formula 1 field of 1980. Colin, knowing he was going to lose Mario, was also in a period of budgetary instability having lost John Player & Son after the champion year of 1978. The Martini association lasted only a year and the Essex deal that followed seemed too good to be true – which unfortunately it was. He could not be out there bidding top dollar for the best driver and knowing in his heart that the current car was not good enough to attract one, so he gave Nigel, whom he had signed initially as a test driver, a chance in Austria and Zandvoort in 1980. Nigel became Elio's number two for 1981 on a retainer that reflected his novice status. After the 'non-championship' South African race (the FOCA teams ran with sliding skirts in defiance of the FIA and the *Grande Construttore* boycotted the event) the Team became mired for the next four races in the controversy and politics of the twin-chassis Lotus 88. At Zolder Nigel finished third and Elio fifth, giving the Team its best result for ages and a much-needed boost. Colin admitted later that when, after the race, he said to Nigel "You're a star!", he never realised that Nigel would take this colloquialism so completely to heart. Nigel reminded him of it many times and ventured that, if he was, he should be paid like one. Early in 1982, in a completely uncharacteristic moment of weakness or lack of concentration, Colin eventually conceded a substantial rise that served only to perpetuate the myth in Nigel's mind.

Early in 1982 Colin called me into his office and gave me the news that for the coming season Nigel was to have exactly equal treatment to Elio. Spare cars, same number of mechanics, a race engineer for each car, all the racing resources were to be split effectively into two camps. This was obviously something else he had been pressed into agreeing with Nigel but, anticipating my aversion to such a divisive way of operating, he had omitted to tell me – or Elio! When I pointed out that Cosworth had agreed only to rebuild sufficient engines for one car and the others would be coming from John Judd's Engine Developments company, Colin suggested that I let Nigel have the choice as Elio was abroad at the time. I duly took Nigel up to look round John Judd's establishment. Persuaded by the special development work they were doing, particularly for Williams, on DFV engines, which came from Cosworth only to a standard specification for all their customers, Nigel chose to use the Judd engines. This story is told only to clarify that, from that moment on, everything that could be done was done to ensure completely equal treatment for the two drivers. This was tantamount to running two teams within a team and created all sorts of inter-group rivalries amongst the staff. The relationship with Nigel had not begun well, for on the first occasion that he came to the factory after my arrival back at Team Lotus he started to tell me which mechanics he wanted working on his car. I had to point out that, whatever his relationship with Peter Collins had been, his new team manager would give him every support as a driver but he was going to have to leave the running of the Team and the assignment of staff to me. Now I had to explain the new arrangements to Elio, who was singularly unimpressed, thus adding to the lack of camaraderie that existed between the two drivers.

Throughout the year Nigel found it more and more difficult to handle Elio. Everything the Italian did, he did with style and a freedom of spirit that irked the man that Elio still considered his number two. Although Elio tended to get knocked back by the vicissitudes of racing and could act like a spoilt child if things did not go well, these black moods would quickly pass. By comparison Nigel was gauche and clumsy, particularly in his relationships within the Team. There were times when it seemed that 'celebrity status' was more important to him than success, and he was often to be seen talking to the press before his Team. What irked more was that, in spite of the equal treatment that was obviously in place, in spite of the so-called 'special relationship' with Colin, and in spite of Elio's carefree outlook on life, Nigel was rarely able to match his pace either in smoothness or, more importantly, in absolute speed.

The final dénouement came in Austria in August at a time in the season when Cosworth took their annual holiday. Elio's engine after practice had more than 300 miles on it and would be out of life before the end of the race. There was no fresh spare in the truck. Nigel on the other hand had a fresh engine for the race and another in the truck. Colin would not agree to let me have a 'Nigel' engine to put in Elio's car. Happily history relates that Elio won the race by five hundredths of a second from Keke Rosberg in a Judd-powered Williams to bring the Team its first victory since 1978.

A Ronnie or a Mario would not have hesitated in agreeing, even offering the fresh engine to Elio, but such graciousness was not part of Nigel's make-up. Unsurprisingly the very powerful

Italian background of the de Angelis family included an ethic that most thought came usually from further south than Rome, namely revenge. If the family honour was impugned it would not be forgotten and Elio never forgave Nigel's churlish behaviour in Austria.

The antipathy that existed between them was soon to rise to new levels. Early in the year Colin held a meeting to discuss the future direction of the Team. With the passing into history of the true sliding-skirt, ground-effect cars and the outlawing of the attempt to revive ground effect with the twin-chassis Lotus 88, the current cars were proving difficult. Without a sliding skirt and with fixed-length flexible appendages strictly regulated, controlling pitch and ride height became increasingly important to gain a stable and constant aerodynamic performance from the tunnels under the cars. Any team still using cross-ply tyres, as we were, suffered from changing ride heights as the tyres grew in diameter with the centrifugal force generated at speed. Our first objective, therefore, was to secure a radial tyre. Michelin were fully committed and were unable to take us on, but a solution was found with Pirelli in Italy. Although they had a long history in competition and had recently been successful in Formula 2, both they and the Team were taking a gamble in tackling Formula 1. The odds against being successful in competition with Michelin and Goodyear were not reduced by the huge retainer I negotiated with Ing. Mezzanotte, their competition chief, but there was no other solution to the engineers' demands for a tyre that did not grow in diameter.

Also on the agenda, inevitably, was a turbo engine. The season had started with Ferrari and Renault using turbocharged engines in their own cars, while Toleman had the Hart turbo and Brabham were to get the new BMW turbo unit. Alfa Romeo was to join the turbo club at Monza at the end of the year. Porsche was building an engine for McLaren. The brief given to me by Colin was simple: "Go get us a turbo." No ground had been prepared, as Colin had been vehemently 'anti-turbo' until there was no chance of reversing the

tide. Casting my net as far and as wide as possible, I held discussions
with several companies. Most were not interested and the one that
was, probably out of politeness, could not have anything ready in
time for the 1983 season. So having gone through the motions and
the same process of elimination amongst engine manufacturers as
had every other team manager, I got in touch with my opposite
number at Renault Sport, Gérard Larrousse.

This resulted in a series of meetings with M Mangenot, Director
at Renault Sport, and subsequently with Georges Martin, a Renault
main board member. A thoroughly charming man, Georges made
our dealings easy. If he recognised that the decision he took was
vital to the future of Team Lotus, hence my nervousness and anxiety,
he did not show it. By Hockenheim at the beginning of August the
contract was signed and it was agreed that at the Austrian Grand
Prix, a week later, a public announcement would be made. Armed
with the Renault news it was not difficult to persuade Elio to re-sign
and both stories were released simultaneously. What neither driver
knew at the time was that the Renault deal only provided the
engines for one race car for the first half of the 1983 season. Nor did
they know that politics in France, Guy Ligier being a friend of
President François Mitterrand, would force the state-owned car
company to commit to supply engines to Ligier as well. So Colin and
I agreed to leave the nitty-gritty details until after the season had
ended.

After the awful news on the morning of 16 December of Colin's
death, it was left to me to tell Nigel that he was to drive a Cosworth-
powered car for the first half of the next season. This provided him
with all the ammunition he needed to tell the world that I was
actively working against him. I had agreed with Elio that he had the
reasonable expectation at the start of the 1982 season of Nigel being
his number two. Out-ranked by the Guv'nor's private deal with
Nigel, I now found myself in the position of having to make a really
serious and far-reaching decision on my own. After carefully
analysing the season just finished, it was completely clear who was

the number one. It was Elio – he was the fastest. He had out-qualified Nigel ten times to three. He had seven points-scoring finishes to Nigel's two and, in addition to the win in Austria, had a tally of more than three times the number of points gained by Nigel. What is more, the margin by which Elio eclipsed his team-mate in qualifying overall was a huge 4.5 per cent. And all this in the year when, as near as can be reasonably achieved, the two drivers were given equal equipment and treatment. In retrospect there was no decision to make. At the time, and though the whole Team concurred with the call, we all took a lot of flak.

The main problem arising from Nigel's belief that the whole world was against him was that it meant he was less than honest with himself, and therefore the Team. This started, I believe, with the over-rapid build-up of his 'star' status. If his apprenticeship had been longer and less hyped, he would have been the first to accept the results of his 1982 season. He had only driven in 29 Grands Prix, but he was already living in cloud cuckooland.

For example, he was "a great street circuit specialist". This myth had arisen at Monaco the year before, when he achieved third place on the grid. At that time I was not yet back at Team Lotus, but was further down the pitlane managing the Fittipaldi effort. Having known each other for more than 20 years and worked so closely together, Colin and I would get together from time to time to chew over things generally. As we trusted each other there were few limits on what was discussed. When I congratulated him on Nigel's position, marking as it did something of a resurgence in the fortunes of the Team, he grinned and said, "If only it were that easy". Asked what he meant by that, he said he had stumbled upon a great ruse. After the South African confrontation with FISA and its autocratic president, no real rules about what was permitted between the bottom of a car's side-pods and the ground had been formulated. Jean-Marie Balestre, tired of the burr under his saddle-cloth that was the Formula 1 Constructors' Association, had for the time being come up with the 6cm ground clearance rule. This was to be 'at all times' but only measured on a 'flat' surface when a car returned to the pits. By sending Nigel out with flexible (but not sliding) skirts of grossly illegally length, virtually sealing the car to the ground in the old ground-effect style, Colin gave the driver massive amounts of extra grip. By going very slowly on the 'out' lap the grip stayed with the car for almost all of the qualifying lap. And by the time the car returned to the scrutineering bay to have the 6cm ground clearance checked, the soft Veethane material of the skirts had worn to a legal level. The driver must have been aware of the scam and had no reason to believe the press when they told him he was good on street circuits, because he knew the real reason. But he did!

No fair-minded observer of Formula 1 could have castigated Nigel for his demoralised attitude for the first half of 1983. Stuck with the Cosworth-engined Lotus 92, the Team had tried desperately hard to give him a Chapmanesque magic ingredient – active suspension. Not enthusiastic, particularly as it added some weight and a small but significant horsepower consumption to a car already giving away a power advantage to the turbo-powered cars, Nigel also suffered a couple of electronic 'glitches'. During these the car gave the impression of having a mind of its own. This was understandably unsettling. But the same fair-minded observer would have seen Elio having a traumatic time in the Lotus 93T with Renault power. Distracted by other matters, Colin made the seemingly mindless decision during the design stage of the car that it should have large flat surfaces of bodywork, ostensibly "to provide maximum space for sponsors". We suspected that the real reason Colin had lost the plot was that for the previous year he had left the head of the design department, Martin Ogilvie, to get on and design the 1982 car by himself with minimal interference. Martin had come up with one of the most beautiful of all Grand Prix cars with smooth, flowing, well-balanced lines that everyone admired. Colin was not used to someone else getting the plaudits.

Because the Team lacked any experience with the whole turbo way of life, the Lotus 93T came to the grid out of step with its rivals.

While other teams pared off weight by having smaller chassis with less fuel capacity, the Lotus was overweight. Our competitors would pit-stop for fuel, running about 80kg of fuel at the start, while the 93T might start the race with 100kg more than them for its non-stop run to the flag. At their fuel stops the other teams took the opportunity to put on fresh tyres, which gave them back some lap time, while we had to stick with the Pirellis that had started the race with all that extra weight and that were now degraded way beyond resuscitation. And because we were limited to a maximum of 250 litres fuel for the race we were watching our fuel consumption, and running lean to the detriment of our engines. The others, with no consumption worries because of their fuel stops, were flooding the engines with fuel in an effort to keep them cool and run higher turbo boost. The Team was trying to cope with being forced to assimilate simultaneously two technologies that were completely new to them and, in the case of the active suspension, new to everyone else as well. And to cap it all there was no Colin to turn to – he would have revelled in solving such a complex set of problems.

So the season that had promised so much to Elio, now with three seasons of experience, turbo power and back to being team leader, turned rapidly into a nightmare. His disappointment was greater than that of Nigel, starting as it did from a more elevated set of expectations. Nonetheless, from having been in the depths of despair around the time of Imola, he quickly struck up a marvellous working and personal relationship with Gérard Ducarouge when the French engineer joined the Team in May. This, and the promise shown by the new car introduced at Silverstone for the British Grand Prix, lifted his spirits. Writing off the 1983 season in his mind, he looked forward with a positive attitude to 1984. At the same time the continual complaining by Nigel was getting everyone down, although he finished the season, for the only time in his stretch at Team Lotus, with more points than his team-mate. Normal service was resumed in 1984 when Elio reverted to his ratio of three times the number of championship points as Nigel, and also finished third in the World Championship.

At this time Alan Henry, a senior and respected motor racing journalist, trying to finish another race report for his column, was provoked to say that Nigel "was the only race driver he knew who needed the cooling-down lap to think up the excuse for why he had not done well in the race." In reply I had to tell him that back at the factory in the fabrication shop they had a blackboard hanging on the wall headed 'The Nigel Mansell Excuse Board'. If ever one was feeling a bit down, stressed or worried by the current situation, an instantaneous mood lifter was to be had by looking at the board. With that uncanny wit and humour so typical of people who work really hard, the 'fabbies' would produce some excruciatingly funny slant on the latest Mansell outpouring. This all came to a head after Monaco 1984 and the dreaded 'white line' incident.

It will be recalled that, in the most appalling conditions imaginable, Nigel had it all going for him in that race. The car's handling was superb and he was on the best wet-weather tyres. After the bad tyre year we had endured in 1983, we had signed for 1984 with Goodyear, who were now making radials. We were even one of their supported teams, and those clever people at Renault had adjusted the engines to make them 'soft' and responsive for the very delicate task of feeding the power to the back wheels on the tricky street circuit. The car handled beautifully and had masses of downforce. Nigel set off and was leading the race comfortably when he threw it all away by crashing, going up the hill to the Casino. While his excuse that he had been caught out by the extreme slipperiness of the white line on the road held up on first hearing, it was also an acknowledgement that he knew it was slippery before going onto it. It also tended to disregard the fact that all the other drivers had also to negotiate it once a lap. But most of all it simply never occurred to him that the race would have been as well won by leaving Prost at half a second a lap as by the two seconds a lap he was gaining, at such risk. As it was, the race was stopped shortly after he crashed and Prost declared the winner.

At that time Goodyear had running on television an advertisement for their latest road tyre with a voice-over by Sir Robert Mark, the then Commissioner of the Metropolitan Police. Sir Robert would say time after time as the advertisement was repeated: "Goodyear – tyres you can trust in conditions you can't. I firmly believe these tyres make a major contribution to road safety." When a thoroughly dejected Team returned to Ketteringham Hall after missing out on what would and should have been the completion of their return to health after the death of Colin, the Nigel Mansell Excuse Board had been wiped clean. On it was a single comment: 'Nigel Mansell says "I firmly believe Sir Robert Mark is a liar"!'

How Nigel went on to be so successful is a source of bewilderment to all those who knew him when he drove for us. Perhaps he was a late developer – unusual in a Grand Prix driver, but not impossible. Perhaps he happened to be in the right place at the right time. As he was almost universally disliked in the very close-knit world of Formula 1 and knowing that he came with quite a lot of baggage, teams were reluctant to take the plunge and hire him. Perhaps the cars he drove later with the addition of the driver aids that Senna was to resent so bitterly served to give him the extra confidence he needed by making the cars easier to drive. The active suspension Williams FW14B that gave him his title was a brilliant and vastly superior car.

But he remained a seriously flawed driver. In fact the over-ambitious driving technique of his earlier seasons was not suppressed when he went to Williams, and his hot-headed approach still got him into difficulties. Picked up by Frank at the last moment when the other driver opportunities he was considering for 1985 evaporated, Nigel threw away two championships while driving Williams cars. One of the most vivid images of 1986 remains that of Nigel see-sawing at the wheel of his Williams down the long straight at Adelaide after his rear tyre exploded. His was a brilliant piece of car control, but Prost managed to get his nearly-out-of-fuel McLaren to the flag and the championship. Only four seconds separated Prost from Piquet, whom Williams had to call in when leading for tyres after seeing what befell Mansell and, earlier, Rosberg. So in 20 short laps the title had passed from Mansell, who needed only third place, to Piquet, who needed a win, to Prost, who was very surprised.

But behind the screaming of Murray Walker and the famous TV pictures lay a more realistic truth. Nigel had lost the championship much earlier than Adelaide. In fact he had started to do so in Brazil in the first race of the year. There, with a car that was over a second a lap faster in race trim, he tried to force his way past Senna halfway round the first lap. Like so many before and after him he discovered that Senna was not usually disposed to give way that easily. He obviously had not yet learned that if you know you have the faster car you have no pressure or reason to try to win the race on the first lap. His team-mate Nelson Piquet went on to win the race with Ayrton second and, yes, Nelson's lap time was also a second a lap faster than the Lotus could manage that day. Going to Mexico early in October, Nigel led Piquet by 10 points and Prost by 11 with only Adelaide remaining. Remembering that in 1986 a win was worth only nine points, the task to tie things up there and then was not a huge mountain to climb. But he forgot to put his car into gear on the grid.

And Elio? Poor Elio had had to reconcile his pride and honour, and the lead place he felt he had earned in six seasons with Team Lotus, with his situation. Some of those seasons had been desperately dour and hard, and just as things appeared to be coming good Ayrton had arrived on his patch. No longer being fastest and conscious that the enthusiasms of the Team were swinging behind the newcomer, Elio decided to move on. He signed for Brabham, where he instantly hit it off with the free spirit that was Gordon Murray, Brabham's great designer and chief engineer. The low-line Brabham was not the best car ever to come out of Chessington but it was making progress as Elio, with a new lease of enthusiasm, threw himself into the testing programme. At the Ricard circuit in the south of France he lost control of the car at very high speed, coming to rest upside-down. Apparently only slightly injured with just a collarbone broken, he died of oxygen starvation when the small fire that broke out was not quickly dealt with by the distinctly inadequate rescue services. So Grand Prix racing lost someone who might honestly be called the last of the 'gentleman' drivers, one who would have raced anyway even if he had not been paid to drive.

A year later, in 1987, Nigel started the season with a car that was two seconds a lap (yes, two seconds) faster than anyone but his team-mate in Brazil, and managed by virtue of a bad start to avoid crashing on the first lap. At Imola his team-mate crashed heavily in practice and was not allowed to start, but Senna was on pole. By Spa (held in May that year) he had forgotten what he should by now have learned. In spite of having a car that the Longines time sheets showed was 10mph faster than that of Senna, he could not wait for one of Spa's long straights and tried to get the race won on the first lap. He knew full well that he had the legs of Senna, because after the first start (red-flagged after two laps) he already had a lead of over 1.5sec by the end of the first lap. Now he tried to go round the outside of Senna through a right-hander, something that was completely unnecessary. The result was instant retirement for Senna and damage that would cause Nigel's retirement within a few laps. Points wasted, and how valuable they would have proved when after Mexico the two Williams drivers, the only ones who could win the championship, headed to Japan with only 12 points between them.

There Nigel threw it all away. Having set the quickest time in Friday qualifying, Nigel returned to the Williams pit, next door to Team Lotus, where we had a grandstand view of what happened next. Nigel's car was checked, topped up with fuel, put up on stands and fitted with new tyres in tyre warmers. Sitting strapped in the car, Nigel watched the times on the TV screen. Suddenly, with more than 20 minutes to go in the session and with no warning, Piquet flew across the line to record a time nearly 2sec faster than Nigel. Having seen the time come up on the screen in our pit, I suggested over the radio that anyone on our crew who wanted to see some excitement should watch the pit next door. Instead of waiting for his team-mate and rival for the title to return to the pits, when he could have discovered the reason for the sudden dramatic improvement, Nigel reacted impetuously and over-excitedly. Waving both his arms furiously in the air he screamed to his crew, "Get the tyre covers off", not once but several times. His car was down on the ground and leaving the pits before Nelson had returned from his 'in' lap. At 2.40pm that Friday he handed the title to Nelson by trying too hard and flying off the track, hurting himself badly enough to preclude taking part in either the Japanese Grand Prix or the Australian that followed.

Almost every time he was interviewed, Nigel would go to great lengths to include somewhere in one of his answers the words "I am a professional". In truth he was on many occasions one of the least professional of drivers. It may be that the lack of professionalism that cost him two World Championships arose from the bitter reality that, throughout his career, he had never been anyone's first choice as a driver. He felt perhaps that he had to go out and prove himself, whatever the circumstances, instead of thinking things through. Perhaps he could not use his brain whilst driving in the same way as a Prost or a Senna.

The fact is that he was not first-choice driver at Team Lotus. He was not first-choice driver at Williams in 1985 when he joined Keke Rosberg, who had already been there five seasons and won a championship. Ferrari had to compensate him financially for preferring Prost in 1990, and when he went back to Williams in 1991 Patrese was starting his fourth season with the team. Even after turning his back on Formula 1 after his championship year (did he really fall out with Frank Williams over the number of hotel rooms included in his contract offer?) he went to CART/Indycar, where Mario was first choice in the Newman-Haas Team. With the same gritty courage that characterised his final years in Formula 1, he did, however, finally prove that he was in fact better on fast circuits with high-speed corners than street tracks, for he took the ovals by storm and added the US Championship to his record.

Elio fell into that category of driver who was liked by everyone with whom he came into contact. Similar guys from his era were Patrick Depailler, Jacques Laffite, John Watson and Gerhard Berger – winners all. Nigel was a winner too, and no-one ever doubted his bravery. To his credit he kept a large number of British journalists in work and their editors happy, and he was also responsible for introducing a large number of new fans to the sport.

AYRTON

Formula 1 has thrown up drivers who, for differing and various reasons and achievements, have been rightly admired. Alain Prost, Nelson Piquet, Jackie Stewart, Jody Scheckter, Alan Jones, Carlos Reutemann and Keke Rosberg are in this group.

Then, at another level, there are the men whose talents graced the track and the world stage, some for too brief a time. Others of this rare breed were stars that shone for longer, but they will all remain forever in the minds of those who were privileged to see them at work – Juan Manuel Fangio, Stirling Moss, Jim Clark, Jochen Rindt, Ronnie Peterson, Mario Andretti, Gilles Villeneuve, Niki Lauda and Michael Schumacher. But perhaps the one whose star shone the brightest, whose outstanding abilities withstood the closest examination, whose strength of character set him furthest apart, and who elicited an emotional and heartfelt response from the largest number of people, was Ayrton Senna.

In October 1983, after watching his progress in the junior formulae for over a year, I invited a very promising young Brazilian driver to visit me in Norfolk to talk about a possible arrangement for him to drive for us. It was a little confusing at the time because no-one knew for sure if he was called da Silva or Senna. After a long session with him, a look round the facilities and a chat with chief engineer Ducarouge about the technical programme, I took the plunge at what was after all our first meeting and offered him a drive supporting Elio in 1984.

To my surprise he agreed straight away, and we even settled on a fee for driving for the year of US $50,000 plus bonuses in line with points scored. I pointed out that as a matter of courtesy to our long-standing sponsors, John Player & Son, as well as Renault/Elf who were now playing such an important part in our programme, I would have to pass this fairly radical change to our line-up before them. The best opportunity to do this would be at Brands Hatch for the John Player-sponsored European Grand Prix in less than a week's time.

But the opportunity to pass it by the Renault and Elf bosses never occurred, because to my astonishment when I raised the matter with Player's in our motorhome on the morning of the race they turned it down flat. When I asked why, they simply produced the Saturday newspapers. Without exception, and in spite of the fact that Elio had taken pole position for the race, they all led with the headline, some bigger than others, 'Nigel Mansell third'! John Player & Son only sold cigarettes in England as their brands were marketed overseas by British American Tobacco, and all they were interested in for their money was coverage in the British papers. Such was the pressure on space in the dailies then that the motor racing correspondents for the various papers could only get their stories included by their editors if their piece had some British interest. This resulted in some strangely weighted reports. The fact that Elio was in a black and gold car on the pole for a black and gold race did not apparently count for much.

With great regret I told Ayrton that things were not going to be possible the way we had planned, and saw him sign for Toleman. We did not have to wait long to see what an opportunity we had missed when he stunned the Formula 1 circus with his times in winter testing. The Team already had in place the sponsorship arrangements with Player's, Renault, Elf and Goodyear for 1984. In a fit of pique I simply told Peter Dyke, Head of Special Events and Sponsorship for Imperial Tobacco, that if they wanted Mansell that badly they could jolly well pay for him, because I was not prepared to do so. This somewhat naïve approach worked. Although Peter was entitled to say, "Sorry, chum, but our deal is done", he realised how profound a wish it was of everyone in the Team not to have to endure Nigel's whingeing for yet another year. The boys in the workshop used to say that Nigel's car was the only one where the whine did not stop even when the engine had been switched off. To his eternal credit, Peter Dyke found from somewhere the £250,000 Nigel wanted as his retainer and paid him.

Ayrton, meanwhile, spoiled everything by starting to score World Championship points in his second and third Grands Prix and by his fifth in Monaco (yes, the wet one where Nigel fell off) he cemented his reputation. In those atrocious conditions he demonstrated his sublime car control, already mature racing brain and terrific will to win, and so nearly pipped Alan Prost to victory in the shortened race. Why had he spoiled everything? Monaco was a key moment when those watching knew instinctively that they were getting a glimpse of something almost supernatural, something so exceptional that it only comes along very rarely. The whole Formula 1 world now knew about this new wonder kid, and they would all be muddying the waters trying to get him to drive for them for 1985.

A concerted effort was immediately started to renew the dialogue that had been interrupted the previous October. A family friend and adviser helped Ayrton with the new proposals. He was Armando Botelho Teixera, and he had been asked to come to Europe by Ayrton's father to keep an eye on the lad. A more friendly and charming man it would be hard to imagine and the advice he gave Ayrton was always sound, well thought through and in the best interests of his young charge. More importantly Armando and Gérard Ducarouge got on very well, and could have the sort of 'non-contractual' chats that helped move things forward. That Ayrton was keen and enthusiastic to join us there was no doubt but he had a contract with Toleman with a pretty steep buy-out clause. Add this to his new-found fame and it was obvious that the $50,000 of the previous year was a fraction of what would now be needed to get the job done.

Things did move forward, albeit slowly. The apparent lack of speed was not to do with either Ayrton, Armando or ourselves, all of whom were keen to get things settled. The exceptionally dour and specific lawyer, Mr A.S. Clare, who had been appointed as their London representative by the Senna family solicitors in Brazil, had broad experience of the Brazilian/Portuguese approach to things legal. Every single item had to be meticulously examined, dissected, re-worded and questioned. Never would he accept that the intentions of what the parties wished to do for each other could be expressed as such. As a result almost every conceivable action that could be envisaged as remotely likely to happen during the duration of the contract had to be put into words, legal words, and spelled out. This led to several monumental sense-of-humour failures on our side, Clare apparently not being in possession of any humour whatsoever. Luckily Ayrton realised that this was the way Clare wished the system to work, and took a fairly relaxed attitude as an apparently innocent bystander. As Team Lotus had a long-standing rule that negotiations to do with driver contracts had to be between the principals themselves and not through their agents or managers, Ayrton had to be present. While pretending to remain remote he nonetheless never missed a trick, our first glimpse of the incredible mind he brought to bear on everything he did. If nothing else, the long and tedious sessions served to strengthen his view that race driving was all that mattered, and ours that we were happier running a race team than being lawyers. If a smile ever passed across the face of Clare it was presumably because he had just completed a mental calculation of the heights to which his hourly fees total had now risen.

By late summer things had firmed up nicely, and on 9 August I met Ayrton in the peace and calm of the Brands Hatch Place Hotel to finalise the details. The then boss of the hotel, who knew perfectly well what was going on in his lounge, was the epitome of discretion although he had a regular through-put of clients who would have been very interested to be a fly on the wall. On 14 August, somewhat coincidentally, I had arranged to meet Martin Brundle at 11am to find out what he was up to for the future. I then raced to London's Ironmonger Lane to meet Clare and Ayrton to sign the contracts. Ever present was the problem of the buy-out clause option from the Toleman contract, but this was something that Ayrton had to exercise, and he and Clare had to handle between them. We all agreed that the formal announcement would be made by press release at Zandvoort during the Dutch Grand Prix meeting ten days later, but that there would be an embargo imposed on the publication of the news until the Monday, 27 August. This meant that all the motoring correspondents and in particular the foreign ones could be given what amounted to a simultaneous delivery of the news.

Embargoes had been used successfully for years. The system allowed the story to be sent out at your convenience but made public when you wished it to be. Embargoes could be as specific as a particular hour of the day. This allowed, for example, the daily papers which went to press the previous evening to have a story in time for their morning editions, while the radio and television news people could handle an incoming story at any time. Sometimes the embargo was timed to miss the print deadline of a weekly so that the story was not swamped by some other news. And in the days before digital imaging and transmission of pictures the 'rags' needed some time to get plates prepared for the printing of pictures that accompanied the story. The journalists consistently respected embargoes, as they got a story with sufficient time to prepare and write their pieces and did not get 'scooped' by other publications. This did not apply to stories they winkled out for themselves, where their aim was to race their rivals into print, but only to those they were fed by press release. The system usually worked well.

For some reason it did not at Zandvoort. There was tension in the air, and most of the journalists were on edge as if expecting something big or wanting something big because there was no other good copy to be had. To handle the developing situation of rumour and counter-rumour we decided with our press officer, Tony Jardine, to issue the press release on Saturday but still with the embargo clearly marked on it. In the very close-knit Formula 1 circus all sorts of relationships exist. Many are symbiotic in the sense that they are of benefit or advantage to both parties. Many of the teams and drivers have links to particular journalists who are a sounding board or source of gossip or information for them.

One of these could not resist the chance to emphasise or strengthen his ties with the Toleman team and its boss Alex Hawkridge. This journalist may have told him 'in confidence' bearing in mind the embargo, but when the mainstay of your team has just been undermined you won't be too fussy about respecting confidences. There was a seismic upheaval in the paddock as Hawkridge lambasted Team Lotus, its sponsors, its personnel and their respective ancestries. By this time the other journalists had come to the view that if the news was out it was out, and so was the embargo – out of the window.

Hawkridge, who had only himself to blame for starting the fuss, took me to task on a very personal basis, but not to my face. His view, broadcast to anyone who would listen, was that by releasing the news in an underhand way I had somehow brought Toleman to its knees. He assumed that, because Ayrton had not chosen to tell him that he was going to be exercising his buy-out option, I had 'engineered' the release to force things through and wreck his relationship with his driver. The truth is that Ayrton could have hardly started negotiating the size of the buy-out fee without prejudicing his relationship. He and his performances had simply, in half his first Formula 1 season, outgrown the team, and Hawkridge must have known that the contract with the buy-out clause exercisable by Ayrton left him vulnerable to just what was now happening. Like others after him, Ron Dennis of McLaren and myself included, he was prepared to concede more contractually than he would for any other driver just to get Ayrton on board. Now he was putting it about that I was personally responsible for the most dastardly behaviour ever seen in Formula 1 and the loss of all his sponsors, not to mention the jobs of all his employees. This was couched in a way that implied that this had all happened in spite of lengthy discussions to try to avert the situation, but that his arguments and pleas had fallen on deaf ears. This was hard to stomach, because when I went up to him on the starting grid for the race the next day to have a word with him about things it was the first time we had ever spoken to each other. His bluster may have been a smokescreen to distract his sponsors and colleagues from the fact that he had been outsmarted and out-gunned. But when he switched tack and said that his driver had been in breach and childishly suspended Ayrton from the next race at Monza, he not only inflicted greater damage on his team but also helped cement the new relationship that Team Lotus was building with Ayrton.

And Ayrton's fee? We settled on US $585,000 for 1985, a little over ten times what he would have been paid a year earlier! There is always a point in negotiations where each party tries to demonstrate that they have the strongest position. I don't know whether Ayrton had included in his fee the cost of buying himself out of his contract at Toleman, some £156,000 sterling as it eventually worked out. What I do know is that, having settled virtually all the terms of his first contract with us at a fee of $550,000, he suddenly came back with a further demand for another $35,000. This did not relate in specific value to any other item or items of his services as a race driver, so I had to assume that this was his way of quietly showing me that his position was the strongest. It was, and I conceded. I neither had the balls nor did Team Lotus have the depth of finances that Ron Dennis at McLaren had later when, in a similar situation, he tossed a coin with Ayrton to settle a similar round of discussions about the last half-million dollars of a contract!

Ayrton needed some time off back home in Brazil after the end of the racing season. His Toleman contract did not leave him free to drive our car until 1 January, and anyway our new offering, the

Lotus 97T, would not be ready until the Rio test that month. He was also suffering from a rare bout of ill health and was convinced that home life, home cooking and home warm weather would put things right. Before he left he came to the factory for a fitting, and drove up in one of the very exclusive new Mercedes-Benz 190E 'Evolution' models. Such was his impact on the racing scene that he had been invited back in May to take part in the inaugural race on the new Nürburgring. The fact that the field, all in identical new Mercedes, included Prost and Lauda and was made up of seven other former World Champions did not impress him a bit. What did impress him was the prize for winning, which was the car he was driving. He duly saw off Lauda and was pretty bullish about his new toy.

It was normal practice at Team Lotus that the race crew would subject all new drivers to an initiation test. This was merely to establish whether they could see the funny side of things, and had the necessary sense of humour to stand them in good stead when things got rough. It also helped establish the limits for pranks and japes that could be perpetrated on an unsuspecting superstar if he got too big for his boots. So at tea break Ayrton handled the Bob Dance "I think the cream is off" trick with great aplomb and not too much cream cake on his face. A reaction was provoked, however, when he came to leave. Jumping in his new car and with all the guys watching, he needed to make an impressive exit from the yard. Hanging a lot of revs on the uncomplaining engine he selected a gear and slid his foot sideways off the clutch no doubt expecting some serious racing driver wheelspin and a bit of dust in the eyes of the onlookers. To his surprise he went nowhere as he had omitted to notice that the lads had put the rear suspension on blocks and the rear wheels, while going round very fast, were not actually touching the ground.

We were not to know until we got to Brazil for the test that the look on his face was not one of embarrassment but one of "I'll get you back, don't worry". The sequel was the sweets. During a lunch break at the Rio test he innocently passed round some sweets that

The launch of the Wolf F1 team: from left, owner Walter Wolf, designer Harvey Postlethwaite, driver Jody Scheckter and Peter. sutton-images.com

Wolf made history by winning its first-ever race. Jody Scheckter on his victorious way in the heat of Buenos Aires, January 1977. LAT

Conference among plastic cups in Austria, 1977: from left, Peter, March driver Ian Scheckter, Max Mosley, Bernie Ecclestone, James Hunt, Ken Tyrrell. LAT

At Wolf, Yvonne Warr had an official role alongside her husband, as timekeeper. Warr family collection

Seven F1 bosses at an awards event in 1979: from left, Chapman, Carlo Chiti of Alfa Romeo, Frank Williams, Teddy Mayer of McLaren, Max Mosley of March, Ecclestone and Peter. Warr family collection

James Hunt's final race, the 1979 Monaco GP, lasted four laps before his Wolf WR7 suffered a possibly driver-inflicted driveshaft failure. sutton-images.com

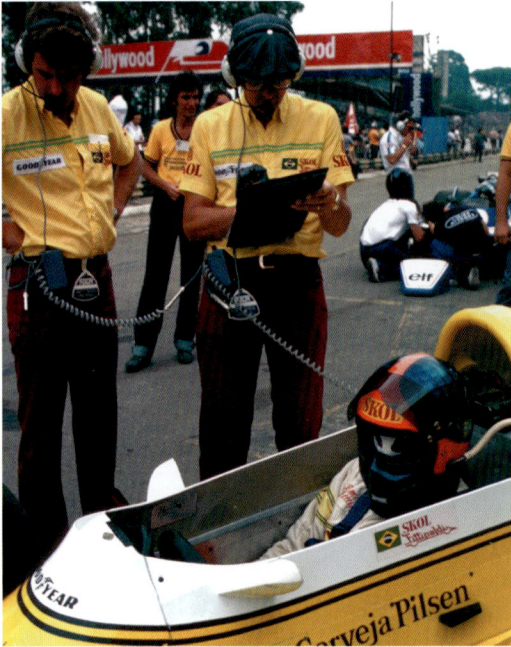

When Fittipaldi Automotive
took over the Wolf team
for the 1980 season, Peter
found himself working
with Emerson again.
Postlethwaite is on the left.
sutton-images.com

Opposite: Back with Team
Lotus, lining up at Kyalami
for the first race of 1982: with
Peter are, from left, Mike
Murphy, Geoff Hardacre,
Peter Wright, Martin Ogilvie,
Paul Simpson, Phil Denney,
Clive Hicks, Dave Crabtree,
Kenny Szymanski, Nigel
Stepney, Steve Davey, Ian
Martin and Bob Dance.
sutton-images.com

Keke Rosberg joined Wolf in
1979 and remained after
the Fittipaldi takeover. Peter
and Harvey could now talk
to their driver by radio in the
pits. sutton-images.com

Opposite: When Peter
returned to Lotus in time for
the 1982 season, Chapman
received him with open
arms. LAT

In one of the closest-ever F1 finishes, Elio won the 1982 Austrian Grand Prix in the Lotus 91 by just five hundredths of a second from Keke Rosberg's Williams. LAT

Elio's girlfriend Ute clowns for this snapshot while Yvonne and Peter ponder the race to come. Warr family collection

'Now, listen here, chap.' Peter's relationship with Nigel Mansell was not a particularly happy one. sutton-images.com

In the sweltering Interlagos pits in 1984 Peter and Nigel confer during practice; mechanics Paul Simpson (right) and Chris Dinnage (with Elio) are also in shot. sutton-images.com

In heavy rain, Nigel triumphantly leads the 1984 Monaco Grand Prix…
sutton-images.com

…until losing control and crashing into the barriers, to Peter's furious dismay. LAT

had seemingly come from the picnic his mother and father had brought along. How he contrived to get 'the' one to Bob Dance we shall never know, but Bob's mouth turned blue and he passed blue water for two days. From then on everyone had to be on their guard, as we knew we had a great fun-loving guy on our hands. We also quickly discovered the inspirational and thoroughly motivating side to his character that helped make him, in my opinion, the most complete racing driver since Jim Clark.

Our next date with Ayrton was early in January when he was to return to England for the final preparations for the season. He had shakedowns to do, seat and cockpit fittings to finalise, and we knew these to be very important. In his Toleman year he had suffered all sorts of cramps, 'dead leg' and discomfort due to his seating position not being perfect. There were also the pre-season publicity shots to be taken for the sponsors and our own press office. Imagine my horror, therefore, when Ayrton arrived in Norfolk and greeted us all with a completely straight face. Not a smile, simply expressionless and with a decidedly glassy stare in one eye. This eye did not close or blink. It was not that he was not pleased to see us: just that his face was paralysed down one side. He had suffered an attack of Bell's Palsy at home. I immediately did what anyone in Formula 1 would do and called Professor Sid Watkins. The publicity photos were a disaster, but had to be used because there were no others of Ayrton in JPS overalls. The visit to Sid was much more successful. Sid, of course, with his inimitable good humour, plain speaking and expert knowledge saw to it that Ayrton got the best course of treatment. Ayrton was very much in the public eye and his condition had the potential to cause him great personal embarrassment. Sid put him at his ease with the reassurance that things might take a little time but he would recover. Though cured, he was to retain a slightly lop-sided smile for the rest of his life.

Denis Jenkinson once said, "Dedicated racing drivers are boring, but Ayrton, now there is what I call a serious racing driver." Ayrton was a man who was frighteningly and single-mindedly devoted to

success. His application to his work was all-consuming, his thirst
for more and more expertise at his work unflagging. Always
amazingly alert and aware and right at the nub of the current
problem to be sorted, he would not let up until he felt he had given
it his best shot. Many were the times that he would leave the circuit
with a nagging thought in his mind only to return later, after dinner,
with a fresh idea for a solution. Many also were the times when
after practice, qualifying and Sunday morning warm-up had
finished, we as a team had to say, "Well, sorry Ayrton, we know the
car is not quite right but this is the best we can do." And off he
would go and give another outstanding demonstration of his skill.
He finished third in his first race for the Team on home soil, and
won his second in Portugal with one of the great drives of the
modern era, in conditions in which most people would not take
their dog for a walk. By this time Gérard Ducarouge had already
made his oft-quoted remark, "It is not a question of *if* he will be
World Champion but *when*."

It is difficult to explain the effect a driver like this has on a team.
Everything they do suddenly seems worthwhile. No effort is too
great to undertake in order to achieve an extra target or to gain an
extra edge. Staff members become light-hearted and the race crew
literally walk with a spring and an added purpose in their step.
Suppliers suddenly become that little bit more keen to deliver on
time. Sponsor negotiations get easier. Even the bank manager seems
more approachable and amenable. Pride goes up by leaps and
bounds and everything that seems difficult and tiresome about
Formula 1 somehow becomes easier to tolerate. But in addition to
his superior driving skills, a truly great driver needs other parts of
his character to get the personal response from those around him.
Like Niki Lauda, who transformed the fortunes of Ferrari when he
joined them in 1974, Ayrton brought these special strengths in
abundance and transformed the fortunes of Team Lotus.

His first great win in Portugal highlighted the difference between
his rigorously honest approach and the compromised one of Nigel

Mansell. In an astonishing display of car control he left the field trailing, beating Michele Alboreto in the Ferrari by over a minute and lapping everyone else in the race. So consistently bad were the conditions over the entire two hours of the race that his fastest lap in the race was 23 seconds slower than his pole position time of only 1min 21sec. Afterwards Denis Jenkinson, having congratulated Ayrton on his flawless drive, said how stunned he was by Ayrton's lightning reaction at catching the car when getting back on the tarmac after an 'off' when he put all four wheels on the grass out at the back of the circuit. Very few others saw this incident. "Rubbish," said Ayrton, "that was pure luck. I was completely out of control and the car just came back." Later he went on to correct any other reporter who said he made no mistakes by repeating his error and his luck.

This completely ruthless honesty with himself and others only served further to enhance his appeal. If he made a mistake, he would be the first to admit it. If you made a mistake he would be the first to tell you. To my surprise I only found out some time after his final race that Ayrton's wet-weather flair did not come entirely from natural ability. A wonderful film, *A Star named Ayrton Senna*, was made by the company G2 Films which was owned and run jointly by François Guiter, formerly of Elf, and his son. This contained many previously unseen clips of film as well as some terrific insights into the man from Sao Paulo. In it Ayrton's sister Viviane explains how upset he had been in his karting days to be beaten once in a kart event in Brazil that was run in the wet. Knowing that he should have won, thereafter he would take out his kart and practise whenever it rained. What may have come from these sessions was the technique he developed to such perfection of rapid and tiny but continuous throttle adjustments that so astounded the Renault and Honda engineers in his Formula 1 cars. What was unarguable was that he had flawless balance in low-grip conditions, and a surreal feel for the very limit of adhesion in changing track conditions.

Also uncanny was his apparent total recall of everything that was happening in the cockpit. It is one of the hardest things to grasp that at the very edge of the performance envelope of the car, say on one of his many pole-position laps with the car dancing on the very edge of adhesion, he could separate so completely the physical requirements of driving the car from his mental processes. Time and again he would astound the engineers by telling them exactly what was happening with the chassis or the engine before they had seen the computer print-outs. Inevitably the latter would confirm the former. If you understand that this was at the beginning of the era of on-board data recorders, electronic fuel management systems and telemetry from car to pit, then you will also understand the astonishment of the engineers at this guy telling them the answers before they had asked the questions of their high-tech new apparatus. To put this into perspective, the active-suspension Lotus 99T would produce 600 million data points in one four-mile lap of the Spa circuit.

A telling example of this ability to separate two or more simultaneous actions is revealed by the following comparison. In 1972 the Team's fuel supplier was Texaco, who wanted to make a television commercial using Emerson driving the Lotus 72. It was filmed at Circuit Paul Ricard, with a camera mounted on the roll-over bar, a tape recorder fixed to the chassis and a microphone fitted in Emerson's helmet just inside the bottom lip of the chinguard. The idea was for Emerson to talk the viewer round a lap. On playback Emerson told us "I am leaving ze pits – now I take ze second gear." There then followed a period where all that could be heard was a regular "thump... thump... thump..." followed by "and now I come back to ze pits." Emerson was not able to drive at full racing speeds and talk at the same time. The "thump... thump...", by the way, was his heartbeat.

Ayrton could drive, talk, analyse the behaviour of the car and recall what the instrument read-outs showed, all at the same time. Testing with Honda once at Monza, he actually talked us through an accident as it happened. Following a Ligier he could see something loose on the back of it. He called us up on the radio to tell us about it when suddenly he said, "Oh shit, it's fallen off, I can't miss it", and then live on the open radio we heard an enormous bang. It turned out that Ligier had been experimenting with a lump of lead on its gearbox to change the weight distribution and had failed to secure it properly. Ayrton returned to the pit with considerable front-end and undertray damage while we had all experienced an accident 'live' on air. But he was still able to tell us how many revs he was pulling in the slipstream of the Ligier compared to those he reached without the tow. Needless to say, the Honda data recorders confirmed his readings.

For the 1986 Spanish Grand Prix we found ourselves at the new circuit of Jerez. There had been no prior testing. On Friday Ayrton qualified with a time of 1min 21.605sec. The next best time was in the 1min 23sec bracket. On Saturday Piquet got down to 1min 22.431sec, Mansell 1min 22.576sec and Prost 1min 22.886sec. Apart from being 1.4sec faster on the first day, Ayrton still had a cushion of 0.8sec. On Saturday his own first run was in the mid-22s. He confirmed what we had already worked out for ourselves, namely that the new track was for some reason a lot slower – it was very hot.

"Well," I said, "you can get out of the car now. No-one can possibly beat your time from yesterday."

"I will just wait in the car," he replied. About 15 minutes later in the session he appeared to be asleep in the cockpit. With about 10 minutes to go he got a mechanic to attract my attention, waved me over and said, "Right, I'll go out again now."

"What for?" I said. "There's no point."

"Ah, but I have just been going round the lap in my head, and I now know I can do a 21.9. I have worked out what I did last time and where I can save a few tenths."

I asked Gérard Ducarouge what he thought and he said that if the guy wanted to go out he should, but to forget about the time. Steve Hallam, Ayrton's race engineer, thought he was in such good form we shouldn't take the edge off his mood. So we let him go. His time?

– 1min 21.924sec!

Before he even signed for Team Lotus, Ayrton already possessed the canny approach that was later to stand him in good stead. Although I offered the number one spot he turned it down and settled instead for joint number one status. He felt that "this would not make Elio afraid of me, he will share more information and I will learn more that way." Notice that he did not say his decision would help him be friends with Elio, as that emotion was not on his agenda. Only years later when his supremacy was undisputed and unthreatened did he find, thanks to the genuineness of Gerhard Berger's character, a real friend in a team-mate. It was this mental clarity, finely developed logic and strength of purpose that allowed him to come off best in his rivalries with Mansell, Prost and, towards the end, Schumacher.

Ayrton's joint number one status did not last long as it rapidly became clear from his lap times that he had relegated Elio to the number two spot. The Brazilian merely confirmed what so many had suspected: he was indeed something very special. But in revealing his outrageous talent by setting seven pole positions, being on the front row ten times, leading eight Grands Prix and winning another two in his first 'real' season in a 'real' Formula 1 team, Ayrton sowed the seeds of the antagonism he engendered in his opponents throughout his career. His so-called 'arrogance' was nothing of the sort. His supreme confidence in his own ability simply served to give that impression to those who did not make the effort to speak to him and attempt to understand him. He became broadly disliked by the other drivers who, perhaps sensing that they might not be able to beat him on the track, thought they might be able to do so off it. His aggressive driving and overtaking style – he would bang wheels with anyone – produced questions about his real priorities.

This poison seeped through to the press, many of whom were being fed all sorts of stuff by their informants in the other cockpits. Ayrton suffered eight retirements, and took a torrid amount of flak that he was abusing the machinery and adopting a completely cavalier attitude with the turbo boost control. It was said he preferred the glory of leading to finishing anywhere but first, constrained as he was by a thirsty Renault engine and the 220-litre maximum fuel tankage (with no refuelling permitted). Nothing was further from the truth, and at that time only those inside the Team and at Renault Sport knew the real extent of the enormous talent that was burgeoning. His sensitivity to things mechanical was such that, several times that season, remarks he made before the event could and should have given warning that some unreliability would strike. Later in the relationship we knew to take everything he said, even the most seemingly casual remark, with complete seriousness if it was to do with the chassis or the engine. In fact he was one of those drivers, like many of the other true greats down the years, who had a quite remarkable ability to bring a sick or broken car home. This requires exceptional sensitivity and Fangio, Moss, Clark, Lauda and Prost all possessed the same gift. It also requires the courage not to park it at the first sign of anything untoward, but to press on – having first quickly evaluated the risk.

In fact the constant adversarial attitude of the press nearly led to the breakdown of the Renault contract halfway through 1985. Renault had several very secret components on their engine and were naturally very worried that, with 'outsiders' such as ourselves and Ligier using their equipment, some of these features would come to the attention of their competitors. One was the DPV, a simply brilliant piece of design from Bernard Dudot's team. Cast housings on the front of the turbo air intakes contained a beautifully and intricately made iris similar to the aperture control on a camera. Every time the car stopped and the body was removed the DPVs had to be quickly covered. Their secret was a linkage coupled to the throttle that shut the iris when the throttle was closed, thus creating a partial vacuum in the air intakes. The vacuum allowed the turbines to spin at undiminished speed and, when the driver accelerated again, virtually eliminated throttle lag, the bane of highly turbocharged engines.

Another was the Renault 'first' of electronic engine management. Not unnaturally these developments were only an advantage if you were the only ones who had them, a Chapman philosophy if ever there was one. But what did you do when it was one of these secrets that caused the car to retire and give the press another chance to have a go at the Team and Ayrton? Things came to a head at Silverstone when, leading as usual, we noticed dark black smoke coming out of the left-hand exhaust pipe. Soon after, and far too early in the race for a liberty with the boost control knob to have caused the car to run out of fuel, Ayrton stopped and, yes, he was out of fuel. The press had a field day. I insisted that Bernard Dudot let me know what the problem had been when he had looked at the engine, and put out a press release telling the truth: which was that a gas temperature sensor in the left-hand exhaust had failed. Every team has them now, but then they were only found on aircraft, from where the Renault ones had been sourced. But it gave away the fact that this was one of the components needed to manage electronically the fuel delivery, richness and throttle response of the engine. Everyone knew Renault had an electronic system but no-one knew how it was done. The Team and the driver were being made out to be a bunch of idiots.

When Renault heard about my press release one would have thought I'd set fire to the French flag on the Champs Elysées in front of the presidential limo. Calls were received from main board members and we feared that we would be without engines at the next race. If nothing else, we had highlighted the complexity of commercial and personal relationships in racing, but we had defended the integrity of our driver. The truth was, so many times that year, that we and Renault had let Ayrton down in his quest for what realistically was a genuine chance at the championship, and any other course of action would have betrayed our driver's inherent and ruthless honesty.

With all Ayrton's subsequent achievements tending to overshadow those early races, we must remind ourselves that in his first full season he finished fourth in the World Championship with 38 points, just 35 fewer than Prost who was first. This was notwithstanding eight retirements, only one of which was due to driver error.

Eventually confronted with the inescapable fact that we were all dealing with someone very far removed from the ordinary, even Bernard Dudot would permit some snippets of information to be laid before the press to stop a false picture of the new star being painted. After Germany, where Ayrton again retired when leading as he pleased and going away from the field, it was discreetly put about that the car's data recorder showed Ayrton being careful with fuel by short-shifting and running minimum boost.

While the run at the championship had been on the cards quite unexpectedly in 1985, such a result would have represented one of the biggest upsets of all time. Ayrton had taken to Formula 1 as if he had been born to it, and put his marker down as the driver all the others had to beat. The following year, 1986, was to be the season when things came together. Renault had abandoned their own race team, leaving Team Lotus as their 'works' effort. Their new engine, the EF15, had an even more advanced technical specification. A superbly clever and original compressed-air valve 'spring' system allowed the engine to be lighter, smaller and less tall, while permitting the revs to reach the heady heights of 12,500rpm. A more sophisticated management system was developed with coils in each of the six spark plug wells, and the drivers now had a fuel read-out that was updated once a lap from the pits by radio signal. If the laps of fuel remaining on the steering wheel display was more than that shown on the pit board the driver could go racing. If it was less he was on a fuel economy run, thanks to Jean-Marie Balestre and his 195-litre fuel maximum.

Ayrton hated the situation that had been forced upon him and the Team. He was a racer and he wanted to go racing. He needed to prove he was the best over a season, and this could only be done by winning a World Championship. He was on pole eight times but he won only two races, and though he led the championship for much of the year he would privately admit that he thought it was beyond him. Too many times did he have to drive with one eye on the fuel meter and see Piquet and Mansell in the Honda-engined Williams cars or Prost and Rosberg in the McLaren-TAGs cruise by in the race. Too many times did he finish with dry tanks even though he was using minimum race boost. Waving his opponents through was not his style, nor the way in which he wished to go racing.

Again with that incessant energy he applied to all aspects of his life, he turned his mind to finding a way out of the dilemma. But this was not halfway through the season, or when relaxing at the end of it. By Spain, the second race of the season, and one in which he used every ounce of his race craft to win by one-hundredth of a second by conserving fuel, by being super smooth and not changing tyres, he already had a plan. This was based on the knowledge and intuition he had already gained from testing and only two races with the latest Renault offering. He would stay with the Team for 1987, he told me, if I could get him the Honda engine. "And what do you think I should do about our ongoing contract with Renault?" I asked him. "Well, we will just have to tell them our reasons. They too are racers, and they will understand the logic of what we want to do." Notice how he said "we".

I flew home to the UK to a meeting in a London hotel with Nobuhiko Kawamoto, head of Honda R&D and the man in charge of the racing programme. Quite fortuitously he had been at Jarama, but getting to see him was hazardous in the extreme. Frank Williams would not have been impressed that I was seeing his engine supplier, and if Renault had found out they might well have dusted off and oiled the guillotine. The paddock is always full of people keeping an eye on who is talking to whom.

As it was, Kawamoto-san, a great enthusiast who had worked on Jack Brabham's Formula 2 Honda-engined car years before and who would go on to become President of Honda worldwide, was not as daunting as one might have expected. Practical and down to earth, he put me at my ease and we talked for ages. He was superbly well informed about what was going on in Formula 1 and we ranged over every topic one could imagine, but I felt that I was still a long way from the nub of the talks. This came towards the end when he introduced his then surprising idea of having a Japanese driver in our second car.

Satoru Nakajima was his suggestion, and I honestly feel the deal was eventually done because I never queried his plan or implied in any way that I thought it was a bad idea. Having talked with him for so long, it occurred to me that he was sounding me out for what my possible reaction might be, and I was on my guard for the moment it hit the table. It would have been a serious personal affront if I had taken it anything less than seriously. What he may not have known at the time was that, after the joint number one year with Elio, it was clearly understood that Ayrton would in future only ever have a number two. What we did have, however, was the commitment from Ayrton that if we had a Honda engine he would stay with the Team, and this was a powerful persuader. Given that Honda and Kawamoto-san could use the arrival of a Japanese driver in Formula 1 for all sorts of political, publicity and commercial purposes he was no more of a long shot than the other young drivers to whom one might have given the chance. All that would hurt would be telling Johnny Dumfries, whom we had grown to like a lot, the same as we would be telling Renault.

By Detroit the Honda deal was done. Now Ayrton had to demonstrate his true professionalism by putting his maximum into what was left of a season that he knew was not going to fulfil his expectations. He did, and ran out fourth in the championship as he had in 1985, but this time with the increased points tally of 55.

Less than three weeks after Detroit the Team mobile home in the paddock at Brands Hatch was the scene for the opening round of negotiations with Ayrton for 1987. Money was the only item on the agenda that day. The outcome was a two-year deal for 1987 and

1988 at a fee of US $2.6 million. By now an old hand at this sort of thing, Ayrton forced acceptance of an option, exercisable by him, to get out of the contract for the second year. In return I managed to get him to concede that the total fee would be split unevenly, with less than half being paid for year one and more than half for year two. His earning power was now so great that he did not care. Our wish to keep him was so great that we had now got him his engines and, within reason, made virtually any concession he requested. He even popped back into the motorhome as an afterthought after his money thing was settled and negotiated a big rise for Gérard Ducarouge. Perhaps that was his way that year of letting us know he once again had the hand with the trump cards.

At this moment we were less than two weeks away from the German Grand Prix at Hockenheim, and Honda told us that they would like to announce their 1987 programme at that race. This surprise news caused a crisis. Renault was going to have to be told, and this was not going to be the best motivation for them to continue making their best efforts for the rest of the season. This was all the more so as with their 'works' Team no longer with them (Ligier's and Tyrrell's engines were supplied by the contractor Mecachrome), our breaking their contract – or asking to be released from it – would almost certainly result in their pulling out of Formula 1. This would entail serious job changes for a lot of guys we liked and respected, and job losses for a lot more. An even more daunting prospect was that there would have to be another marathon session with the dreaded lawyer, Clare, who from previous experience could not be relied upon to agree in less than a fortnight that the year was 1986.

Ayrton and I went to see Renault, and as usual Ayrton turned out to be right. Horrendously disappointed and feeling let down, they were nonetheless true racing people. They could not fault Ayrton's reasoning and agreed to release us. Gentlemen that they were, there was no suggestion of any recourse against us, and to their eternal credit they kept giving it their very best shot until the last lap of the season, when we had a simply enormous party with our friends from Viry-Châtillon. All of Team Lotus felt that in the Renault guys we had found some kindred spirits. They worked very hard, were good at what they did and had enormous fun doing it.

But to get back to the case in hand. After the relief of the Renault reaction I managed to persuade Ayrton to do an 'Emerson'. We sat down in a room at the Holiday Inn in Waldorf, where we were staying for Hockenheim, and on one sheet of A4 paper I wrote out the Heads of Agreement of our deal for the next two years. We agreed we would get into the tedious detailed contracts when the season was over and we were back at the ranch in December. In any case Ayrton, like all race drivers, was a company – or more than one company – for taxation and accounting purposes, and the real contracts would be in those names. Nonetheless he was able make commitments for himself provided they were replaced later by the formal documentation. The piece of paper, which I wrote out in duplicate and we both signed, was essentially single-line statements under the heading:

The Team confirms that:

1) it has a sponsor, JPS, for 1987;

2) it has a contract to use Honda engines for 1987 and 1988;

3) it will continue to have the services of Ducarouge;

4) it will continue to use Goodyear tyres in 1987...

And so on. Then there was a section headed:

The Driver confirms that:

1) he will take part in all Grands Prix and tests for which he is required;

2) he will wear the Team uniform;

3) he will do so many sponsor days...

And so on.

Not very complicated and legally binding, but a big mistake as it turned out. We proceeded to join the folks from Honda and a seriously out-of-sorts Patrick Head of Williams (who was not by any means delighted with the new arrangements) at a press conference in the hotel under the grandstand on race morning. It was big news at the time.

Quite a lot of water passed under the bridge before I finally got together with Clare on New Year's Eve, and Ayrton a few days later. In the meantime Imperial Tobacco had been taken over by the Hanson Group. One of the first things the new owners did was to cancel their support of Team Lotus. With the aid of a minor miracle and some diligent work by our marketing manager, Ekrem Sami, we had within a month a new title sponsor in the shape of Camel, at double the JPS money.

But, to my horror, Clare's and Ayrton's view was that the new deal with Camel broke and invalidated the Hockenheim agreement and that a new deal was to be negotiated.

"You confirmed in writing and signed that you had a sponsorship contract with JPS. Now you do not. So we have to have a new contract."

"But Ayrton," I pleaded, "surely you can see that the Hockenheim agreement using the name JPS was true at the time, was made in good faith, and simply served to confirm that we had a sponsorship funds in place for the next year. Now all we are saying is that we have replaced JPS with a better sponsor, but we still have a sponsor, which was what we wished to convey in the Hockenheim document."

"You will recall from earlier negotiations that we do not deal in intentions," responded the lawyer.

"And now that you have broken the contract, about my fee!" said Ayrton.

To cut a long story short, the new contracts, which contained all but no more than the original Heads of Agreement, had one fairly significant modification. The driver's fee that had been $2.6 million now read $5 million.

In 2011 Duncan Lee provided a fascinating account of the contractual negotiations between Lotus and Senna. At the time Duncan was International

Sponsorships director for the owners of the Camel brand, R.J. Reynolds Tobacco International Inc, based in Winston-Salem, North Carolina. More than 20 years later, his recall of the sequence of events is finely detailed.

"In late 1986 I had a telephone call from a man I'd never heard of called Ekrem Sami. He said he worked for Team Lotus, and asked if I would be interested in hearing a sponsorship proposal. I knew that Lotus was sponsored by John Player Special, and I said to myself, 'Is this guy for real?' He insisted, in his calm, quiet way, that he was serious and asked to arrange a meeting. (Ekrem, of course, went on to become a vice-president of McLaren International, and one of the top Formula 1 marketing managers of all time. We remain friends today.)

"Then I had a call from another stranger, Andrea Secchi, who said he represented Brabham. He asked if I could meet Bernie Ecclestone to discuss sponsorship of the Brabham team, which Bernie still owned at the time. Of course, I said 'yes'.

"So in December my immediate boss Howard Banwell and I met in a London hotel restaurant with Peter Warr, Fred Bushell and Ekrem Sami of Team Lotus. Ekrem gave a quick presentation using some flip charts. The deal was for Ayrton Senna as number one driver, Saturo Nakajima as number two, Honda engines and, of course, the long, rich history and legend of Team Lotus. Howard and I were excited about it, but the $7.5 million price tag was far more than any of us at RJR had planned on.

"The next day, in another restaurant, I met with Ecclestone and Secchi. There was no presentation, no photos or illustrations: just Bernie saying, as only he can in his direct, succinct manner, that Camel could sponsor the whole Brabham team, with BMW engines and Riccardo Patrese as number one driver, for $3 million.

"This presented a predicament for me, because I knew the benefits that would come from sponsoring the team of the guy who ran all of Formula 1's business. It would make life very easy, but in my gut I knew that for the Camel brand to have any chance of competing in Formula 1 with its number one competitor, Marlboro, we had to be on a team that could challenge and, hopefully, beat the Marlboro teams of McLaren and Ferrari. I didn't feel that the BMW engine and Brabham chassis were up to the task.

"Back in Winston-Salem, Banwell and I described the meetings to RJR Chairman and CEO Lester Pullen. An Englishman originally hired by the company as a marketing manager for Europe, Pullen was a keen supporter of motor sports sponsorships. He got me to prepare a presentation to the executive board. So on 11 December I presented to the highest-ranking managers in the company, but support from expected sources did not materialise and the mood was generally negative about spending so much money on one sponsorship.

"That evening Pullen charged into my office and asked for all the back-up material I had on Team Lotus and Senna. 'I'm not going to let this opportunity get away,' he said. He had dinner that night with some key company vice-presidents, and at 8am next morning he was back in my office. 'Get Team Lotus over here fast, we're going to do the deal.'

"Soon after that Pullen told me he wanted to meet Bob Tyrrell again. I had met with Bob several times: he had been the first of any Formula 1 team representatives to contact me, and at that time he was the only Formula 1 consideration we had, but we did not consider them championship contenders. But he and Pullen had got on well, and Bob had been patient. So I got Bob in to see Pullen on 16 December, and a sponsorship of small proportions was quickly agreed. There was only one decent hotel near our headquarters, and both Bob Tyrrell and the Lotus people were staying there. I was worried that Bob would be checking out just as Peter, Fred and Ekrem were checking in, so I arranged for one of my staff to escort Bob back to his hotel and get him to the airport quickly. All that cloak-and-dagger stuff was quite fun.

"The next day the meeting in the RJR boardroom with the Lotus people started at 1.30pm, and by 5pm a draft contract had been drawn up and signed by the appropriate individuals. Five days later I flew to London with my wife for a brief Christmas holiday before going on to Paris for the start of the Paris-Dakar Rally on 1 January. Ekrem met me at Heathrow and we drove to Ketteringham Hall. There Peter showed me the 1987 Formula 1 Lotus in Camel livery. It was outstanding, especially as it had been done in less than a week!

"I was back in North Carolina by 6 January, and during that week

Fred Bushell called asking if we could change the contract so that RJR paid Senna's fee direct to him, and the Team's fee to the Team. He explained that Senna wanted it that way, and that his retainer was now $5 million. Shocked, I asked if the Team could operate efficiently on the remainder of the sponsorship, and he said that with some supplemental sponsors they would be able to make it. So I arranged for Peter Van Every, our chief legal counsel, to make the necessary changes.

"Then, about a week before the February press conference to announce the Camel Team Lotus relationship, Peter called me to say that Senna and his lawyer had requested (demanded) a meeting to go over the contracts to make sure everything was perfect. There were three contracts: between RJR and Team Lotus; between RJR and Senna; and between Team Lotus and Senna. Nakajima's part was included in the RJR-Team Lotus contract, and his accommodation in the Team was strictly between Team Lotus, Nakajima and Honda.

"The meeting took place the day before the press conference. Van Every and I represented RJR, Warr, Bushell and the Team's lawyer were there for Lotus, and Ayrton Senna brought his lawyer, a man named Clare. Clare went through every single sentence in each contract, and it was immediately obvious that this was going to be a long meeting.

"At one point Senna asked the Team Lotus folks to leave the room, which they did. He then asked that any dispute or conflict that might arise between him and the Team that was not racing-related should be handled through me. I was honoured, shocked, dismayed, confused and worried all at once. But I agreed. Shortly after that, Fred Bushell and I decided we were no longer needed, and left the meeting. It was 2am when Van Every called me at my hotel and said that all parties had agreed on final versions of the contracts, and the press conference could go ahead. I thought to myself, 'Welcome to Formula 1.'

In the new bright yellow colours of Camel we arrived in Rio for the early pre-season test. Ayrton had two cars to try. One was a new Lotus 99T, an evolution of the Ducarouge family of cars but now propelled by Honda horsepower with conventional passive suspension using normal springs and dampers. Also in the garage was the first result of the expanded R&D programme that was part of our commitment to Ayrton. This was the same basic 99T but with fully active suspension. The computer-controlled suspension system, using an on-board 'brain' and hydraulically powered wheel movements, was an advanced development of the system first tried on Mansell's racing car in 1983. The brain was, of course, a computer, capable of thousands of calculations a second. Potentiometers measured wheel, steering and other movements, about 20 in all, and sent the data to the computer, about half a billion inputs per lap, which instantly, according to the programme pre-loaded into it, returned the compliment by telling the wheel what to do next. The problem was that, while the computer components were readily available (provided you had someone seriously clever like Dave Williams of the Cranfield Institute of Technology to put them together in the right order), the rest were not. The measuring devices to our specification were on ten weeks' delivery while the Moog valves, the very tricky wheel movement hydraulic components, were aircraft industry parts and normally on 26 weeks' delivery after order.

So we were somewhat taken aback when early on in the Rio test Ayrton calmly announced that he was not going to drive the passive car again, and that the way to go was unquestionably to have two active cars ready for him for the beginning of the season. As we had planned the second car for June, we thought we might have had the chance to do enough development on the system by then. To have to produce and prepare not one but two production (not experimental) cars in the next four weeks was a reprise of the sort of challenge the Team had faced when they produced the two completely new Lotus 94T cars in six weeks. But this is the effect that a driver like Ayrton has on a team. For the opening race in Rio we managed the one race car for him with sufficient spares to be fully operational, but his spare car was a passive one. For the San Marino race three weeks later, Ayrton had both cars actively suspended, and he never raced a passive one the whole season. His infectious enthusiasm had even invaded the staid, conservative and very systematic production departments of the aircraft industry.

Who is to say he was not right? In 1984 Mansell had rejected out of hand the chance to use carbon brakes. The excuse was that they had caused him to fly off the road. A seasoned observer with over 250 Grands Prix under his belt told us that he had gone off purely and simply because he was going too fast and appeared to have had another attack of the red mists. All year we used steel brakes. All year with the data we had available we found it hard to work out why the McLaren was consistently half a second a lap faster than we were on a circuit of average length. When we fitted carbon brakes at the end of the year in preparation for the next season we found that half-second. It was what the composite material brakes saved by better braking performance.

Not so with Ayrton. He could see, sense or feel the potential of the active system, and committed to it straight away. He retired in Rio, was second in Imola and was taken off by Mansell at Spa. At Monaco he won in style to go second in the championship to Prost, and at Detroit three weeks later he overtook Prost in the standings with another superb win.

However Spa, Ricard and Silverstone confirmed what he already had worked out for himself. The Lotus was a seriously complex car that incurred a weight penalty with the mechanical components needed for its suspension system. Additionally the pump for the high-pressure hydraulics driven off the Honda engine soaked up some horsepower. The Williams car, with none of these deficits and the same engine, was seeing him off on a regular basis, particularly on the high-speed circuits. What he needed was to put in place the set-up that would give him the consistent results needed to take the World Championship.

His relationship with Honda had quickly become extremely close. Japanese companies operate in the main on two principles. The first is consensus: if everyone agrees to do something, it will be easier to achieve. The second is to gather as much information as possible so that the decision that follows is based on the broadest possible knowledge of the subject. One can imagine the awe in which they held Ayrton, giving them as he did a humanised, accurate and just as comprehensive set of data of what their engines were doing as their inhuman computers that simply punched out numbers. What is more, from their human driver/computer they got an opinion on how to solve problems or improve performance. Ayrton got to work on putting Honda engines into McLaren cars for the next year, something that was not difficult to achieve. The Honda hierarchy were just as much slaves to his wishes as everyone else was. On top of that, Ron Dennis had been enticing him for ages. Honda would go where Senna went, and Dennis was presented with the strongest package in Formula 1 on a plate.

Once more, Duncan Lee's detailed description of the sequence of Senna's departure and Piquet's arrival from Camel's point of view is fascinating:

"Senna came to me during the French Grand Prix at Magny Cours in July 1987 to tell me he was looking to move to another team for 1988. Sure enough, by the end of the month Peter Warr called me to say that Ayrton was sure to go to McLaren, and he had talked to Nelson Piquet as a replacement. At the time Nelson was second in the championship behind his team-mate Nigel Mansell, and he was familiar with Honda.

"Peter asked me to talk to Piquet, and I did the entire negotiation with him in a day-long saga of discussions, calls to Japan for assurances that the Honda engine would continue to be available, calls from Senna saying he had not signed anything with anyone yet, and calls to Lester Pullen to report progress. In the end, Senna said he would stay with Lotus for $7 million, and Pullen told me to tell him 'no'. I called Peter, and told him we would sign a deal with Piquet for $5 million for two years, with a $500,000 bonus if he won his third World Championship that year,

which of course he duly did. We then renewed our sponsorship with Team Lotus for two years and upped the payment to, I think, $8.5 million, including Nelson's fee, but not the bonus.

"The Team retained Nakajima and the Honda engines, but the engineer who agreed to supply the engines to both McLaren and Lotus lost his job. I suspect that Honda wanted to stay with Senna and supply only McLaren with engines in 1988, but I don't know that for sure."

What did happen after the news broke with our announcement that we had signed Nelson Piquet for 1988 was that Ayrton applied himself to driving races in a way that consistently scored points. He had discovered that this was how the World Championship rules worked, and he simply trained himself to score points rather than win or bust. That is not to say that when a victory was possible he would not grab it. But after the Mansell incident at Spa, he finished the next eight races in the points. One of his more brilliant but less heralded races was Hockenheim, where the active hydraulics failed. With no pressure in the system, the chassis lowered itself onto the helper springs. These were only sufficient to support the weight of the car at a ride height sufficient to pass scrutineering when the engine was not running, and to allow the car to be wheeled about with the ignition off. At the highest top speed circuit in Europe, with the belly dragging on the ground, he brought the car home in third place. Only his disqualification from second place in Adelaide for a technical infringement by the Team stopped him being second in the World Championship.

So how does one summarise this astonishing man? In 1985 a French journalist, Lionel Froissart, when asked what he thought of the latest impressive outing of the Brazilian, replied: "Magic!" This nickname stuck with him through all his time at Team Lotus, and it was entirely appropriate. Though my contacts were inevitably less frequent once he was driving for McLaren, we did chat occasionally. It seemed to me that his target, once he had his first championship title under his belt, was simply to equal if not exceed the five World

Championships of Juan Manuel Fangio. He did not appear to be interested in individual race wins, although they still excited him. He believed that the only way he would be recognised and accepted as the greatest ever was to achieve or beat what the Argentinean had done.

I further agree with those who believe that he was unfairly robbed of his victory in the Japanese race in 1989 when most observers believed that (a) Prost, aware of the cushion of his 16-point lead with one further race to come, deliberately turned in early on Senna at the chicane; and (b) push-starts generated when being pushed by the marshals to a place of safety were permitted. In my experience cutting a chicane, the other reason given for his disqualification, was rarely if ever a cause for exclusion, particularly if the driver had gained no track advantage by doing so. His spectacular recovery to win the race was erased by the autocratic and partisan interference in the duties of the stewards by Jean-Marie Balestre, President of the FIA. Formula 1 was demeaned. Ayrton's outraged reaction was to cost him a $100,000 fine and nearly his racing licence for the following year. Whether in the atrocious conditions that followed in Adelaide Ayrton could have clawed back the deficit, which would have been seven points had the Japanese win been allowed to stand, will never be known. Prost never admitted whether he would have raced had the World Championship still been alive. As it was, he withdrew because of the conditions, and Ayrton crashed because of the conditions. In any event Ayrton felt he had been robbed of the chance at the title, if not the title itself.

What so nearly could have been four in a row became a total of three in 1991. His truthfulness in admitting that he had taken Prost off at Suzuka in 1990 was his way of confirming his abhorrence of the politics and double standards that he felt were being applied more and more frequently in racing. He knew he had been right about the location of pole position. I like to believe that the way he would have preferred to handle the 1990 situation would have been to visit Balestre in his office before the race. He would have left a blank signed cheque and said, "Fill that in for whatever you want in the way of a fine, but if Alain turns in on me at the first corner he is off." Knowing he could not hope to get away with that he dropped one or two hints, so that what happened was not entirely unexpected.

On paper at the start of the 1994 season it looked like another World Championship for Ayrton. Few would have bet against it. Prost was in retirement and the Williams-Renault had just delivered two championships on the trot and still looked the class of the field. Then the dreadful events at Imola intervened.

There is hardly a serious follower of Formula 1 who would deny that in Ayrton existed a racing driver who could have won five, six or, who knows, even seven championships. Unlike Mansell, who had thrown away two world titles with mistakes, people felt and perhaps still feel that, like Jimmy Clark before him, Ayrton was deprived of two titles by factors out of his control. What is true is that his passing probably touched more people worldwide than that of any previous sportsman in history. His brilliance shone into the lives of hundreds of millions and uplifted their spirits. His ability was perceived by those in Formula 1 to be on a higher level than all of his contemporaries. He possessed an innate goodness, and such a strong sense of injustice that he went to great lengths to alleviate the lot of underprivileged children in his own country. Those close to him knew him as a great fun friend, those more remote could not help but stand and admire. Throughout he was true to his principles. One of the first of those principles was honesty with himself, and with everyone else.

Magic.

CHAPTER 4

ENGINEERS

"Don't confuse me with the facts – my mind is made up"

At this point we leave Team Lotus, as I did at the end of 1976, to pay a brief visit to another racing team. Since 1972 Frank Williams had been based in a small 3,500sq ft industrial unit at 36 Bennet Road, Reading. When the Hesketh Grand Prix effort folded in 1975 Frank acquired the assets from Alexander Hesketh. A wealthy Canadian enthusiast called Walter Wolf funded the acquisition and the partnership took part, unsuccessfully, in the 1976 Grand Prix season. Much of the problem stemmed from the recalcitrant Hesketh 308C cars that came with the deal. Not even James Hunt had managed to come to terms with the Hesketh's unpredictable handling and when Jacky Ickx, Frank's lead driver, failed to qualify for the British Grand Prix at Brands Hatch in front of Walter's influential guests, Walter was not amused. He had, however, got a real taste for Formula 1 and the role of team owner, and desperately wanted to stay on the grid. In the paddock at Brands Hatch he approached me to see if I might be interested in managing his team for him in 1977. Walter was not a person to take 'no' for an answer for, like all wealthy self-made men, he was used to getting his own way. On the Sunday evening after the race he took my wife and me to dinner at Trader Vic's at the London Hilton. There he started an expansive and voluble campaign to persuade me. While my wife was impressed with the huge leap forward in our standard of living that would be possible with the numbers mentioned as a salary, I found myself impressed for another reason. It seemed to me that this rather loud and brash guy, who was really far too showy for our tastes, did indeed have a burning desire to do well. He was happy to leave the running of the team to me, was prepared to get the best driver that we could find in the market, and recognised in some of the personnel at the team the ingredients of a strong unit. Frank was to stay as the marketing and sponsorship man and, given that he had survived in Grands Prix as long as he had, was probably pretty good in this area. Thus I found myself in December 1976 working out of this small unit in Bennet Road, Reading.

To start with we were just over 30-strong, entering a one-car, privately owned Formula 1 team against the big boys. Jody Scheckter was the driver, fresh from his time at Tyrrell. The team made history by winning its very first Grand Prix, in Argentina in January 1977. To this we added the prestigious Monaco event and, as if to complete the fairy tale, the team owner's home race in Canada. The team finished fourth in the World Championship for Constructors with only one car and driver and, more amazing still, Jody was second in the Drivers' Championship to Niki Lauda of Ferrari. The last private entrant in Formula 1, Walter Wolf Racing had really turned the establishment on its head.

Arriving at each race with two cars (a race car and a spare) and having a third chassis that was used extensively for testing, the season cost £585,000 in total. Obviously the team had got it pretty nearly right. Much-needed expansion to cope with the onset of the ground-effect era followed, and the team grew to 45 people over a period of time. Nowadays a serious team is perhaps 15 times that on the personnel head count. The premises were too small, and the design office was already housed in a Portakabin in the back yard. Now this was joined by a second Portakabin for the administrative offices, and the lock-up garage behind the main workshop was turned into a glassfibre shop. Further expansion took place with the renting of the rear half of the adjoining unit, and a door was knocked through the connecting wall to what became our new gearbox shop and development area. This is not an obsession with irrelevant geographical details but an attempt to put you, the reader, in a position where you might see what I could see.

Head of Design and Engineering and housed in the first Portakabin was Dr Harvey Postlethwaite. Number two to Harvey, and taking the leading role in the design of the chassis and mechanical components, was Patrick Head.

To make our own body panels and particularly to gain experience with the new lightweight woven-cloth glassfibre technology, we asked someone who was working in the machine shop to help out in the lock-up garage. His name was Ross Brawn.

And finally, to provide help to Harvey with his aerodynamic work in the wind tunnel, we hired straight from Southampton University a young graduate who took up residence in the new development shop. His name was Adrian Newey.

All four of those names went on to become major stars in Formula 1's technological firmament. Harvey Postlethwaite, having got Hesketh and James Hunt into the winner's circle, came with the package when Frank Williams acquired the Hesketh assets in 1976. He went on to Ferrari (twice) and was responsible for introducing all the new chassis technologies to that team. He then went to Tyrrell, where he was working when Ken Tyrrell finally sold that team to the new BAR operation. Retained by Honda to oversee their return to Formula 1 as both a chassis and engine constructor, Harvey was stricken with a fatal heart attack in 1998 while overseeing a Honda test in Barcelona. It was rumoured that such was his importance to the project that it caused Honda to revise their position, withdraw as a chassis manufacturer and return only as an engine supplier.

Patrick Head was invited by Frank Williams to join him at his new team when Frank, totally unsettled by not running his own outfit, parted company with Walter Wolf. By mid-1979 Williams Grand Prix Engineering had won its first Grand Prix. Since then, cars for which Patrick has had overall responsibility have won nine World Championships for Constructors and seven World Championships for Drivers. To do this his cars have been first across the line in more than 100 races.

Ross Brawn really came to public notice when, as Head of Engineering at Benetton, he guided Michael Schumacher to two World Drivers' Championships. Persuaded to follow the German ace to Ferrari, Ross masterminded the Italian team's transformation and returned them to the level of champions after an intermission of 21 years. After steering Ferrari through six consecutive Constructors' titles and helping Schumacher to five more Drivers' Championships, Ross left Ferrari and, after a year's sabbatical, joined Honda. When the Japanese manufacturer withdrew at the end of 2008 he set up a management buyout and turned it into his own team. Brawn GP made history by winning the Drivers' and Constructors' titles in its first season, and was then bought out by Mercedes-Benz.

Adrian Newey quickly became the most successful car designer and engineer in CART/Indycar racing, winning several championships. Returning to Formula 1 he produced an exceptional March car for the struggling Bicester team before joining Patrick Head at Williams. There his designs continued the run of successes enjoyed by the pure Head cars. Persuaded to join McLaren at the least competitive period of their history, he produced cars that won two World Drivers' Championships in as many years. He moved to Red Bull in 2006, and by 2010 was winning Championships all over again. He is recognised as the leading aerodynamicist in the single-seater world.

With those four on board, it's not surprising that Walter Wolf's little private team did really rather well in 1977. There must have been something in the water at Bennet Road.

At Team Lotus, of course, we were all under the influence of Colin Chapman, who was not only the leading race car engineer of his time but also the boss. The role of the staff engineers was therefore rather different. Design engineers working in the Drawing Office interpreted Colin's initial car schemes, improvements or rectification ideas. During periods of high activity or anticipation he would visit the Drawing Office several times a day. Standing at the shoulder of a designer he would look at what was on the board and point out where he felt his idea had not been correctly interpreted. Or he might be prompted by what he saw to develop his idea still further. Many of the original drawings of Team Lotus cars carry his hand-sketched annotations. His greatest feel for things, however, appeared to come when he was actually handling a part. Then, it seemed, he could visualise most succinctly where the finished item had departed from his original brief. Or seeing it in reality, rather than the two dimensions of a drawing, might prompt some further process in his mind to take the design to another level. Sometimes, it has to be said, he saw in the finished item a flaw in the design that he had missed in his sketch, or even in the proper drawing.

Walking through the stores one day I asked our buyer what was on the new shelves he had erected. "I call them the Guvnor's shelves," he said. "The first one is fabricated scrap. The second is fabricated, heat-treated scrap. The third one has the fabricated, heat-treated and machined scrap. The fourth shelf is for fabricated, heat-treated, machined and plated scrap. And the final one is for parts that have had all that done to them and then been assembled but still not made it onto the car before he decided that they were not what he wanted." If nothing else the story illustrates how much of a hands-on engineer he was, but it also highlights another problem. The designers rarely got out of the Drawing Office and, though they spent time, lots of time, in the workshops, they rarely got to see the cars run. This left them short of some vital areas of engineering experience, not the least of which was the role of managing people in a way that got the best out of them.

From the earliest days of competition outings of Lotus cars, through the formation of Team Lotus in 1956 until the day in 1962 when he left the company, Mike Costin had been the perfect foil for Chapman. From a part-time start (he still had a day job at De Havilland Aircraft) to his eventual position as Development Director of the whole Group, he was the engineering rock on which the fortunes of Lotus were built. Only he was close enough to Colin to constrain the worst of the early excesses and the manic schedule. Only he had the standing to say that he could see a better way to sort out a problem. No mean driver himself, he could jump in a race car and get the feed-back for himself. Not content with just testing cars, he would sometimes race himself. He drove the development Lotus Elite at Brands Hatch in the Boxing Day meeting in 1959, racing against – and keeping up with – Jim Clark and Colin Chapman in similar cars. For much of 1960 he was Jim Clark's mentor as Jimmy started his single-seater career in the Formula Junior Lotus 18 run by Mike's department. Mike also raced a Formula Junior Lotus at Mallory Park in 1961.

His first experience of a single-seater had come in 1959. The Series 4 Lotus 16 (the baby Vanwall-shaped Formula 1 car) was due to test for the first time. An incredibly lightweight space-frame chassis housed a Coventry Climax FPF engine, now canted over to the opposite side compared to the earlier series of cars. Angled across the centre line, the propshaft connected to a Lotus sequential gearbox, known inevitably as the 'queerbox', in unit with the differential. An elliptically shaped aluminium undertray helped stiffen the chassis by being riveted to its tubes. A straight back or forward, pull or push gearchange selected the gears. The car appeared out of Mike Costin's development shop, above which was the Drawing Office in the old Hornsey works. Halfway up the ramps of the trailer onto which it was being pushed, the rear wheels locked up. Investigation revealed that the chassis had flexed so much during this simple manoeuvre that the car had put itself into gear.

"Well, don't hang about, you lot," said Mike. "Let's get it back in the shop and fix it."

The undertray was wrinkled, and some chassis reinforcing was needed. A little while later in the front office that had been created from the showroom built into the ground floor of the Hornsey frontage, the telephone on Mike's desk rang. In amazement we listened as we heard him tell the lads to warm up the car: "We'd better make sure it's OK before it goes testing." A little while later

Mike settled his 6ft 3in frame into the sculpted driver's bucket seat and set off, in a Formula 1 car, down Tottenham Lane, Hornsey, London N8. We could hear the engine revs rise and fall as he did a lap around the nearest block or two. Occasionally we could hear the engine being 'blipped' as he was held up in the traffic or by traffic lights. This would be followed by a rising crescendo of noise as the clutch bit once more and the car shot up the next bit of urban north London. Finally the windswept haircut and Mk8 flying goggles of Mike appeared back in the yard. By the time the police arrived the car was in bits, up on its trestles in its workshop, with Mike studying some part or another. The coppers were bamboozled and went away, happily not having thought to touch the still hot engine.

An immensely pragmatic and down-to-earth engineer of wide experience, Mike brought aircraft industry technology to cars. Not someone who was afraid to get his hands dirty or work through the night alongside the mechanics, he was hugely popular with the staff and respected throughout racing. He was largely responsible for seeing through the transition of the company from a bunch of enthusiastic amateurs to some semblance of a proper business. This additional attribute was to stand him in good stead later in his career, when he was Chairman of Cosworth Engineering Ltd. In 1958 he had formed Cosworth in partnership with Keith Duckworth, and it was to give that rapidly growing organisation all of his time that he left Lotus. The partnership he formed with Keith was to become perhaps the greatest success story of all time in motor racing. Who knows to what heights the fortunes of Team Lotus and Lotus Cars might have risen had that partnership remained with Colin?

After the departure of Mike Costin no position to duplicate his existed within the Team for 15 years. The design work was carried out in the Drawing Office with such luminaries as Len Terry and Maurice Phillippe in the 1960s and early 1970s. Team Lotus had won races in every one of the previous 11 Grand Prix seasons, so 1971 was a serious blot in the copybook with not a single victory.

Emerson had his fearful road accident mid-season, which effectively ruined his year, and Maurice Phillippe was tempted to the US by Parnelli Jones to design Indianapolis cars. He returned to haunt his old team with the beautifully engineered Parnelli Formula 1 car which Mario drove, and which was everything that Chapman so wanted the successor to the Lotus 72, the Lotus 76, to be but was not.

Now there was a mini-crisis. With no traditional in-house designer I was charged with poaching one from somewhere else. The McLaren team had built a very interesting and quite successful car, the M19, which had a rising-rate front suspension system of some intricacy. Though Gordon Coppuck was the Chief Designer at McLaren, the story was that Ralph Bellamy had actually designed this suspension in his capacity as Chief Designer – Formula 1. Ralph was an Australian who had come to England and worked under Ron Tauranac for three years before deciding to return to Australia. Teddy Mayer and Phil Kerr of McLaren heard of this and persuaded him to stay. Ralph worked with Gordon Coppuck, whose first responsibility was the CanAm and Indianapolis McLarens. After one short year he decided to return to Brabham to join Gordon Murray at Bernie Ecclestone's revamped team.

In his interview he further told me that he had been responsible for the elegant new triangular Brabham chassis that was due to race the following season, and that the last thing he had done prior to joining us was to hand to Gordon Murray the completed roll of drawings. The problem with this sort of statement is that it has to be taken at its face value as, if you are trying to poach someone else's staff, you can hardly ring them up and ask for a reference. Similarly if you are after something you have to demonstrate some trust. The sense of trepidation and anxiety about the worth of Ralph's reputation hardly improved when, after he had joined us, I asked Teddy Mayer of McLaren for his view. Whether Teddy was only too pleased to see some discomfort in a competitor or whether he had a serious point to make I'm not certain, but his opinion was forceful and to the point. "He certainly did the drawings for that suspension, but whether he or Gordon actually designed it I am not sure. In any case the car did not start handling properly until we had thrown it away!"

This damning with faint praise was not good for my peace of mind, as I had sold Colin a pretty big bill of goods about his new engineer. Happily the dramas lay some way in the future, because the Lotus 72 was still so far ahead of the field that Ralph and Martin Wade had to concern themselves mainly with updates. Between them they produced a series of wing, oil tank and suspension developments that kept the car at the front throughout 1972 and 1973. This even included the somewhat unnerving change to the small and very stiff-walled Goodyear 13-inch front tyres of 1973, Firestone having withdrawn from Formula 1. These tyres had been developed for the less radical cars like the Tyrrell and the McLaren, which carried much more weight on the front wheels than the miserly 33 per cent of the Lotus 72.

This experience with suspension, aerodynamics and systems led Colin to give Ralph Bellamy his first brief for a complete Lotus racing car. But the Lotus 74 was not called a Lotus but a 'Texaco Star'. The fuel sponsor had been getting more and more enthusiastic about its involvement in motor sport through the Formula 1 Team and its close ties to Emerson, who was the reigning World Champion, and Ronnie, the new arrival. But they fretted over the all-enveloping black and gold identity that had established itself so firmly, positively and quickly in the minds of the public. Texaco had fought hard to get a concession that their logos on the Grand Prix cars should be in red, white and black, having started that way in Argentina in 1972 and then mistakenly having agreed to adopt the same livery as the other sponsors. With even the churns that held their fuel appearing in black and gold, they needed to undo the potential damage which was being done to their world-wide image by appearing most frequently on TV and in the press in distinctly non-corporate colours. Anxious to give them what they wanted without compromising the

After John Player blocked Peter's efforts to sign Ayrton Senna for his first F1 season, he kept a close eye on him while the new rising star was driving for Toleman in 1984… sutton-images.com

…and was able to get his signature on a contract for 1985. Ayrton stayed with Lotus for three seasons. LAT

The French designer Gérard Ducarouge (left), who joined Lotus in 1983, with Anglophile F1 journalist and perennial Lotus supporter Jabby Crombac, and Peter. Elf

Post-qualifying debrief in the motorhome with, from left, Elio, Ayrton, Peter, Steve Hallam and Bob Dance. Warr family collection

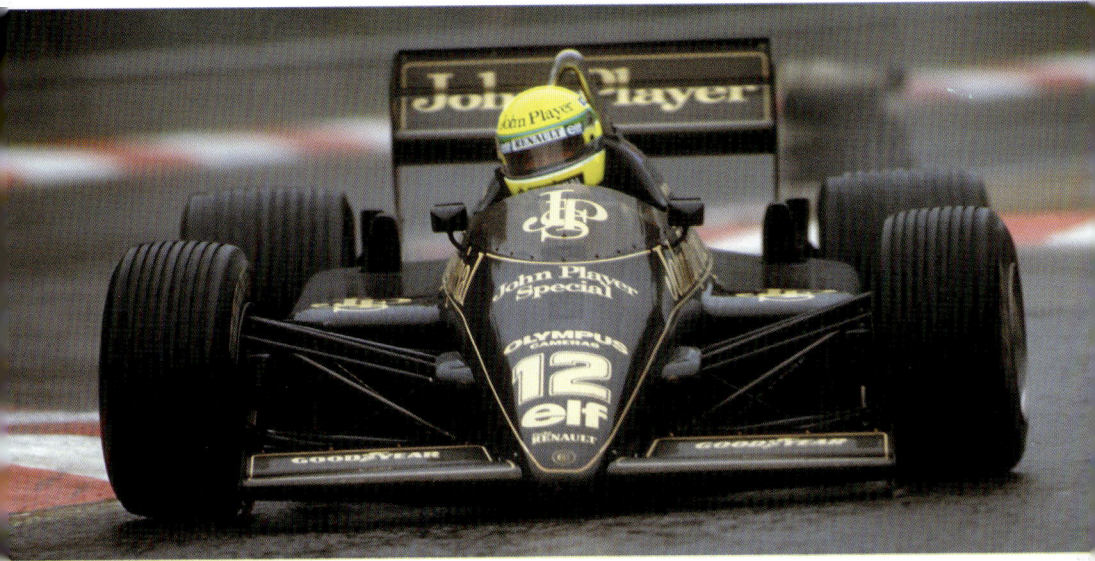

Ayrton's second F1 victory came at Spa in 1985, in difficult track conditions and despite a misfire. LAT

Among the Detroit skyscrapers in 1986 Ayrton scored his fourth Grand Prix win. With him, from left, are Renault's Bruno Mauduit, Steve Hallam, Gérard Ducarouge and Peter; behind them, at far left, is Kenny Szymanski. LAT

Monaco 1987 brought a classic Senna victory with the Camel-yellow Lotus-Honda 99T turbo. Elf

Ayrton, ecstatic over his Monaco victory, made sure Peter got his share of the champagne. Elf

Peter with Bob Dance, the most respected of all Team Lotus mechanics, who is still working for Clive Chapman's Classic Team Lotus today. Bernard Cahier

Team members crowd onto the pit wall to cheer Ayrton Senna to the flag in the 1987 Detroit GP, the last of his six Lotus Grand Prix victories. Norio Koike

Having fun in Monte Carlo outside the famous Tip Top Bar in 1988. Peter, Fred Bushell and Hazel Chapman are with two drag artistes in the form of Lotus tyre men Clive Hicks (brunette) and Kenny Szymanski (blonde). Courtesy of Kenny Szymanski

Hazel Chapman remained great friends with Peter and Yvonne after Colin's death. Here she is during the late 1980s with Peter in the Seychelles, where it was so hot that she joked about frying an egg on the tiles around the pool – and duly tried it. Warr family collection

Peter gives a detailed brief to Japanese driver Satoru Nakajima, who arrived at Team Lotus with the Honda engines in 1987 and stayed as number two for three seasons. sutton-images.com

Peter and his son, Andy, with his beloved Mercedes-Benz 300SL 'Gullwing', during his two-year spell as Secretary of the British Racing Drivers' Club. Warr family collection

The last time Peter drove a race car came when he was reunited with a Lotus 23 at the re-opening of Suzuka circuit on 12 April 2010 Sid Ogura

Peter's last visit to a race circuit was for the Classic Team Lotus Celebration at Snetterton on 20 June 2010. It was two days after his 72nd birthday and here he is with his favourite car – the Lotus 72. Sid Ogura

relationship with Players, and equally keen to give our two drivers a full season of racing, we persuaded Texaco that the best destination for some additional funds would be in a dedicated Formula 2 team. That way they could have the livery exclusively, use their personal sponsorship of the drivers effectively, and build their own motor sporting image. They went for it and the result was Ralph Bellamy's first Lotus.

A really tidy chassis and the first-ever race car with side- rather than forward-facing radiators, the little chassis was a fine piece of work. The engine, however, was a disaster. Colin, determined to use racing to improve the breed and get some publicity for the road cars, insisted the car use a racing version of the 900-series Lotus road car engine. Originally using a Vauxhall block with Lotus-designed and manufactured cylinder heads, the engine had progressed into an all-aluminium block that was now produced fully in-house and used throughout the road car range. The contract to do a 'Cosworth' on it was given to Novamotor in Italy, who had built a formidable reputation in Formula 3. Unfortunately, in spite of having what was perhaps the most spotlessly clean engineering factory ever, the Pederzani brothers failed to come to terms with the inclined lightweight engine. Always underpowered, never very reliable and prone to arrive for each race in a different configuration, it gave the mechanics nightmares when changing engines. It caused the reputation of what was actually a well thought-out and sound chassis to suffer unfairly, and the programme was discontinued after one season.

Happy with what he had seen from the first Bellamy attempt at a complete car, Colin now gave Ralph the oft-reported brief to start work on the successor to the Lotus 72 that was to be ready for the 1974 season. Unfortunately what was to be a better version of its famous predecessor but '100lb lighter' was neither better nor lighter. Ralph continued the design philosophy of the Formula 2 car with its angular, tapered but flat panelled monocoque, which was far easier to manufacture than the double-compound-curvature chassis of the

72. He also included the successful side radiators of the smaller Formula 2 car, but on both sides of the bigger car to meet the requirements of the much more powerful 3-litre Formula 1 engine. But there he seemed to run out of steam. Perhaps there was too much pressure from Colin to include items like the electric clutch that would allow Ronnie to brake with his left foot. Or perhaps it was the bi-plane rear wing arrangement, together with the complex structure to mount it and support it where it needed to be, that took Ralph's mind off the job. The result was that some glaring omissions occurred with the remainder of the car.

Ralph's drawings were always drawn with what appeared to be a 14H pencil. The lines were incredibly fine and the poor old ammonia-fuelled print machine in the Drawing Office seemed to have permanent problems finding and reproducing the marks on the original drawing film. So not unnaturally when the moment came, one of the mechanics building the first car asked him to come into the shop and answer a few points on the latest drawing to arrive. The object was to discover whereabouts within the chassis the wiring loom was to go. It turned out that the designer had forgotten all about this quite important item. It eventually found itself housed under a triangular bolt-on aluminium channel sitting on top of the monocoque by the driver's elbow, completely spoiling the clean lines of the chassis. Under the regulations, if the electrics were not concealed within the chassis they had to be fireproof. And so some more weight was added.

With these thoughts and the complaints of the workshop personnel ringing in my ears, the next time I saw Bernie Ecclestone, who had been Ralph's previous employer, I asked him, "What did you think of Ralph's drawing?" Sensing my discomfort and seeking a laugh at my expense, Bernie, as quick as ever, spluttered, "Draw? Draw? The only thing that bloke could draw was his wages!"

This story is not repeated to cause Ralph any embarrassment, but to highlight the relationship that existed between Colin and the engineers/designers that Team Lotus employed, and how this was very different to how it had been with Mike Costin. It was also very different to that which existed in every other team. No other team had the situation where its chief engineer was also the team owner. As Colin became more and more involved in the ever-expanding and demanding business that was Group Lotus (he had even started in the boat-building business by now), less and less of his time was available for the racing team. But, as the best engineer in the business, he could not bring himself to delegate the racing responsibilities as completely as Bernie Ecclestone had been able to do at Brabham. This left people like Ralph in an impossible position, knowing that whatever they did was likely to be criticised as being less well-engineered than if "I had done it myself". It also meant that if Colin failed to spend enough time designing, his own reputation would suffer – and it did. The other unsatisfactory side of this approach was that huge amounts of the hard-won budget were soaked up making parts more than once.

In retrospect Ralph Bellamy's greatest achievement was to stay the course for as long as he did. His input into the revolutionary ground-effect car for the 1977 season was important. He was an easy-going chap, and his worst failing was perhaps his reluctance to stand up to Colin. That was never an easy thing to do, but the odd battle toe-to-toe, when convinced that he was right, might have given him the stature he needed to thrive in such an atmosphere. The more rarefied air of the newly formed Development Area at Ketteringham Hall, away from the daily stress of the Formula 1 workshop and race track, was perhaps the environment he needed to produce his best work. By the 1980 season he was working with Mo Nunn and the Ensign team, having first gone to the Fittipaldi brothers' newly formed Grand Prix team.

Colin, having been kept in the winner's circle through the sheer brilliance of Ronnie Peterson's sublime and heroic driving of the ageing Lotus 72 during 1974, became severely depressed with Formula 1 during 1975. This was due partly to the lack of budget, which would eventually lead to the departure of Ronnie, and partly because the engineering of the 'Formula Ford' era of Formula 1, which was coming up to its tenth year, had in his opinion become boring. With two of the best drivers in the world, the entire season was spent fire-fighting the inadequacies of the now outdated Lotus 72. Crippled by its putting on weight like a middle-aged lady and handicapped more and more by the tyre company making tyres suited to cars with very different weight distributions, the Team was going nowhere.

The famous treatise that Colin wrote whilst on holiday at his villa in Ibiza at the end of July, and that ultimately gave birth to ground effect, was the product of his frustration at no longer being in the spotlight of championship success. It was also the product of the boredom that would set in if he did nothing for longer than a day or two. His internal dynamo simply did not allow him to sit still for that long, even if he was on holiday with his family.

First he needed to get to grips with the upcoming problems of the next race, the German Grand Prix at the Nürburgring at the beginning of August. Then he came up with his recommendations and job list for that race. This mental process led him inexorably into further design and philosophical thoughts.

In the long handwritten document, produced mainly on a sun-lounger next to his swimming pool, he bemoaned the fact that the then current racing philosophy was what he called the "do nothing wrong policy". If a team concentrated solely on making fewer mistakes than the others they would ultimately have some success in an era where everyone was using similar equipment, and the regulations had been distilled over and over again. This left little room for individual expression by the average designer. And Colin was not an average designer. He committed himself there and then to raising the performance of the race car above those presently in use.

The thesis he set out started from the premise that what was needed to put right the now inherent faults of the Lotus 72 was to support the front end of the car by a very wide track. This was achievable mechanically. However, he saw the need to complement this improvement in turn-in and stability with a non-pitch-sensitive aerodynamic system. By preventing the front downforce from increasing dramatically under braking, the rear end of the car could be stopped from stepping into violent and sudden oversteer. The required lack of pitch sensitivity also demanded a very long wheelbase. It was the rear-end requirements that taxed him the most, and the search for a logical and unarguable solution led him to continue the thesis. What he was really searching for was the means to maintain a low-drag configuration while, if it was possible, not reducing the aerodynamic downforce on the rear of the car when it squatted under acceleration and reduced the angle of incidence of the rear wing.

After copious calculations, theories and even posing a series of questions that needed to be answered, which he equally set out in the document, he attempted to sketch how he thought the resulting car might look. This was a long way from the ground-effect Lotus 78. Only short, stubby and cambered sponsons in front of the rear wheels revealed a new approach. These were inspired by the full-width noses used by some Formula 1 cars at the time. The other radical difference would be an extremely slimline nose/monocoque frontal section that maximised airflow to the rear pods. By being able to pass through the gap created by the wide front track/narrow tub, the devices ahead of the rear wheels would receive the cleanest possible air. The very small frontal area of the chassis, little wider than the driver's legs, provoked the requirement that the entire fuel reservoir should be sited behind the driver. This would in turn help to limit the change in handling from full to empty tanks.

Returning from holiday bursting with enthusiasm to investigate the new theory and answer some of the questions posed, he asked me to set up a section of Team Lotus within the Group Research & Development facility. The only space available was in the workshops used by Lotus Cars and Tony Rudd, Group Engineering Director, to build the prototype model Lotus Esprit. Prior to that the buildings had been a boys' school and before that it had been used as the Headquarters of the Bombardment Group of the US Eighth Air Force. That was, of course, during the Second World War, before which it had been a country house or a stately home depending on who you were speaking to at the time. Subsequently it was to be renovated and used as Group Headquarters, that is to say where Colin and his Head of Finance, Fred Bushell, had their offices away from the hustle and bustle of the main Lotus Cars offices. By the end of 1976 the whole of Team Lotus would move to the new premises. It was there at Ketteringham Hall that the work now started that would produce the revolution that was ground effect.

Ralph Bellamy was assigned to the R&D programme. This left a gap in the engineering strength of the race team. As previously mentioned, I had been involved in a fairly serious road accident in the spring of 1975 while driving to Silverstone for a test, when the lead driver of an army convoy drove his Land Rover out of a side turning and into my Lotus Elan Plus 2. My injuries were to keep me in hospital and recuperating for 14 weeks. Nigel Bennett, who was later to become chief engineer of the very successful Roger Penske CART/Indycar team, was taken on to fill the gap in the ranks. His role was partly the one that I had been doing and partly race engineer, the first to fill that role since Mike Costin. Nigel was not employed as a designer. When by mid-1976 the new R&D department, due to its increasing work load, had swallowed up some more of the staff at the Potash Lane racing workshops, more engineering reinforcements were needed.

The Shadow racing cars built by Don Nichols' team had impressed everyone with their outstanding speed and terrific handling in 1975. The designer and engineer responsible for them was Tony Southgate. He had also been in charge of the excellent-handling P160 series of 12-cylinder BRM cars. With such a reputation we hired him to help recover from the difficult start to the 1976 season. This he did to such good effect that by the end of the year the Lotus 77, which had a dismal early season, was developed into a competitive and eventually a race-winning car.

It was curious that he came to work on the infinitely adjustable Lotus. His own suspension design, and particularly the BRM, was so right straight off the drawing board that it did not even have the adjustment possible by incorporating threaded spherical bearings in the suspension links. This man obviously knew what it took to make a car handle. What he had never previously experienced was the frenetic pace of life that existed at Team Lotus, and in particular the Chapman way of going about things. Hired primarily to engineer the cars at the track, he had input from the Drawing Office only into the endless list of modifications that are the lifeblood of keeping a racing car reliable or capable of going faster. When we got back to the ranch after the first race he attended and had the usual meeting to discuss and settle the forward work programme, we were impressed with his calm and measured approach to the list of 'mods' required by the 'Guv'nor'.

He had his own quite forceful but quietly stated views on things, and even managed to persuade Colin that his ideas on a couple of items were preferable. Was this, we asked ourselves, finally the engineer for whom Colin would have the respect needed to begin to delegate the routine engineering responsibility? Could we get on with things without having to wait for the few moments that Colin could spare the Team in a working day at the office when he had so much else on his plate? Yes, we had him to ourselves at the circuits, but the engineering work was mainly done at the factory. It did not help if a decision was not forthcoming because of his other engagements. And Tony Southgate was easy in his relationships with the other designers and got on well with people throughout the organisation.

Tony handled his part of the meeting with aplomb, contributing when he needed to and letting others have their say. The next and most urgent step was to get the work list typed and circulated so that all departments were aware of their roles and programme in getting us to the next race. A couple of days later Colin dropped by to check on progress or perhaps add something he had thought about since the meeting or, as was his habit, change something entirely. Standing with Tony Southgate at the drawing board he started running through the list.

At exactly which point things became clear is not known, but the rumblings of thunder were felt. The Drawing Office was separated from the main office only by a glass and plasterboard partition. It seems that Tony, perhaps used to a different pace, had indicated to Colin that only the first six or eight items on the list were on schedule to be finished by the next race. The rest would be done in due course. When the dust and debris from the explosion had settled no-one, least of all Tony, was under any illusion that it mattered not one iota if there were a hundred items on a job list; they were all to be finished by the next race. It was my fault for not having got this simple truth about Team Lotus across to Tony before he fell foul of the 'Guv'nor' and his wrath. But while Tony quickly got himself up to speed with the way things were, I felt that Team Lotus never got the best out of him as a result of their way of doing things. Perhaps the BRM with its beautiful handling and non-adjustable suspension was because Tony's style was to work things through very carefully and methodically. He was openly critical of what he saw as the complete panic approach, and reflected frequently that it was hardly a surprise that we fell flat on our face with some experiment or other.

What his period at the Team did mark was the end of an era in which the business of going racing had transformed itself from something of a black art into a truly scientific and measured approach to ever more complex engineering problems. Tony Southgate left Team Lotus by the end of 1977 to return to Shadow, which was later to become Arrows in a reincarnation questioned in the Law Courts. A quarter of a century later Tony was still a chief designer and engineer. His post-Formula 1 work has perhaps been his most spectacular and successful, concentrating mainly on sports-racing cars. With winners of the Le Mans 24-Hour race to his credit and many other successes with some of the biggest names in the sport, he has carved out a real place for himself as one of the leading engineers of his time. The only reason his loss was not felt more keenly was because of the advent of the next Lotus Grand Prix car with a magic ingredient.

As the flow of results from the R&D guys at Ketteringham Hall increased, a new group of designers/engineers was formed. The leading one of these was Martin Ogilvie. As a very young graduate he started as a design draughtsman and was involved in everything that was designed and produced throughout the 1970s. Together with Geoff Aldridge and Mike Cooke, Martin had already been primarily responsible for the Lotus 77. Now Mike was moved to strengthen the new R&D department, and was to build the rolling chassis test rig that had also been sketched in the Chapman missive from his holiday in Ibiza in 1975. Martin and Geoff were therefore left to do all the detail design of the new wonder car, the Lotus 78.

Quite the most remarkable thing about Martin was his ability to produce drawings at speed. Once settled at his drawing board he could produce designs for individual components at the drop of a hat. Complete assemblies only took a little longer, and he was a priceless asset in maintaining the tempo of the entire organisation. Unfortunately this was also in a way his downfall. There was no engineer keener to branch out onto the wider stage of chief engineer at circuits: but year after year he was simply too valuable to be unchained from his drawing board. This caused him to fret a little, and there is no doubt that he rarely received the credit for the enormous volume of very good work that he produced. A Lotus man through and through, he only wandered as far as the Engineering division of Group Lotus for a period before he was again to be found back with the racing team.

Having shared in the great times of the Lotus 78 and 79, Martin had reason to feel a bit a bit bruised by what followed. Starting with the Lotus 80, a supposedly wingless but totally skirted 'step forward', he was involved in the disaster season of 1979. The Lotus 80 was abandoned halfway through the year and entries reverted to the 79s from the previous year. Carlos Reutemann, who could be out-psyched by another driver just suggesting that he was pulling a taller top gear than the one he was using, was completely unable to handle the setbacks and simply gave up. Mario, always keen to get on with development, persevered but was increasingly frustrated.

Having resurrected in Colin's mind all his original thoughts about loads of stable downforce but with less drag, by producing the Lotus 81 with its pitiful straight-line speed, Martin was pleased to move on to Colin's next leap of imagination, the twin-chassis Lotus 86. By the time the rules had been arbitrarily changed by Balestre to foil this dastardly Chapman plot, Martin had to pen the second 'legal' version, the Lotus 88. With this car now allowed to run, now not, Martin's labour of love continued with the hasty but enormous modifications to turn the Lotus 88 into the back-up Lotus 87. This was a concession Colin had had to make given the ongoing controversy, black flags and disqualifications. Otherwise there might have been no Lotus on the grid for the first time since 1957. And in the blink of an eye the all-conquering season of 1978 had turned into three winless years.

So the era of sliding skirts, twin chassis and protracted disputes with the governing body came to an end. What was needed was a 'sensible' car with fixed skirts, using the aerodynamic lessons learned in the heyday of ground effect to the fullest degree allowed by the regulations. Colin was by this time going through another of his 'fed up with whole business' troughs. He had blown a fortune on legal fees on a lost cause, fighting Jean-Marie Balestre over the twin-chassis car. He was in the throes of his business relationship with John DeLorean on the road car to be built by the American in Belfast, and had partaken of the tantalising 'high life' that David Thieme with his Essex Petroleum sponsorship had invited him to share.

Now one might think that someone like Martin Ogilvie would be concerned first and foremost with his salary and continuing employment. This was patently not true. As competitive as most others in the organisation, he felt deeply aggrieved at the lack of success.

When he was given the brief for the 1982 car he realised that, because of Colin's other preoccupations, he at last had a chance to do a car virtually on his own. The result was the stunningly beautiful Lotus 91. With the advantage of several seasons' experience with the carbon/kevlar honeycomb sandwich chassis construction that had been used on the previous four cars, he utilised the versatility of the method brilliantly. The suspension, which was mounted as before on machined-from-the-solid aluminium bulkheads, was strong and elegantly incorporated into the requirements of the aero package. The systems were just about as refined as they were going to get on a Cosworth-engined car, and the whole was clad in a shapely and slippery set of body panels.

The Lotus 91, by winning the 1982 Austrian Grand Prix in the hands of Elio de Angelis, scored the final Formula 1 victory for a Cosworth-powered Lotus, and the Team's only Grand Prix win during the six-year period up to 1984. Martin Ogilvie went on to design the first turbocharged Formula 1 Lotus, the Renault-powered 93T. In 1983 Peter recruited the former Matra, Ligier and Alfa Romeo designer Gérard Ducarouge, who produced the 94T in an incredibly short time and continued as Chief Designer through the great Ayrton Senna years.

CHAPTER 5

Bernie

"If you're absent you get screwed"

Driving south along the main street of Bexley in south-east London late in 1969, it was noticeable that among the usual array of High Street shops a much smarter building intervened in the mish-mash of frontages. It stood out, quite frankly, because it was bigger and more elegant than its neighbours. After some searching for the address for which I was looking, it dawned on me that the smart building was the one I was seeking. I had come to meet Bernie Ecclestone to talk to him about the arrangements for the works-supported Formula 2 team that he was to run in 1970 for the racing driver whose interests he managed, Jochen Rindt.

Entering the showroom it was obvious that this was at the cutting edge of design and layout. The floor was made of black and white tiles laid in a chequered flag pattern. Around the perimeter of the space were various cars on display, each with acres of their own space and spotlessly clean. Only the floor was more immaculate than they were. The overall lighting effect was somewhat subdued for the norm in car showrooms, but there appeared to be a multiplicity of high-specification lights that were not used. Central to the whole floor space but elevated above the level of the rest by a designer staircase was what seemed to be a hexagonal self-supporting mezzanine area, but having the appearance of a stylish balcony. At the top of the stairs, surrounded by an extensive and, for those days, very high-tech set of consoles, I found Bernie. There were no other staff to be seen, and where Bernie sat reminded me of the command controls of a spaceship as seen in Hollywood movies.

The opening chat, after introductions, was to do with his

impressive place and the extensive but rather mundane stock of Ford, Rootes Group and BMC products on display. He was keen to demonstrate the state-of-the-art aspects of the premises, and turned to the consoles from where he could, with concentrated and deliberately targeted spotlights, illuminate any individual car in which a customer showed interest.

"Very nice," I commented, "but one thing worries me, Bernie. There don't seem to be many customers around."

"Oh," he replied, quick as a flash, "I don't like them coming in here. They get the floor dirty!"

After we'd had our discussions my head was reeling. I had never before met anyone whose grasp of things was so instant, whose mind worked so fast and whose responses were so quick and to the point. Not only to the point but, if you had not picked up on any little variations to the deal that he included in his reply, you were basically too late. In the absence of a response as quick as his own, his interpretation was that you had accepted his counter-proposal and it was a done deal. You needed to proceed with a great deal of caution and force yourself to work at your own pace, in spite of his tactic of letting you feel his impatience. The caution was needed because you were the one likely to make the slip, not Bernie.

I was quickly to come to understand that few people could keep up with him. This did not mean that he was 'sharp': just that he was very clever, his mind worked at a pace that others found hard to grasp, and he could see a deal where few others could. This meant that he could have multiple things going on all at the same time, and he could switch from one to the other without losing the thread of any of them. But our negotiations were also to demonstrate to me that, if Bernie ever gave an undertaking, that was it. His word was his absolute bond. Even if he had reason to think he had drawn the short straw you never, ever heard him complain, and to ask for a concession was just not in his vocabulary. All of this is still true today, 40 years later.

After completing our business that day he asked if I would like to have a look round the rest of the premises. He took me over to some sliding concertina doors and opened them. I was confronted by a huge warehouse-type area, no showroom gimmicks here, filled with closely packed Ferrari, Lamborghini, Rolls-Royce, Bentley and Aston Martin cars. Never had I seen so many luxury, exotic and desirable cars under one roof. This was obviously where the serious business happened. In the yard was the four-wheel-steer coach chassis that was later to become well-known as the Brabham transporter, and all manner of crates, boxes and machinery. When I asked what they were, Bernie, who at that time had his own British-made twin-engined aircraft, told me he was worried that the manufacturer was going out of business. So he had simply bought up all the remaining spares, including all the engines, so that his parts requirements would be met for the foreseeable future.

"But what about the other owners?" I asked. "Won't they need spares for their aircraft too?"

"Yes," he said. "I suppose they will."

During 1970 we had occasion to speak primarily about the Formula 2 programme, which under his guidance was not only doing well but needed little factory input. Once he had his 'deal' he just got on with things in a completely self-sufficient way. Bernie was at Monza in September and suffered, as we all did, the dreadful despair of Jochen's accident instead of what should have been his crowning as champion.

Nothing much passed between Bernie and Team Lotus through 1971, but he resurfaced in all our lives at the end of the year. Jack Brabham, who had retired from driving at the end of 1970, had passed on the running of the Brabham team to his long-standing colleague and design chief, Ron Tauranac. Jack still retained an interest in the racing activity of the team and a financial interest in the company. They decided to sell at the end of 1971, and Bernie was the buyer. It would be hard to say whether, at that moment, he had a vision of the way he would like Formula 1 to develop. It is more likely that, applying himself with his usual energy and standards to his new enterprise, he found Formula 1 to be seriously lacking in areas that he considered of absolute importance. Finance was certainly one, and image and presentation was another. Sensing quickly that the other teams and their principals were completely tied up in their own little worlds, some competing, some satisfying their egos, some simply struggling to survive, he moved decisively to put order and structure in place.

Now admitted, as a team owner, to the inner circle of FOCA (Formula One Constructors' Association), he realised that the meetings were essentially a bunch of individuals defending their own self-interests. Dealing with the immediate problems with organisers, circuits and safety, ticket allocations, the governing body and the race purse, these individuals were suspicious of anything that could be interpreted as joint action for the benefit of all, thinking that this might in some way undermine their competitiveness with each other. Bernie, able as always to see the wider and longer-term picture, started quietly introducing proposals that were not contentious but, with some calm explanation, demonstrated that his way would give a benefit for all. Careful to steer clear of things that could be seen as threatening to a team's individuality, his proposals suggested an easier, more organised way of going racing. Gone would be the stupid and endless wrangles with the Automobile Club de Monaco about pit credentials for our tyre companies. We had even 'gone on strike' and refused to go out to practise until our Firestone guys had their tickets. Now there was Bernie who said "I'm not having that", and not only volunteered to go and do something about it, but got it sorted.

"Bernie," someone else would say. "Now these cars are more complex, we like them up on trestles in our pit garage. And it doesn't help to keep these new slick tyres safe if we have to push the cars around the paddock."

"Well, let's get something done about it," was his reply. And all of a sudden the scrutineers were coming round to our garages to check the cars. Notice the "Let *us* do something about it." Never one to say "I", Bernie also had this very astute way of making all these disparate and strong-willed people think that they had been responsible for getting something done. The reality was that only Bernie would apply his time and his effort to this sort of thing, and he knew that it only happened because he was the driving force. But it suited him to have them think otherwise. Next, we no longer had to traipse up to the control tower to show licences.

"These people know we've all got licences. If they don't, they shouldn't be running a Grand Prix," was Bernie's comment.

And then it was, "What we have to do is get the paddock layout and garage allocations sorted out. Leave it to me, I'll have a word with these guys." Bernie's tone would imply he was going to make them an offer they couldn't refuse. Which was, of course, precisely the impression he wished to give. Then, when these things started to happen, the belief in his infallibility was germinating very nicely in people's minds.

Earlier in the 1960s, when the first mutterings of the teams getting together had been mooted, there was little progress towards a common perspective, mainly due to the inequalities of the financial system. It was this inequality that gave rise to the first ideas of an 'association', but it was also the stumbling block to progress. Throughout the decade the existing appeal and historical status of Ferrari and the exceptional success of Team Lotus had meant that these two between them cornered most of the appearance or 'start' money offered by the various organisers of World Championship races. This was a negotiable incentive to the participants to come and take part and make up a field. Needless to say, the two teams that represented the greatest attraction to the paying public, who could therefore guarantee the commercial success or failure of a Grand Prix meeting, held the whip hand. They were happy to be racing for peanuts in prize money. By threatening not to come they had the best negotiating sanction of all. A balance would eventually be struck by the organiser, who knew the threat was to be taken in the context of the loss of championship points. The rest of the teams fought over the scraps, and on many occasions appeared for nothing.

Before any worthwhile progress could be made towards a uniform arrangement for all teams and all races, Ferrari and Team Lotus had to give up their pre-eminent position for the greater good. The greater good was not the type of philosophy to be found sitting easily among the intensively competitive and ambitious world of racing teams. The trade-off that was eventually accepted by the two big guns was the proposal that all prize funds in future would be huge by comparison with the average £750 first prize of the time. And, being the type of people they were, the big guns, Enzo Ferrari and Colin Chapman, were confident that between them they would continue to share the biggest slice of the pie. Not entirely obvious at the time was the fact that, by making hitherto unavailable riches accessible to the other teams, those teams would try harder to share in them. The extra stability of the environment of which they were now a definite rather than an uncertain part also helped them put their businesses on a firmer footing.

So, while everyone around the FOCA table was finding that things were going rather better on the organisational side, Bernie was experiencing for himself the blotting paper characteristic of a Formula 1 team when it came to soaking up money. In place were arrangements covering ticketing, paddock layouts, freight arrangements and pit allocations, and first steps were being taken to have an input into the regulations, both sporting and technical. The original FOCA prize fund had been negotiated at 66,000 Swiss francs, it being considered at the time that the Swiss franc was the most stable currency and one that was least likely to be the subject of exchange rate swings or, worse still, devaluation. But at a sterling value of about £40,000 and annual increases linked to price indices, the pot would start to look decidedly lean as the explosion in technology and development made itself felt. And then there was the ever-present strife over how the pot should be shared out among the members, all of whom now considered themselves fully fledged and of equal rank.

Colin Chapman used to say that any meeting that lasted longer than an hour would become counter-productive. Bernie, acutely aware of the sensibilities of meetings with eight or ten well-inflated egos present, let his FOCA meetings go on for as long as it took. In fact, such was his patience that he would allow the discussions to cross back and forth across the table until the protagonists had worn themselves out. Pausing only to order more coffee, tea or smoked-salmon sandwiches, he would gently introduce his proposals seemingly as counters to some insoluble conflict of opinions elsewhere around the table. After a whole day's discussion or late on into the night, when two or three had perhaps left to go to more urgent appointments, the meeting would collapse. What would be left would be a general view of, "Well, if nothing better's available we'd better accept this – but we don't like it." And as one left, tired and bewildered and sometimes on the wrong end of a savaging from one of the other team chiefs, it would suddenly dawn that what had been agreed was exactly what Bernie had proposed hours ago. At the time it seemed like the compromise expediently produced by a fertile brain to solve a conflict between two opposing views. Now it was obvious that it was what he wanted all along. How he managed it also added to the aura building up around Mr Ecclestone.

And now he had the prospect of handling the financial negotiations on behalf of all the teams. The fact is that no-one else wanted to do it. Mostly they were too wrapped up in their own world of crisis. Whether in performance, personnel, supply or finance, there was always a crisis going on in a team. Only Bernie had contrived to surround himself with people he could trust so implicitly that the art of delegation came easily to him. He was free to spend enormous amounts of his working days – which comprised, needless to say, all seven in each week – concentrating solely on the general problems of organisation, promotion, image and finance of the sport. This in turn allowed him to see the bigger picture and where it might lead.

The others in FOCA were essentially happy to let him get on with it. He delivered when he said he would, had a bold and fearless streak that recognised no door as being closed, and was certainly never going to be outsmarted by the people with whom he was dealing. They were frequently almost amateurs, putting on a Grand Prix once a year. He was the consummate professional with years of business success behind him and was now in possession of an intimate and hands-on insight into the workings, requirements and structure of a modern Formula 1 team.

That is not to say that the other members of FOCA failed to contribute. Around the table sat the leading lights in Grand Prix racing, and every subject under the sun was raised and discussed. Fixture lists, circuits, safety, drivers and their contracts, regulations, the FIA, testing, tyres, transportation, air travel and much else came in for the most minute dissection. It follows that where things technical or financial were discussed, and especially where future driver choice was concerned, things were played pretty close to the chest. There was nonetheless a continual jousting that took place on the off-chance that perhaps someone around the table would be so provoked that he would let slip something advantageous to the rest. But from this multiplicity of different outlooks and ideas would come some form of consensus. Again it was Bernie who had the ability to pick up on those things that would move us all forward, and who did something about it.

For now the formative years of FOCA were taking up enormous amounts of time in seemingly endless meetings. Finance, and the prospect of more of it, guaranteed the full attention of members, and no-one rang up and pleaded a prior engagement if this item was on the agenda. Again Bernie had this technique of being able to deal with his notes on all sorts of sundry matters whilst keeping the meeting in total suspense. Then when he had covered what he knew to be less interesting but still necessary for him to complete his current projects, he would casually slip in the result of his latest negotiations. He rarely failed to surprise us.

It was at about this time that he asked for the members to consider a proposal from him personally. He pointed out that, while he had been happy to help out with matters to do with FOCA, he did also have a Formula 1 team to run. If we wanted him to continue he was going to have to put in place the beginnings of an organisation that could do this work. He could no longer expect members of the hard-pressed Brabham staff to deal with these extra-curricular items. The two or three staff he envisaged would have to be paid, and he wished the FOCA members who benefited from this work to consider a way of paying for the new people. Needless to say he already had a solution in mind. After the usual two hours of round-the-houses discussions with everyone showing a marked reluctance to get out their cheque books, he said, "You don't have to give me a cheque. Why don't we fund this work from the prize fund? Give me a percentage of that and I will take care of everything. There will never be anything extra to pay." After a further two hours discussing the percentage the meeting voted to allocate to Bernie a figure of four per cent of the prize fund. From this grew the initial FOCA staff of Ann Jones and Alan Woollard, and later the huge empire of the 21st century.

The FOCA meetings were also a great source of humour, banter and gossip. There was usually a period of bemoaning the perennial shortage of money, without which one just could not do all the things that one knew would make the team super-successful. The lack of assets of the typical Formula 1 team was a continuing barricade to accessing funding, and bank managers were very stringent with their favours, thinking (as they did at that time) that motor racing was an entirely frivolous pastime. When Bernie mentioned that he was having a bit of grief with his bank manager, we could not resist asking why.

"Well," he said, "the Brabham overdraft got to £1.5 million, so he called me in to see him." This was really heavy stuff, because most of us were operating on overdrafts of £50,000, and under the sort of pressure where in some cases we had to ring the bank for permission to write the next wages cheque.

"So what happened?" we asked incredulously. "I told him that if he didn't like my business I would take it elsewhere!" You somehow knew with Bernie that this was the way it happened.

He told me once, "In this life you have to get on, get rich and then get honest." This implied that in stage one you did not worry too much about business ethics. In stage two it was an enormous bonus to be liquid when everyone else was strapped for cash. Buying when everyone else wanted to sell was good business. In stage three not much really mattered any more, because you could get away with anything. This I did take to be a 'Bernie story', for in over 30 years I have never met anyone who said anything derogatory about his business ethics. In fact the reverse is true, for he is and always has been scrupulously fair and correct in his dealings. In stage two he obviously applied some of his skill to acquiring things at the right price. But my experience is that, being in the position that his skills have enabled him to be, he has used his liquidity without hesitation and with rare generosity of spirit to help others. There is not one team in Formula 1 that he has not at some time helped out, even to the extent that ensured their survival. There are some that have been indebted to him time and time again. If ever a driver or team member of any team was injured or ill, all his facilities and any others he could bring to bear were immediately put at their disposal. He is suggesting that in the third stage, which is somehow the result of the first two, things get easier because people trust you. This self-deprecating assessment is wholly at odds with reality. Bernie has always been someone who was trusted implicitly for his honesty. But the reality is that, as he has got older, his workload has increased rather than decreased. And because of the respect and trust that people have for him he has often been asked to be the 'honest broker' in this or that dispute, or to help bring two sides together. This he does willingly and in addition to his other responsibilities. His clarity of mind and expertise in finding solutions often surprises and jolts the opposing factions into the realms of common sense.

Throughout the remainder of the 1970s Bernie worked hard at

building a stable platform from which Formula 1 could operate in a professional, well-organised and financially equitable way. Systems were thrashed out for the distribution of the steadily growing prize funds. To reward the 'regulars', the longstanding big-name teams which constituted the main appeal of individual events, 35 per cent of the prize fund was set aside based on the last two years' performances. Stalwarts were rewarded thus for the continuity they brought to the grid. The top ten teams in the championship shared this chunk that represented their old 'start money'.

The second 35 per cent was awarded on a sliding scale based on performance at specific races. The results of the previous season's championship races counted until the halfway point of the present season. Then the division of this second one-third of the fund was calculated on the results of the last half of the previous year and the first half of the current one. This kept everyone on their toes and rewarded them broadly in line with how well they were doing currently. This portion was particularly important to teams trying to get into the top ten, or in their first couple of seasons. It also provided solid income to the top teams doing well on a consistent basis. Most importantly it reflected movements in payments to teams on the way up or down, within a short enough period of time to be relevant. It penalised new teams who were trying to break into Formula 1 with inadequate resources, and also those teams who were simply not doing a good enough job.

The final 30 per cent of the fund was set aside for true prize money. However, because the stars might lead a race nearly all the way through and then perhaps fall out near the end, it was felt that the winner-takes-all system was not a proper reflection of what happened in a race. Very often the real spectacle came from the excitement of the initial sorting out of protagonists, and not the actual result. Therefore the split of the prize money was made down to 20th place only, with grid positions, positions at quarter distance, half distance, three-quarters distance and the finish determining

each individual car's earnings. This meant that any team entered –
and there was a long period when pre-qualifying was needed to
whittle the number of starters down to 26 – could race for the same
prize money as any other. The regulars, if they just happened to have
a bad day, could absorb the loss because they were receiving money
for just being there.

If there seemed to be a Machiavellian slant to these financial
goings-on, that was probably true. The two FOCA members who
delighted in helping Bernie with these sorts of calculations were
Teddy Mayer of McLaren and Max Mosley of March. While Max
often gave the impression that for someone of his superior intellect
(barrister and all that) this was just a game to see who could be the
most devious and clever, Teddy had a deep-rooted feel for the special
status of the major teams. He felt that their presence year after year,
successful or not, and their commitment to supporting all the
championship races, set them aside from the 'Johnny-come-lately'
outfits. These had suddenly found Formula 1 was accessible to them,
purely because of the universal availability of the Ford DFV engine.
Teddy felt they should have to earn their place at the table in order
to share the benefits that had been put in place by the hard work of
the regulars and now, in particular, Bernie. This was a feeling shared
strongly by BRM, Ferrari, Lotus and Tyrrell, the other main players.
Ferrari did, from behind the lofty desk that was occupied by Enzo
Ferrari, consider themselves more equal than others in many
respects, and one of Bernie's essential skills was to keep them happy
while not ruffling too many feathers at home.

The story at the time that did the rounds of the journals, put about
mainly by the disgruntled, was that to get into Formula 1 you had
to be a member of FOCA. To become a member of FOCA you had to
do a full season in Formula 1! This glib set of words was purported
to be the reality, the dark side of the cartel and definitely not a joke.
In fact it was just a journalistic play on words. Anyone could enter a
Formula 1 race. If a team had the resources to stay the course and
do a whole season then their membership of FOCA was automatic.

What was not automatic was receipt of all the financial benefits. These had to be earned either by stability and continuity, or by results. Because Bernie was by this time recognised as the leader of FOCA he came in for the most criticism. He was 'running a union or a closed shop' and 'using his strength to force organisers into submission'. As usual he kept his counsel and did not respond to the growing sets of rumours and press stories, knowing that to reply only gave them the legs to run for longer. Instead he created agreements that were fair and beneficial to all parties involved in the business.

Now, in return for the increased prize funds, the teams had to undertake to turn up to all the races. No more could they retire to their factories in a sulk if they were not doing too well and miss a couple of races, putting a race organiser in the position of letting down the fans. Another favourite trick had been to give the last two races of the year a miss if they were in the USA and Canada or Mexico. These were very expensive to attend and not cost-effective, especially if the team concerned had no remaining chance in the championship.

In time Bernie put in place a complete package that included the calendar, the grid, the circuit, the racing programme, the paddock, the pits, the ticketing, the car parks and, in the case of the long-distance events, the transportation. The organisers, the entrants, the press and the spectators gradually came to accept that this was a better way. Everyone knew where they stood, what they were committed to doing, how things were going to work and what the financial implications were. And throughout, Bernie's inherent good humour with his critics remained intact.

Asked by the BBC once if they could film a 'fly on the wall' bit of one of these FOCA meetings that everyone was talking about, he agreed to let them in at one held at Brands Hatch during a Grand Prix weekend. Ever the ringmaster, he realised that by doing it there, rather than in one of the London Airport hotels in which they usually took place, the team chiefs would be wearing their sponsor labelling and would gain some extra TV exposure. He also knew the TV people were after some juicy bits of 'inside story' which they would then probably edit to make up part of a sensationalised exposé. Having got circuit boss John Webb to let us use his boardroom, Bernie explained that to make it authentic he would admit them, but for the first few minutes only. By way of a sound bite he would give the members an 'opening report', which was not at all the way meetings usually worked. With all the lights and crew installed and the cameras whirring, he started completely calmly and with a straight face.

"Welcome everyone, and thanks for coming. Just before we start the agenda, I have to report that last month the drugs produced £50,000 and the loan sharking realised £35,000, but we had a poor month with the prostitution which made only £20,000." The TV crew carried on filming without noticing anything amiss until the whole meeting burst into laughter. Bernie told the director that that was all he was getting, and perhaps he had better look at the tape. In a few minutes the director was back in the room pleading for a re-run, which was seriously done.

One of the characteristics of most very successful businessmen is their innate sense of value. They can always, it seems, assess the worth of something accurately, and Bernie was no exception. Since Team Lotus had started the era of commercial sponsorship in 1968 there had been a period when several other major companies, having seen what their competitors were doing, joined in the fun. By the late 1970s there had been an increase in the number of teams participating in Formula 1, and the costs were rising steadily year by year at what was rapidly becoming an alarming rate. The frenzy to get a sponsor or sponsors quickened in pace. The pool of companies with large enough budgets to support this type of promotional activity was small. Bernie stood his ground and remained true to his principles. If a company would only sponsor his Brabham cars if he reduced his offer, he would turn them down. He would rather run the team from within his own resources than sell something for less than he thought it was worth. This attitude, coupled with his everyday attention to detail, style and image, meant that his Brabhams were simply the smartest cars in the paddock year on year. They either carried no advertising, or what they did carry was stylish, never garish or intrusive, and never out of keeping with the overall colour scheme, which was generally white. The same was true of his drivers and team personnel. The rest of us were amazed at the sponsors he turned down!

By the time 1979 started there was much that Bernie could look back on with pride. His Brabham team had been in the top five in every year but two since he bought it, and FOCA had gelled into the most powerful lobby in Formula 1. Max Mosley had given up on team ownership at the end of 1977 and was spending much of his time advising and helping Bernie on things legal, as well as being a second set of forward-looking eyes on the bigger picture of the future of Formula 1. But it is not Bernie's style to look back, and it was just as well that he was not looking over his shoulder. If he had been he might not have seen an out-of-control juggernaut coming over the hill towards him in the shape of Jean-Marie Balestre.

The French have always been political animals, and their priorities have long had a different emphasis to the rest of Europe. In the absence, with a few important exceptions, of a legion of sporting heroes, they quickly realised that the way to power and influence in sport was through the governing bodies. In Paris they had the environment of good communications, impressive addresses and stylish living that would always be attractive to the blue-blazer brigade. As many sports burgeoned through the 20th century, one after another contrived to locate their headquarters in the French capital. You will have noticed how many governing bodies start with 'Fédération Internationale de...'. And if the sport is governed in French, the rules are written in French and the HQ is in Paris, then surely it should have a Frenchman at its head.

Bernie had had some pretty easy years dealing with the CSI (Commission Sportive Internationale), a commission delegated by the FIA (Fédération Internationale de l'Automobile) to look after and regulate motor sport, for it was distinctly amateur and low-key in outlook and behaviour. Now Jean-Marie arrived on the scene. With a grandstand seat from his position as President of the French Motor Sport Federation, he had witnessed as the nominal organiser of the French Grand Prix the inexorable advance of the FOCA systems introduced by Bernie. Contemplating with horror the loss of face that would be incurred if he were no longer in a position to hand out leather armbands to his mates, he stirred emotions at the FIA. With a mixture of canny lobbying and Gallic bluster, he persuaded the powers in Paris to abolish the CSI and create a new body – FISA (Fédération Internationale du Sport Automobile). To this new body was delegated the authority to govern motor sport. He contrived to get himself elected as its first President, with the pledge that in the new commercial world of motor sport he would get stuck into these Formula 1 guys (who did they think they were?) and show them who was boss.

Confirmed in his new position, Balestre arrived in Argentina for the first race of 1979 showing all the symptoms of the megalomania that characterised his time in office. Often interrupting his own officials and those of the national organising club, he interfered with most aspects of the event and decided arbitrarily, without offering any chance for a word in his own defence, that John Watson should be hit with a monster fine. Most observers considered the accident soon after the start to be merely a 'racing incident'. FOCA considered the summary justice a direct and undisguised threat to the wellbeing of all that they had striven to achieve. There now started a stand-up, knock-down, drag-out fight that was to last three years.

Hindsight shows that the fight was worth it, but it did not seem like it at times during those fraught years. Drivers were being fined for things they did on the track; organisers were being castigated for things they did not do on and off it. New rules were arbitrarily introduced for teams and officials, and every event seemed to contain a confrontation. Balestre worked the 'divide and rule' card for all it was worth, and now that Renault had established themselves as a serious contender a wedge was driven politically between the 'grands constructeurs' (Ferrari, Renault and Alfa Romeo) and the disparagingly named 'garagistes' (the British kit-car builders). Things were not helped by the arrival of turbo engines, as this served only to concentrate the minds of the teams using the less powerful Ford-Cosworth engines to try for even more controversial and provocative interpretations of the rules to maintain their competitiveness. The 'grandees' were constrained on the one hand by the fact that their real business was global, huge and subject to fickle market influences if they suffered adverse publicity generated on the race track, especially if it smacked of foul play or cheating. On the other hand they were pioneering a new era with their engines and could not give an inch on performance while they were getting the new technology up to speed. So we had the skirt saga, the water-cooled brakes saga, the Lotus 88 twin-chassis saga, the drivers' briefing saga, the superlicence saga and many others.

In this quagmire Bernie knew that to reach the future he envisaged he had to stick to his guns. This was in his nature and not, therefore, a difficult stance for him to take. What was incredibly tricky was to keep the group that made up FOCA united. "If we don't hang together, we'll all hang separately," he would say as yet another member showed signs of straying from the flock. Additionally he had to keep the 'grandees' on side on a vast range of matters, while being portrayed as their mortal enemy on others. He also had to explain the subtleties of the FOCA position clearly enough to teams from France like Ligier, and teams from Germany like ATS, to make sure they were with him. No-one will ever know how one man managed all this, but he did.

We also had a new member in the shape of Jackie Oliver of Arrows. Although Alan Rees had represented Shadow for some years, it would have taken him a lifetime to relate to his new partner all that had taken place in meetings. When Jackie arrived on the scene his team achieved the rare distinction of getting into the top ten in its first year. But he had other problems with lawsuits from Don Nichols of Shadow and the perennial ones of making ends meet and securing his sponsors for the following season. Somehow getting in place the start-up package was always easier than getting it renewed, and by then you were aware of how much it really cost and your sponsors were aware of how well you were fulfilling your promises to them. In any case, one or other of these pressing problems seemed at the time to Jackie to be more important than attending the next FOCA meeting. To his horror, at the following meeting he found that something had been agreed that he felt mitigated against him and his team, and he made the most frightful stink. Coming from a new member this was a bit strong and one of the brethren, I cannot remember who, pointed out to Jackie that there was little in life more important than a FOCA meeting. "And anyway," he continued, "he who is absent gets screwed." There and then we had a motto that stuck.

When the dust of the FISA–FOCA wars had settled there was surprise from some FOCA members that Jean-Marie Balestre was still there. Many assumed that Bernie would have hung him out to dry. The public, through clever handling of the press coverage of the outcome, believed there had been a stand-off and that neither side had 'won' and a middle-of-the-road compromise had been reached. The truth is that Bernie, while keeping us posted about the merits of communal hanging, was also wont to say "Don't get mad, get even." And that is what he did. He actually supported Jean-Marie through further terms of office, including his elevation to the Presidency of the FIA itself. Jean-Marie was now President of everything – but Bernie was still the boss. Although the FISA–FOCA wars had ultimately been fought out over the territory of the technical regulations, from 1982 onwards nothing happened in Formula 1 without the approval of Bernie. He was clever enough to realise that a breakaway championship was not worth the hassle of getting it recognition and acceptance world-wide when there were so many pre-existing connections to the FIA to be severed. So he simply left things as they were, and made sure that he had people and committees in place to put forward the Ecclestone way of running Formula 1. The blazers and armbands were kept happy by being made to feel important, elected to lots of committees and regularly dusted down and put on display on some VIP balcony or function. And, like so many astute characters, Bernie was not averse to feeding one of his own ideas to Balestre, who then instantly put it about as one of his own and promoted it like mad. So he had control of a President he knew, rather than taking the risk of ousting him and perhaps getting one he did not.

Of course it has to be said that Bernie did not always come to the next FOCA meeting with a success to report. Often our hopes may have been built up by dreams of further coups either financial, political, technical or organisational, and perhaps we were to blame, for having shared in most of his triumphs it was easy to take these too much for granted. Honest as always, he would let us down gently by telling it the way it was. Often, if asked to explain a particular setback, he would say, "There comes a point when if you know you are going to get f***ed, you might as well lie back and enjoy it!"

Now the way forward was clear. The vision of a global televised World Championship could become a reality. As always Bernie threw himself into it with fervour. While there were the two or three financially strong events that did not even have to try – Monaco, Silverstone, Monza – yet made serious profits, there were also some lame ducks. Some events needed their government's support; some needed sponsorship; others needed spectators. Several of the races came in and out of fashion, depending on whether there was a national driver involved. In much the same way that Bernie had earlier guaranteed starting grids to organisers of first 18, then 26, cars with weighty penalty clauses if he did not deliver, he now set about rationalising the calendar and circuits.

But he needed something else first. He once more approached his fellow members in FOCA to explain that if we were to enjoy a regular season of 16 championship races all over the world, some of the weaker organisers would have to be supported by the stronger. This meant in effect that for us to race for a guaranteed purse of the same amount everywhere we went, the money paid out from some would have to be less than that received from the organiser. The surplus would be used to top up the purse of an organiser whose race we wished to attend but who could not afford the fee. In extreme cases we might have to promote the races ourselves. There were indeed at this period several events that were not financially viable but important to the calendar. The fact that such a course of action could, if an event was unsuccessful, incur a loss scared the living daylights out of some the teams, whose day-to-day existence was already precarious.

"Well," said Bernie, "there is another way. I could take it on myself. That way the risk would be mine but also the rewards, if there are any."

This was not a trap, simply a statement that the way ahead was not a smooth one, but it was nonetheless the way. Utterly convinced that he was right, Bernie was not going to be diverted when the goal was in reach. We gave him an additional four per cent of the prize fund for taking on this huge amount of extra work, mainly to pay for the organisation that would need to be in place to run things. Also assigned and formalised in the early 1980s were the television revenues.

Though some income was being generated by the sale of the rights to televise Grands Prix, it was small beer. Bernie proposed and obtained agreement from FOCA that, in return for negotiating all the TV deals that he could, he would keep 70 per cent of the revenue, and that 30 per cent would be shared equally amongst the qualifying members. At a time when some TV companies had to be begged to cover a race and some carried no live coverage at all, this did not seem a bad deal. The extra income required no work to be done by the teams whatsoever.

What did become a landmark event, however, was the evening that Bernie invited us all out for dinner after the season had ended, usually to the St James's Club. In addition to being a great fun evening with everyone relaxed and much joking and mickey-taking, not to mention a very fine dinner, there would be a certain moment of high tension. This was when Bernie dipped into his briefcase and got out each team's cheque for their share of the TV kitty. Those with mental arithmetic skills would go quiet and could be seen struggling to grasp that, if his team's cheque represented one-tenth of 30 per cent, then Bernie's 70 per cent was worth 23 times as much. Now, "Do I know my 23 times table?"

In fairly quick order, and to everyone's pleasure, the revenues increased substantially. Of far greater concern to FOCA members, particularly those who had been involved since the start, was the fact that in equally quick order Bernie's new organisation was now also the promoter for 11 out of the 16 races. Coupled with the fact that the Brabham team had been sold and now the circuit advertising and corporate hospitality rights were contracted to Bernie's organisation, this caused some worries. Ron Dennis had taken the place of Teddy Mayer and had brought with him a fresh, if slightly abrasive, attitude to the business. Max Mosley was head of an FIA committee busy building the launch pad for his own go at the Presidency. This slightly altered and less traditional balance of FOCA was not helped by the fact that it seemed as if Bernie called you only when it suited him, and only when he wanted your agreement for something. And he was not even a team owner any more. The sums of money were getting sufficiently large that, human nature being what it is, jealousy and greed were in danger of being visible.

Bernie's view, as always short and to the point was, "You were all free and over 21 when you agreed the deal, so why are you now moaning?" Our income streams had hugely improved, but so had our costs. We were now, in the turbo era, in the midst of the greatest technological explosion ever seen in Formula 1, and our costs were rising exponentially. The danger, as it was perceived, was that if one person controlled all the most important financial aspects of the undertaking then we, the participants, would lose control of our own destinies.

And so was born the Concorde Agreement. A hugely complex document involving the signatures of entrants, organisers, promoters and the governing body, it became the Magna Carta for the world of Formula 1, the ground rules for everything from the sporting regulations to the code of business practice. A period of calm followed for the duration of the first agreement. The second one followed pretty smoothly on the first. There was a growing acceptance that things were working well; stability had been achieved with the calendar and the prize funds; the TV coverage was building very nicely and producing stronger income; circuits were coming to heel with the upgrading of facilities; and by and large sponsors were happy.

All that was really needed was to write in the new numbers in dollars, pounds or whatever, pay the lawyers' bills and get on with the racing. And so it was. But when the time came around for the third renewal there was once again some dissension in the camp. This had arisen mainly because of the two-tier nature of Formula 1 at the time. There were the turbo teams, mostly supported by engine manufacturers, and the atmospheric-engine teams that were hopelessly uncompetitive. We had become a group of 'haves' and 'have-nots': teams that cornered the majority of the funds, and teams that had to feed off the scraps. This situation led to a similar juxtaposition of interests and was a corrosive and divisive issue.

For the first time in its history a sub-group of FOCA members held meetings (shock, horror!) without Bernie being present. We wanted a bigger, better and different deal to what he was offering, and we felt we should stick out for it. For weeks and months Ron Dennis, Frank Williams, Ken Tyrrell and I would have meeting after meeting to study the latest draft of the proposed new Concorde Agreement from Bernie and return it with our counter-proposals.

Due to the nature of our driver contracts we all employed some pretty high-powered city lawyers, some of the best-known firms in the land. Heaven only knows what the composite total of their bills for this period was. Certainly a back-of-the-grid team could probably have run for half a season with that much money.

It all finished with another stand-off. We were refusing to sign, and Bernie had given us an absolute ultimatum. Either it was signed by a certain time (6pm as I recall) or it was all over, and things would return to the bad old days. Ron, Ken and I were holed up at the McLaren offices in Woking, and Frank was on a personal mission to sort Bernie out. Ours were the only signatures missing. For whatever reason, and we shall never know how or why he managed to pull it off, when the telephone in the McLaren boardroom rang not long before the deadline, it was Bernie to say that Frank had signed! This rupture of our unanimity brought about an immediate collapse of our position, and there followed a race far more intense than any Grand Prix to get our signed copies to Bernie before the deadline. His deadlines were non-negotiable. Ken Tyrrell delivered the signed documents with minutes to spare.

We shall never know how or why it came to be that Bernie got Frank to sign and break the deadlock. In truth the remaining items in dispute were few in number and did not go to the essence of the contract, the new Concorde Agreement. What this round of negotiations did do, however, was to confirm to those involved that the business was now truly global and that the sport was now driven by money. As had happened in football, golf, tennis and particularly the major American sports, business decisions would henceforth determine the future direction of the sport. Television schedules would impose themselves on Grand Prix timetables; races would be run to a format that fitted satellite transmission times; image became so important that oil or grease was no longer to be tolerated in pit garages; and the money became so huge that all the fun was eradicated from the pit lane, lest the big-spending sponsors and TV companies got the impression that their money was not being spent on a serious endeavour.

The first FOCA prize fund had been for 66,000 Swiss francs. The 1992 British Grand Prix contract was for $4.5 million. And this was not the whole story. An earlier era had seen a 'free' transportation allowance to the qualifying teams of two race cars and 1,500kg of spares weight when they went to a 'long-distance' overseas race such as Brazil or the US. To this were added ten 'free' air tickets for the crew. By the end of the century a team would not be able to go to such a race with less than three cars, 20 tons of spares and 40 personnel. This huge increase had to be paid for from somewhere. Television was the answer. The huge global audience of over a billion viewers in a season meant that, for an advertiser, Formula 1 had become without question the most effective way of reaching the largest number of people at the lowest cost per head. And once again Bernie was responsible.

He was responsible for the common format for all television presentation of races. He produced the lavish brochures that publicised the viewing figures. He demonstrated the value of TV exposure on cars, drivers and circuit hoardings. He got the advertising spenders flocking to be on board. He put in place the lavish hospitality possibilities that gave a new meaning to 'a day at the races'. And he negotiated the rights for the Grands Prix to be televised world-wide. This produced more revenue for the teams, but also for him. While the teams suddenly found that sponsors did not blanch at numbers of a size not dreamed of just a few years earlier, the sponsors now recognised that the Formula 1 season, which lasted from March to November, was up there with the Olympic Games and the Football World Cup in terms of viewer attraction. But the motor racing season lasted for much longer than the month of the other two.

Bernie, meanwhile, turned his attentions to the next step: his own TV production capability. Funded by the continuously rising revenues, he started pouring huge sums of his own money into his vision of the future. The result was his digital TV product. A line-up of 30 immaculately turned-out trucks turned up for each race to combine together to make a major production studio. Known as 'Bakersville' because it was operated by Eddie Baker, another of Bernie's trusted ex-Brabham people, the huge complex could send digital pictures with all sorts of inter-active features direct from the paddock of every race. When 'Bakersville' needed to be in Australia, no less than 280 tons of airfreight took it there. Sadly, because of Bernie's principle of not compromising on the value of anything, Formula 1's own digital service was a step too far. The response of pay-per-view purchasers failed to justify the huge investment, and at the end of the 2002 season Bernie closed it down.

The biggest political step-change in Formula 1's huge growth came after the Balestre era had ended. Max Mosley slid smoothly from head of the Manufacturers' Committee of the FIA to President, in succession to the Frenchman. For some time Bernie had already been a Vice-President (responsible for all things commercial), and now he had in place his old ally. Max turned his four-year first term into a five-year stint by offering himself for re-election after only 12 months. By the time his next campaign started he was entrenched in all aspects of the responsibilities of the FIA and playing a grand role in Europe particularly. His alliance with Bernie fell foul of the EEC anti-competition rules, but between them they satisfied those who sought to tumble the edifice, or more likely wished to share in some of the good fortune.

So Bernie's success seemed to be complete. For more than 30 years he had toiled ceaselessly for what he saw as the true way. Now, instead of having to guarantee grids of 26 or more cars, the field was reduced and exclusive. As in NFL football in the US, to get to play in the awash-with-money Formula 1 arena you needed to hold a 'franchise'. If you didn't have one, you had to buy one of the existing teams. How the FOCA brethren must have been smiling. Their race team assets were finally worth a fortune. Stock exchanges, finance houses and motor manufacturers all began to flex their muscles to get a part of the action.

And it has all been due, without any doubt whatsoever, to the efforts of one man, Bernie Ecclestone. On his own he has done 100 times more than any other individual to build Formula 1 into what it is today. He deserves whatever success and rewards his efforts may have brought him. And, well into his ninth decade, he is still effectively at the helm. No individual successor has been groomed; it is hard to see where a person of similar calibre would be found. However, Bernie has surely put in place the means by which the huge business may continue when he is no longer there.

But just remember, Bernie: "If you're absent, you get screwed."

Epilogue

LEAVING LOTUS
By Simon Taylor

Peter worked in Formula 1 uninterruptedly for 20 years, from October 1969 to July 1989. Over that period Team Lotus won three Drivers' titles and four Constructors' titles, and he shepherded his Formula 1 charges on to more than 300 starting grids. He was a central player in the Grand Prix circus, and most notably he shouldered the responsibility of leading Team Lotus back to winning ways after the crushing loss of its charismatic leader.

Then in July 1989 he abruptly left Lotus, where – with a couple of interruptions – he had worked for over 30 years. The official release said: "At an extraordinary meeting of the shareholders of Team Lotus International, Chairman Fred Bushell and Team Director Peter Warr have both stood down from Camel Team Lotus Grand Prix. Group Lotus plc has been requested to second Group Technical Director Tony Rudd to act as Executive Chairman of Team Lotus with effect from July 24."

When I talked to Peter in 2008 about his departure, he explained it thus: "We were working on good sponsorship deals for 1990. One was with Coca-Cola: we'd presented to them in Atlanta and had a reasonable expectation that they were going to sign for $45 million over five years. Another was with BP, which was also going well, so things were looking really good. Then suddenly Fred Bushell was arrested over the DeLorean affair." This happened on 10 July. Bushell, as Lotus's finance director since the early days and Chapman's close confidant in all money matters, went on to serve a three-year prison sentence for irregularities connected with the deal between Chapman and John DeLorean to develop the latter's sports car for production in a new factory built outside Belfast, with the help of a massive grant from the Irish Development Agency.

"As soon as the news broke of Fred's arrest, Coca-Cola and BP not surprisingly both withdrew at once. I went to Hazel Chapman and said, 'I'm sorry, but I don't think I can go on working under these circumstances.' I left the following week."

Duncan Lee, once again, has a very detailed recall of the circumstances leading up to Peter's departure, and from Camel's viewpoint the circumstances were slightly different.

"Unfortunately, from 1988 the Lotus chassis had become less and less competitive. The team abandoned the active suspension system that Senna had insisted on, and the resulting package was not up to McLaren's speed. Senna and Prost dominated the 1988 season for McLaren and for Marlboro. Towards the end of that year Peter Warr invited me to a dinner with him, Nelson Piquet and Frank Dernie, who was then aerodynamicist at Williams Grand Prix. Peter said he was offering Frank the job of technical director of Team Lotus, at a salary of $500,000 per year. Nelson then chimed in and said, 'And I will pay Frank another $500,000 to sign on!' That was the bonus we'd paid Nelson for being World Champion when he arrived at Lotus. Dernie accepted, and resigned from Williams – which resulted in a law suit against him for breach of contract. A lot of lawyer talk followed, and finally Dernie was able to join Team Lotus.

"However, the results were not what we had all expected. The chassis did not improve over the Gérard Ducarouge design, and the team's performance continued to decline. A lot of bad feelings went around during the 1989 season, and my company was putting extreme pressure on me to make things better. How, I had no clue! I spoke to Nelson, saying my company was pointing blame at him, even if I wasn't. But during that summer my new boss, my fifth in four years, decided to get involved and said he wanted to speak to somebody in a high position at Lotus. So I arranged a meeting with Tony Rudd, who was Technical Director of Group Lotus, working on the road car side and not directly connected with the Team.

"We met at a dinner in London, and my boss Joe Sherrill came straight to the point and told Tony Rudd that R.J. Reynolds was not happy with the team's performance. Sherrill said that, as a long-time corporate manager, he always placed the responsibility for any problem on top management. Therefore the blame must be placed on the shoulders of Peter Warr, and Camel would no longer sponsor the team if he remained.

"I was dumbstruck, blind-sided, shocked and dismayed. I had no idea this was going to happen, but I was out-ranked, and could only sit there silent. Within two weeks, Peter had left Team Lotus. Tony was named Team Director, a job I know he took reluctantly. Camel remained with Team Lotus through 1990 and then left for Benetton and Williams.

"I was able to discuss the issue with Peter some time later, and explained my role in it. He said he understood completely, and we remained friends until the end of his life.

"In my opinion, the real problem at Team Lotus in those final years was that the Chapman family was keen to see the Team continue in Formula 1 in memory of its founder, but that the necessary funds were not available to remain competitive with the likes of McLaren, Ferrari and Benetton. The discontinuation of active suspension is an example. Peter Warr was financially hamstrung in his efforts to improve the technical performance of the team. World Champion drivers are not enough to overcome lack of technical advancement.

"Every Formula 1 team director and owner I dealt with was different in his own way. Peter stood out amongst them all because he came into Formula 1 not as a team owner, or as an engineer, or as a driver, although he had raced in his younger days. He was hired by Colin Chapman to help organise and manage the operations of the team. Chapman was a genius at spotting talent, and he didn't fail with Peter Warr. With his military schooling and experience, Peter was a master at organisation and discipline, much to the dismay of some of his employees. In spite of this strict demeanour on the job, he had a sense of humour that belied his serious side. He loved to carry on the Chapman tradition of the crème caramel-eating contests in restaurants, and was not shy about pulling elaborate practical jokes, such as his surprise birthday party for Ron Dennis in Detroit – complete with dominatrix. Peter Warr was a presence in my Formula 1 experience who will remain a highlight and a pleasure."

After 20 high-pressure years at the absolute heart of the frantic hubbub that is Formula 1, it can't have been easy for Peter, a few weeks past his 51st birthday, to turn his back on everything that had motivated, nourished, infuriated and driven him for most of his adult life. He parlayed his huge experience into a spell on the other side of the Formula 1 fence as a permanent FIA steward, and he also accepted an offer to be full-time Secretary of the British Racing Drivers' Club, based at Silverstone. He stayed there for more than two years before the internal politics of that organisation, at a somewhat fluid time in its history, drove him away. He got involved in a high-end garage business in Hampshire, and also returned briefly to team management, looking after a BMW touring car team racing in Australia, New Zealand and Macau, with Tim Harvey and Justin Bell as drivers. He and Yvonne found time to enjoy classic car events with his superb gull-wing Mercedes-Benz 300SL, and he was also able to become more of a family man: "Through working too hard I had missed a lot of my children growing up, and I didn't want to make the same mistake with my grandchildren."

There must have been something in the Warr genes that drew the clan to motor sport. Peter's sister Ilma had married ERA, Cooper and Lister racing driver Bill Moss, and Peter and Yvonne's two children did not escape involvement either. Son Andrew remembers, as a schoolboy, getting himself to Grands Prix around Europe by train, and on one notable occasion thumbing a lift home in Nelson Piquet's plane. He now works for Cosworth in their Electronics company in Cambridge, and over the past few years his responsibilities have involved him in powerboat racing, superbikes, international rallying and Champcars. Daughter Susie is married to historic racer David Morris.

In 2002 Peter and Yvonne bought their beautiful house in south-western France, on the edge of a little hamlet near Sainte-Foy-la-Grande, surrounded by the Bordeaux vineyards. After much contemplation Peter pulled together his thoughts, memories and papers and started to write this book. A very fit 72, he was just off to Biarritz on a golfing holiday with Yvonne when, on 4 October 2010, he suffered a totally unexpected heart attack, collapsed and died.

As the news of his passing spread, the tributes rolled in. Colin Chapman's son Clive, whose Classic Team Lotus keeps his father's marque alive in historic racing with beautifully restored examples of charismatic Lotus single-seaters, said: "Peter always put more in than he took out. At Team Lotus he not only managed the team, the sponsors and the drivers, but also, and perhaps more importantly, he managed my father. He played a vital role in enabling him to realise the potential of his engineering brilliance. After my father's death he stepped up to lead Team Lotus back into the winner's circle with Ayrton Senna, a fantastic achievement in difficult circumstances."

Bernie Ecclestone, referring to Peter's role in the foundation and growth of FOCA, said with typical brevity: "He helped me to build Formula 1 to what it is today."

Peter Warr was, in every way, a strong character. If he hadn't been, he could not have survived working so closely for Colin Chapman, could not indeed have survived being part of Formula 1 for so long. He was a man of high intelligence and a man of integrity: determined, outspoken, a natural leader and a disciplinarian, impatient with people who, in his view, could not rise to the occasion. But he was also a man whose humour – if you could expose it, just below the surface – could be uproarious. And, despite his toughness and his single-minded drive, there was a generosity, almost a humility, which he expressed when he said to me, summing up his life:

"It was a huge privilege to work with all those blokes, and live through it all. I had a hobby that became my job, and then my entire life. That makes me a very fortunate human being."

INDEX

Page numbers in *italics* refer to illustrations.

Absalom, Hywel 'Hughie' 53
Adelaide 144–4, 174–5
Alboreto, Michele 155
Aldridge, Geoff 42, 201
Alfa Romeo 127
Amon, Chris 82
Andretti, Mario 36, 44–5, 63, 94, *110–12*, 14–20, 136–7, 183, 202
Andrews, Chris 18
Argentinean GP: 1973 94; 1977 *145*, 177; 1979 219
Arrows F1 team 200, 220–1
Ashcroft, Michael 38
Australian GP: 1986 133–4; 1989 174–5
Austrian GP: 1970 83, 88; 1971 91; 1973 95–6; 1982 45, 126, 127, *150*, 203
Austrians, the 74–5
Automotive Products 103
Avus, Grosser Preis der Nationen (1962) 19

Badcock, Roy 14, 20
Baker, Eddie 227–28
Balestre, Jean-Marie 129, 161, 174, 204, 218, 219–20, 228
Banwell, Howard 167, 168
Barber, Chris 25
Barcelona, Montjuich circuit 77–8, 100, 103
BBC 216–17
Beaulieu, National Motor Museum 37
Belgian GP: 1973 100, 101–2; 1977 118; 1981 125; 1985 *188*; 1987 135, 171
Bell, Justin 232
Bellamy, Ralph 40–1, *107*, 116, 182, 184, 193–4, 195, 198
Beltoise, Jean-Pierre 82
Bennett, Colin 14
Bennett, Nigel *110*, 198
Berger, Gerhard 74–5, 137, 158
Best, George 62
Bexley, Kent, car showroom 204–5, 206
Blash, Mike 'Herbie' 52, 53, 55
Bolster, John 16
Bonnier, Joachim 77
BP 230, 231
Brabham, 'Black' Jack 75, 81, 82, 83, 162, 206
Brabham F1 team 75, 76, 127, 134, 167, 183, 195, 206–7, 212, 217–18, 224
Brambilla, Vittorio *112*
Brands Hatch 13, 58, 82, 93, *106*, 138, 163, 176, 216–17; Boxing

Day meetings 16, 17, 181; Cooper Racing Drivers' School 14; Drivers v. Team Managers celebrity Ford Escort race (1978) 20, *111*; Rothmans 50,000 *Formule Libre* race (1972) 93
Brands Hatch Place Hotel 140–1
Brawn, Ross 178, 179
Brawn GP team 179
Brazilian GP: 1973 94, 100; 1976 114, 117–18; 1985 154; 1986 134; 1987 135, 171
British American Racing 54
British American Tobacco 138
British Car Auctions 38
British GP: 1969 77, 78; 1970 82; 1971 91; 1973 95; 1975 *108*, 1976 43; 1992 227
British Racing Drivers' Club (BRDC) *191*, 233
BRM F1 team 215; P160 car 198, 199, 200
Brookmans Park, Herts 17
Brundle, Martin 141
Bucknum, Ronnie 19
Bueb, Ivor 13
Bunwell, Norfolk 90
Bury St Edmunds hospital 41
Bushell, Fred 25, 35, 39, 167, 169, 170, *190*, 198, 230–1

Camel (R.J. Reynolds Tobacco International Inc) 166, 167–70, 172–3, *188*, 231–3
Campbell, Ian 53
Canadian GP: 1973 97, 100–1, 102; 1977 177
Cesenatico 73
Cevert, François 95, 97, 118
Chapman, Clive 39, 234
Chapman, Colin (Anthony Colin Bruce) *73*, *108*, *110*, *147*: ability to go straight to core of problem 28–9; and Andrew Ferguson 24; appearance 29, 30; blame for Jochen Rindt's death 84–5, 89; as businessman 35–6; children 39; and criticism of build quality or cost-cutting 37, 38; and customers ('lunatic fringe') 37–8; death of 25–6, 30, 45–6; as decision maker 28, 29, 31; depressed with F1 during 1975 196–7; difficulties of working with 42–3; early cars 31–2; energy of 30, 180–1; engineering design skills 179–80; engineering philosophy 31–2; events leading up to death 25; as family man 39; four-wheel-drive development 77; generosity 39–40, 41, 43; Heathrow Airport incident 39–40;

house 22, 39; influence of car designs on GP racing and road cars 35; as innovator 27, 31, 32, 33–4; and Jochen Rindt *70*, 76, 77, 78–9; last time in pits with his cars 45; last World Championship 34; Le Mans 24 Hours trip (1958) 14, 26; legal battle over Lotus 86 'twin-chassis' car 203; loss of Jim Clark 76; and Lotus Elite 27; management technique 28; and Mario Andretti *112*, 115; the mind of 27, 28, 34; motivational skills 15, 27, 29; and Nigel Mansell 125–6, 129, 130; offers Peter a job 24, *148*, 232–3; 'Oxford' note pads 43; period of budgetary instability 124; and Peter's racing 18; philosophies 15, 27, 31; photographic memory 29; plans for 1973 season 93–4; plans for 1982 season 127; preoccupation with weight 78, 80; and prize funds 209; in races 13, 29–30; and Ralph Bellamy 184, 193, 194; relationship with engineers/designers 194–5, 199–200; and restrictions on race car design 32; and Ronnie Peterson 96, 97, 113–14; and sale of obsolete cars 36–7; skill at spotting race driving talent 115; temper 28, 30–1, 42, 78, 113; thesis and design for Lotus 78 ground effect car: 43–4, 196–7, 201; and Tony Southgate 199–200; and turbocharged engines 127–8; utilises monocoque construction 33; and 'wings' 76–7
Chapman, Hazel 22, 25, 39, 43, *190*, 231
Chapman family 232
Cheshunt, Delamare Road 17, 20–1, 23, 35–6, 64, *66*, *69*
Chimay circuit, Belgium 17; Grand Prix des Frontières (F3) 18
Chiti, Carlo *147*
Clare, A.S. 140, 141, 164, 166, 169
Clark, Jim 17, 21–2, 23, 62, 63, *73*, 76, 90, 115, 137, 153, 175, 181
Classic Team Lotus *192*, 234
Clermont-Ferrand circuit 82, *105*
Coca-Cola 19, *68*, 230, 231
Collins, Peter 123, 126
Concorde Agreement 226–7
Cooke, Mike 42, 201
Cooper cars 13, 18; Formula Junior 73
Cooper-Maserati F1 team 75
Coppuck, Gordon 183

Costin, Mike 16, 19, *69*, 180–2, 194, 198
Cosworth Electronics 234
Cosworth Engineering Ltd 16, 55, 125, 126, 182; Ford DFV engine 93, 100, 125, 215, 220; engines 43; experimental engine 83, 84, 86, 88
Courage, Piers 82
Cowley, Fred 91
Crabtree, Dave *148*
Crombac, Jabby 19, 22, 91, *186*
CSI (Commission Sportive Internationale) 218–19

Dance, Bob 48, 49, 53, 55, 59, 144, *148*, 153, *186*, *189*
Davey, Steve *148*
de Angelis, Elio 45, 122–9, 131–2, 134–5, 137–8, *150–1*, 158, *186*, 203
DeLorean, John 44–5, 203, 231–2; sports car 202, 230–1
Denney, Phil *148*
Dennis, Eddie 53, 56–7, 58, *106*
Dennis, Ron 75, 142, 143, 172, 224, 225, 233
Depailler, Patrick 137
Dernie, Frank 231
Design Auto 118
Detroit *187*, *189*
di Montezemolo, Luca *107*
di Waldkirch, Rudi 18
Diggins, Paul 59
Dinnage, Chris *151*
Donington circuit 45
Doodson, Mike *72*
drivers, racing: best driver debate 61–2, 64; categories of 62–4
Ducarouge, Gérard 131, 137, 139, 154, 157, 164, 165, 170, *186*, *187*, 203, 231
Duckworth, Keith 16, 182
Duckworth, Ursula 16
Dudot, Bernard 159, 160, 161
Dumfries, Johnny 163
Dutch GP: 1970 *70*, 82; 1971 93; 1973 95, 96, 100, 103
Dyke, Peter 138–9

Earls Court Motor Show (1959) 17
Ecclestone, Bernie 55, *107*, *146*, *147*, 167, 183, 194, 195, 204–29; as Brabham owner 206–7, 212–13, 217–18; builds stable platform for F1 to operate on 213–14, 218, 219; car showroom 204–5, 206; complete FOCA package put in place 216; and Concorde Agreement 225, 226; end of season dinner with FOCA members 223–4; and filmed FOCA meeting 216–17; and FISA threat to wellbeing of F1 220; as FOCA spokesman 207–8, 209, 210–12, 213–14, 216, 221–2; generosity 213; innate sense of value 217–18; and Jean-Marie

Balestre 221, 222; as Jochen Rindt's manager 75, 79, 204; and Peter 234; philosophy 213; and prize money improvements 214–15, 216; as promoter for F1 races 224; quick mind of 205, 213; success of 228–9; trustworthiness of 205, 213; and TV coverage of F1 222–3, 224, 227–8
Elf 138
Elsworth, Stan 58
Endruweit, Jim 58
Engine Developments 125
engines: 900-series road car 193; turbocharged 127–8
Ensign F1 team 195
Essex Petroleum 44, 124, 202
European GP (1984) 138
Evans, Bob 42

Fangio, Juan Manuel 61–2, 63, *69*, 137, 159, 174
Ferguson, Andrew 14, 24
Ferrari, Enzo 34, 209, 215
Ferrari F1 team 76, 116, 121, 127, 136, 168, 178, 179, 208, 209, 215; cars 84
FIA (Fédération Internationale de l'Automobile) 218–19, 221, 224, 228; prizegiving 41
Firestone 80, 184, 207; tyres 92, 94
FISA (Fédération Internationale du Sport Automobile) 219–20, 221; ground clearance rule 129–30
Fittipaldi, Emerson 59, *72*, 83–4, 88–98, 100, 102–3, *105–6*, *148*, 156, 182–3, 184
Fittipaldi, Maria-Helena 90, 91
Fittipaldi, Wilson 59, 98
Fittipaldi F1 team 98, *148*, 195
FOCA (Formula One Constructors' Association) 125, 129, 207, 209, 210–12, 215, 234; and Bernie Ecclestone's vision of global televised World Championship 222–3, 224; complete package put in place by Bernie 216; Concorde Agreement 225–6; end of season dinner 223–4; and FISA threat to wellbeing of F1 219–20, 221; initial staff 212; Jackie Oliver upset by decision at meeting 221; meeting filmed 216–17; meetings 207, 210, 211, 212–13, 216–17, 221, 222; membership benefits 215–16; success story under Bernie's leadership 228; teams' undertakings in return for prize funds 216; transportation allowance 227
Ford 33, 43; Anglia van *66*; Cortina 41; Escort *111*
Ford-Cosworth DFV engine 93, 100, 125, 215, 220
Formula 1 GP racing: four sequential periods 35; team

personnel 53–4; team specialists 54; world TV audience 226, 227
Formula 2: 92, 93, 193, 204, 206
Formula 3: 52, 93
Formula Junior *67*, 73, 17, 20, 181
four-wheel drive development 77
Foyt, A.J. 120
French, the 218
French GP: 1970 82; 1971 91; 1972 *105*; 1973 95
Froissart, Lionel 174
fuel calculations 78

G2 Films 155
General Motors 38
German GP: 1970 82–3; 1973 95, 96; 1975 196; 1985 161; 1987 173–4
Goodwood circuit 18, *107*
Goodyear 132, 133, 138; tyres 94, 102, 132, 165, 184
Goossens, John 97
Granatelli brothers 116
Griffiths, Willy 58
ground-effect car design 196–7
Group Lotus sale to General Motors 38
GT racing 52
Guiter, François, and his son 155
Gurney, Dan 115

Hall, Keith 13
Hallam, Steve 157, *186*, *187*
Hanson Group 166
Hardacre Geoff *148*
Harris, Ron 20
Hart, Rex 59
Harvey, Tim 233
Hawkridge, Alex 142–3
Hayes, Walter 33, 52
Head, Patrick 34, 165, 178
Henry, Alan 132
Herd, Robin 79
Hesketh F1 team 176, 178; 308C car 176; 308E car 118
Hethel factory 23, 24, 35–6, 80, 81
Hicks, Clive *148*, *190*
Hill, Graham 15, 16, 21, 24, 51–2, 73, 76, 77, 90
Hill, Phil 115
Hillman Minx 14–15
Hockenheim circuit 82–3, 165–6, 173–4
Holman Moody team 120
Honda 19, 170, 172, 173, 178, 179; engine deal 162–3, 164, 165, 167; S800 19
Huckle, Gordon 58
Hulme, Denny 75, 86, 100
Hunt, James 62–3, 121–2, *146*, *147*, 176, 178
Hunt, Peter 121–2

Ibiza 43, 196, 201
Ickx, Jacky 82–3, 88, 102, 104, *108*, 114, 176
Imola circuit 175

Imperial Tobacco 138–9, 166
Indianapolis 22, 33, 36, 52
Interlagos circuit 100, *110*, *151*; F2
  race 59
Ireland, Innes 23
Irish Development Agency 231
Italian GP: 1971 89, 91; 1973 96–7

Japanese GP: 1963 (sports cars)
  19, *68*; 1964 (sports cars) 20;
  1976 45, *112*; 1987 qualifying
  135–6; 1989 174; 1990 175
Jarama circuit *112*, 162
Jardine, Tony 142
Jenkinson, Denis 61–2, 64, 153,
  155
Jerez circuit 157–8
John Player & Son 52, 104, 124,
  138, 165
Jones, Alan 137
Jones, Ann 212
Jones, Ian 15
Jones, Parnelli 116, 183
journalists, motoring 141–2
Judd, John 125

Kawamoto, Nobuhiko 162–3
Kermanshah, Persia 13
Kerr, Phil 183
Kettelberger, Ute (Elio de Angelis's
  girlfriend) 123, *150*
Ketteringham Hall 26, 35–6, 44,
  169, 197–8; Development Area
  195; Drawing Office 179–80, 182,
  184, 200; fabrication shop 131,
  132; Group R&D facility 197, 198,
  201
Knight, Mike 20
Kyalami circuit *148*

Laffite, Jacques 137
Lake Garda 73
Lamplough, Robs 37
Larrousse, Gérard 128
Lauda, Niki 63, 74–5, 102, 104,
  113, 137, 144, 154, 159, 177
Le Mans 24 Hours (1958) 14, 26
Lee, Duncan 166–70, 172–3, 231–3
Leighton, Brian 'the Broom' 57–8
Leighton, Keith 58–9, *107*
Levin circuit, New Zealand 77
Leyland Leopard transporter 56–7
Ligier, Guy 128
Ligier F1 team 159, 164, 221; car
  156–7
London: Cosworth premises,
  Southgate 16; Heathrow Airport
  39–40; Hilton Hotel 176; Hornsey
  182; Lotus works, Hornsey 14,
  15, 16–17, 21, 27, 30–1, 35–6,
  181; Radford coachbuilders,
  Hammersmith 24; Railway Hotel,
  Tottenham Lane, Hornsey 14,
  16–17; St James's Club 223–4;
  Team Lotus workshop,
  Edmonton 26, 27
Long Beach 122, 124

Lotus 72: 34, *70*, *72*, *73*, 80–1, 82,
  83–4, 90, 93, 94, 101–2, 103, 104,
  108, 116, 156, *191*, 184, 195, 196;
  brake shafts 85, 88; design 85;
  and Jochen Rindt's death 85–8;
  problems with 80–1; suspension
  92; testing 99–100; wing 84
Lotus cars: Six 29; Seven 15–16,
  20, *66*; Eight (Mk VIII) 13, 29,
  32–3; Nine (Mk IX) 13, 29, 32–3;
  Ten 32–3; Eleven 13, 29, 27,
  32–3; Twelve 33; Fifteen 29,
  32–3; Lotus 16 Series 4: 182–3;
  Lotus 18: 17, 18, 20, *66*, 182;
  Lotus 20: 17–18, 20, *67*; Lotus 22:
  17, 19, 20, 73; Lotus 23: 19, 20,
  68, *192*; Lotus 24: 33; Lotus 25:
  33; Lotus 26 (Elan) 33, 36; Lotus
  27: 20; Lotus 29: 33; Lotus 38:
  33; Lotus 49: 33, 37, 52, *70*, 76,
  77, 90, 115; Lotus 49B 24, 51–2;
  Lotus 56: 22; Lotus 56B 89, 91,
  93; Lotus 63: 77; Lotus 64: 36,
  52; Lotus 72 *see* Lotus 72; Lotus
  74 'Texaco Star' 184, 193–4;
  Lotus 76: 103, *107*, 116, 183;
  Lotus 77: 42, 44, *112*, 114, 117–
  18, 193–4, 198–199, 201; Lotus
  78: 34, 43, 44, 195, 197, 201;
  Lotus 79: 34, 201–2; Lotus 80:
  201; Lotus 81: 202; Lotus 86: 202;
  Lotus 87: 202; Lotus 88: 125, 127,
  202, 220; Lotus 91: *150*, 203;
  Lotus 92: 45, 130; Lotus 93T
  130–1, 203; Lotus 94T 171, 203;
  Lotus 95T *152*; Lotus 97T 143–4;
  Lotus 99T 156, 170–2, *188*; Lotus-
  Cortina 20, *69*; early Chapman-
  designed 31–3; Eclat 38; Elan
  (26) 33, 36; Elan Plus 2: 40–1,
  103, 198; Elise 38; Elite 20, 27,
  33, 36, 181; Elite (second series)
  38; Esprit 38, 44, 197
Lotus Cars (company) 15;
  Cheshunt works 17, 20–1, 23,
  35–6, 64, *66*, *69*; Hethel factory
  23, 24, 35–6, 80, 81; Hornsey
  works 14, 15, 16–17, 21, 27,
  30–1, 35–6, 181; Stock Exchange
  flotation 38
Lotus Components 15, 20, 23–4
Lotus Engineering Ltd 15
Love, John 18

Maggs, Tony 18
Majorca 41
Malvern College 13, *65*
Mangenot, Max 128
Mansell, Nigel 62–3, 122–5, 154–5,
  158, 173, 175; 1981 F1 season
  124–5; 1982 F1 season 126, 127,
  129; 1983 F1 season 130, 131;
  1984 F1 season 131–3; 1986 F1
  season 133, 134, 157, 162; 1987
  F1 season 135–6, 171; antipathy
  with Elio de Angelis 126, 127;
  character 123, 126; complaining

manner 123, 132, 133, 139; equal
  status to Elio 125–6, 128; feels
  whole world against him 123,
  124, 129, 136; Imperial Tobacco
  sponsorship 138–9; lack of
  professionalism 136; later success
  133, 136–7; and Monaco GP
  'white line incident' 132, *152*;
  parents 124; performance
  compared with Elio 128–9; and
  Peter 128, 129, *151*; rejects
  chance to use carbon brakes 171;
  salary 124–5; as seriously flawed
  driver 133
Mansell, Roseanne 123–4
March F1 team 79, 94, 114, 116; cars
  112, 179
Mark, Sir Robert 133
Marlboro 168, 231
Martin, Georges 128
Martin, Ian *148*
Martini 124
Matthews, Sir Stanley 62
Mauduit, Bruno *187*
May, Stevie *106–7*
Mayer, Teddy 97, *147*, 183, 184,
  215, 224
McCarthy, Vic *106*
McCormack, Mark 117
McLaren cars 172, 183, 184; M19
  184
McLaren F1 team 54, 97, 103, 121,
  127, 168, 171, 172, 179, 183, 231;
  Woking offices 226
McLaren-TAG cars 162
Mecachrome 164
mechanics, racing: attraction of
  working as 50; character of 50;
  chief 58–9; dedication of 57; pay
  dispute by 52; salary of 52, 55;
  stamina of 51, 55; typical
  working week of 54–5; variety of
  backgrounds of 49–50; workload
  of 47, 48–9, 51, 53, 54–5
Melbourne 54
Mercedes-Benz 179; 189E
  'Evolution' 144; 300SL *191*, 233
Mettet road circuit, Belgium 18
Mezzanotte, Ing. 127
Michael of Kent, Prince 45
Michelin 127
Miles, John 77, 79, 84, 88, 90
Mitterrand, François 128
Monaco, Automobile Club de 207
Monaco GP 223: 1970 81; 1971 91;
  1973 94–5; 1974 103, 104; 1977
  177; 1979 122, *147*; 1981 129,
  130; 1984 132, 139, *152*; 1987
  171, *188*
Monkhouse, George 13
Monte Carlo 81, 222; Tiptop Bar
  58, *190*
Monza, Hôtel de la Ville 84, 89
Monza circuit 73, 83–6, 89, 91,
  96–7, 121, 156–7, 222; Jochen
  Rindt's death at 86–8
Morris, David 234

Morris (*née* Warr), Susie
  (daughter) 233, 234
Mosley, Max *146*, *147*, 215, 218,
  224, 228
Mosport Park 100–1, 102
Moss, Bill 233
Moss (*née* Warr), Ilma (sister) 13,
  16, 233
Moss, Stirling 62, 63, 137, 159
Motor Racing with Mercedes-Benz 13
Motor Show (1959) 17
Mower, Derek 'Joe 90' 53
Murphy, Mike *148*
Murray, Gordon 134, 183

Nakajima, Satoru 45, 163, 167, 169,
  173, *191*
National Motor Museum, Beaulieu
  37
Nazareth, Pennsylvania 116
Newey, Adrian 178, 179
Newman-Haas Team 136
Nichols, Don 113, 198, 221
Nilsson, Gunnar 42, *111*, 114,
  118
Niven, David 29
Nordic Racing 53
Novamotor 193
Nunn, Mo 195
Nürburgring 16, 17, 95, 96, 144,
  196; Eifelrennen (1962) 18

Oberon, Jean-Pierre 64
Ogilvie, Martin 42, 130, *148*, 201,
  202–3
Oliver, Jackie 220, 221
Oulton Park 18, 56

Paris 218; FIA headquarters 25;
  Hôtel de Crillon 25
Parnelli F1 car 116, 183
Patrese, Riccardo 136, 167
Paul Ricard, Circuit 99–100, 134–5,
  156
Pederzani brothers 193
Pelé 62
Peterson, Barbrö 101, 114
Peterson, Nina 114
Peterson, Ronnie 42, 58, 63,
  94–104, *107–8*, *110*, 113–15, 117,
  121, 137, 184, 194–5
Phillippe, Maurice *70*, 88, 116, 182,
  183
Phipps, David 16, 123
Pickles, Jim 53
Piller, Michel 64
Piper Cherokee 39–40
Piquet, Nelson 133–4, 135, 137,
  157, 162, 172–3, 231
Pirelli 127; tyres 131
Player's (John Player & Son) 52,
  104, 124, 138, 165
Porsche 38, 127
Portuguese GP (1985) 154–5
Postlethwaite, Dr Harvey 43, *145*,
  148, 178
Pratt & Whitney 91, 93

prize money 208–10, 212, 214–15,
  216, 223, 226
Prost, Alain 62–3, 97, 132, 133–4,
  136, 137, 139, 144, 157, 158, 159,
  174–5, 231
Pryce, Tom 113
publication embargoes 141, 142
Pullen, Lester 168, 173

Raby, Ian 13
race car preparation 47–8
race crew initiation test for new
  drivers 144
Racing Engines Ltd 15
Radford, Harold 24
Red Bull Racing 179
Rees, Alan 79, 94, 113, 220
Reims circuit 16, 17, 30
Renault Sport 127, 128, 132, 138,
  159, 161, 164–5, 220; DPV
  (Variable Pre-rotation Device)
  159–60; EF15 engine 161;
  electronic engine management
  160
Repco engine 75
Reutemann, Carlos 103–4, 137,
  202
Revson, Peter 100–1
Reynolds (R.J.) Tobacco
  International Inc (Camel) 166,
  167–70, 172–3, 231–3
Richardson, Ron 36
Rindt, Jochen 24, 52, 63, 64,
  73–89, 137; accident in Spanish
  GP 77–8; Austrian GP (1970) 83;
  blame for death 84–5, 87; with
  Brabham team 75–6; British GP
  (1969) 77, 78; cause of death
  87–8; and Colin Chapman *70*,
  78–9; with Cooper-Maserati team
  75; death of 58, 73, 86–8, 206; as
  enigma 88–9; F2 team 204; first
  F1 win (US GP, 1969) 24, 79–80;
  Jochen Rindt Show 80, 84; life
  and career before F1 73–4, 75;
  and Lotus 72: 80, 81, 82, 83–4; at
  Monza 83, 84, 86; night before
  death 84; plans for own team 79;
  posthumous World
  Championship win 88, 90;
  rebellious nature 75; signs for
  Team 76; talent of 74–5; wins
  British GP (1970) 82; wins
  German GP (1970) 82–3; wins
  Monaco GP (1970) 81
Rindt, Natascha 80
Rindt, Nina 80
Rio de Janeiro 51, 170
Rolex Oyster Perpetual wristwatch
  40
Roma football club 123
Rosberg, Keke 45, 126, 134, 136, 137,
  148, *150*
Rouen circuit 17, 18
Royal Horse Artillery 14, *65*
Rudd, Tony 197, 230, 231–2
Russell, Jim 13

Sainte-Foy-la-Grande 234
Salvadori, Roy 75
Sami, Ekrem 166, 167, 169
San Marino GP: 1987 171; 1994
  175
Scammell, Dick 53, 58, *72*
Scarfiotti, Lodovico 22
Scheckter, Ian *146*
Scheckter, Jody 43, 95, 104, 121,
  137, *145*, 177
Schlesser, Jo 22
Schumacher, Michael 62, 137, 158,
  179
Seaman, Trevor *106*
Secchi, Andrea 167
Senna, Ayrton 39, 62, 63, 85, 133,
  137–44, 153–76, *185*, *186*, *188*,
  231, 234; 1984 F1 season 139;
  1985 F1 season 154–5, 158–9,
  160–1, *187*; 1986 F1 season 134,
  157–8, 161–2, 163, 164–5, *187*;
  1987 F1 season 135, 171–2,
  173–4, *188*, *189*; 1989 F1 season
  174–5; 1994 F1 season 175;
  ability to bring sick or damaged
  car home 159; as complete racing
  driver 139, 153, 158, 159, 175;
  contract for 1987/1988 163–4,
  165–6, 169–70; death of 175;
  effect on Team of 154; honesty
  with himself 155, 176; innate
  goodness 175–6; inspirational
  side to character 153, 154;
  Japanese GP (1989) 174;
  Japanese GP (1990) 175; karting
  days 155; leaves Lotus 172–3;
  and Lotus 99T 170–2, 173–4;
  motivational side to character
  153, 154; practical joke on and
  reaction by 144, 153; relationship
  with Honda 172; sensitivity to all
  things mechanical 159, 172; signs
  for McLaren 143; signs for Team
  141–3, 158, *185*; single-
  mindedness 153–4; suffers attack
  of Bell's Palsy 153; supreme self-
  confidence perceived as
  arrogance 158–9; talking whilst
  driving ability 156–7; target to
  beat Fangio's record 174; Team
  attempts to sign 137–8, 139–41;
  throttle control 155; total recall
  skill 155–6, 157
Senna, Viviane 155
Shadow F1 team 113, 198, 200,
  220, 221; cars 198
Sherrill, Joe 232
Siffert, Jo 'Seppi' 19, 64–5, 77
Silverstone 77, 78, 103, *108*, 160,
  222; *Daily Express* Trophy meeting
  117, 118; International Trophy
  (1972) *106*; Six-Hour Relay Race
  16
Simpson, Paul *148*, *151*
Sims, Dave 'Beaky' 53
slot car racing 24
Snetterton 26

Solitude circuit, Germany 16
South African GP: 1971 91; 1975
    108; 1982 148; prize-giving
    dinner 21
South African 'non-championship'
    F1 race (1981) 125, 129
Southgate, Tony 112, 198–201
Spa-Francorchamps circuit 16, 23,
    76, 156, 171, 187
Spanish GP: 1969 77–8; 1971 91;
    1973 100, 103; 1977 112; 1986
    162; 1986 practice 157–8
Speedwell 21
Spence, Mike 22
Stacey, Alan 13, 22–3
Star named Ayrton Senna, A (film) 155
'start' money 208, 214
Stepney, Nigel 59, 148
Stewart, Jackie 62–3, 77, 81, 92,
    95, 96–7, 117, 118, 137
suspension: active 130, 131,
    170–2, 173–4; Chapman strut
    rear 33
Suzuka circuit 19, 175, 192
Swedish GP: 1973 94, 95; 1975 108
Szymanski, Kenny 148, 187, 190

Tasman series 52, 76, 77
Tauranac, Ron 206
Taylor, Richard 59
Taylor, Simon 13–24, 230–5
Taylor, Trevor 23
Team Lotus: achievements 59; and
    Colin Chapman's death 26;
    design engineers 179–80;
    Edmonton workshop 26, 27;
    factory cleaner 57–8; F2 team
    193; Gold Leaf team 52;
    inspector 57; Ketteringham
    Hall see Ketteringham Hall;
    'The Nigel Mansell Excuse
    Board' 132, 133; Peter given
    manager's job 24, 232–3;
    profitability 39; race shop 20;
    successes during Peter's time as
    manager 24
Teixera, Armando Botelho 139, 140
television coverage of F1 226,
    227–8
Terry, Len 15, 118, 182
Texaco 97, 156, 184, 193
Thieme, David 44, 202
Times, The 18
Toleman F1 team 127, 138, 139,
    141, 142–3, 153
Toyota 38
transporters 55–7
Tyrrell, Bob 168
Tyrrell, Ken 78, 107, 146, 178, 225,
    226
Tyrrell F1 team 164, 178, 215; cars
    94, 95, 184

United States GP: 1968 115; 1969
    24, 51–2, 79–80; 1970 72, 88, 90;
    1986 187; 1987 171, 189
United States GP West: 1976 42;
    1979 122

Van Every, Peter 169, 170
Vanwall 29–30
Villeneuve, Gilles 137

Wade, Martin 184
Waldorf, Holiday Inn 165
Walker, Dave 93
Walker, Murray 134
Walter Wolf Racing 43, 44, 121,
    145, 176–8, 179; Bennet Road,
    Reading factory 176, 177, 179;
    TR7 car 147
Warr, Andrew (son) 191, 233–4
Warr, Ilma (sister) 13, 16, 233
Warr, Peter Eric 69, 72, 73, 106, 107,
    108, 110, 111, 150, 186, 187, 189,
    190, 191: and Ayrton Senna
    137–8, 140, 141, 142–3, 157, 162,
    165, 174, 185, 186, 187, 188; and
    Ayrton Senna's contract for
    1987/1988 164, 165, 166, 169;
    and Ayrton Senna's departure
    172, 173; and Bernie Ecclestone
    204–6, 234; birth 13; buys house
    in France 234; car accident 40–1,
    108, 198; and Colin Chapman 14,
    26, 27–9, 35–6, 39–40, 41, 42–3,
    44, 78, 110; 180; Colin
    Chapman's death announced to
    team 26; and Concorde
    Agreement 225–6; and Dave
    Walker 93; death from heart
    attack 234; and driver deaths
    22–3; early fascination in motor
    racing 13, 14; early years 13, 65;
    and Emerson Fittipaldi 89; father
    13; F1 career 230; first job 13–14;
    first meets Colin Chapman 14,
    26; generosity 235; gives up
    racing 20; and Gunnar Nilsson
    118; Honda engine negotiations
    162–3; and James Hunt 121–2;
    and Jim Clark's death 90; after
    Jochen Rindt's death 90; and
    Jody Scheckter 121; Le Mans 24
    Hours trip (1958) 14, 26; leaves
    Lotus for first time 24; leaves
    Lotus for good 230, 231, 232;
    leaves Lotus to join Wolf 43, 44,
    112, 121, 176–7; life after Team
    Lotus 191, 192, 233; and Lotus
    72: 88, 92, 99–100; and Lotus
    Elite sales 36; and Lotus Seven
    15–16, 66; as man of integrity
    234; as manager of Lotus
    Components 20–1, 23–4; marries

Yvonne 20; National Service 14,
    65; and Nigel Mansell 128, 129,
    151; and Pirelli contract 127;
    qualifying skills 100–1; races at
    Goodwood 18; races Lotus 20 in
    Europe 17–19, 67; and Ralph
    Bellamy as designer 183, 184,
    194; and Renault secret
    components 160; returns to Team
    as manager 24, 232–3; returns to
    Team in 1981 44, 45, 148; and
    Ronnie Peterson's car testing
    99–100, 103; and sale of obsolete
    cars 36–7; second in Japanese
    sports car GP (1964) 20; as
    Secretary of BRDC 191, 233;
    sense of humour 233, 234–5;
    starts working for Lotus 14–15,
    26–7; tributes after death 234;
    and turbocharged engines 127–8;
    wins Formula Junior race in
    Lotus 18: 17; wins Japanese
    sports car GP (1963) 19, 68; with
    Wolf F1 team 121, 146, 147, 148,
    177–8
Warr, Susie (daughter) 233, 234
Warr (née Bell), Yvonne (wife) 20,
    23, 25, 41, 146, 150, 176, 233, 234
Watkins, Professor Sid 153
Watkins Glen 24, 51–2, 72, 79–80, 88,
    97, 115
Watson, John 137, 219
Webb, John 217
Wickins, David 38
Williams, Dave 170
Williams, Frank 118, 133, 136, 147,
    162, 176, 177, 178, 225, 226
Williams cars 150, 172; FW14B
    133; ground-effect 34–5
Williams F1 team 125, 126, 134,
    135–6, 176, 178, 179; Bennet
    Road, Reading factory 176, 177,
    179
Williams-Honda cars 162
Williams-Renault cars 175
'wings', arrival of 76–8
Wisell, Reine 90, 91
Wolf, Walter 43, 44, 146, 147, 148,
    176–7
Wolf F1 team see Walter Wolf
    Racing
Woollard, Alan 212
World Championship Trophy for
    Constructors 41
Worldwide Racing 89
Wright, Peter 148
Wroxham Hotel 25

Zandvoort circuit 70, 82, 93, 95, 96,
    100, 103, 141–2
Zeltweg circuit 45, 83, 88
Zolder circuit 100, 101–2, 125